Russia transformed

Since the fall of communism, Russia has undergone a treble transformation of its political, social, and economic system. The government is an autocracy in which the Kremlin manages elections and administers the law to suit its own ends. It does not provide the democracy that most citizens desire. Given a contradiction between what Russians want and what they get, do they support their government and, if so, why? Using the New Russia Barometer – a unique set of public opinion surveys from 1992 to 2005 – this book shows that it is the passage of time that has been most important in developing support for the new regime. Although there remains great dissatisfaction with the regime's corruption, it has become accepted as a lesser evil to alternatives. The government appears stable today, but will be challenged by constitutional term limits forcing President Putin to leave office in 2008.

RICHARD ROSE is the Director of the Centre for the Study of Public Policy at the University of Aberdeen. He is the founder of the Barometer series of surveys of popular response to transformation in sixteen post-communist countries and the author of dozens of books on comparative politics and public policy.

WILLIAM MISHLER is a Professor in the Department of Political Science at the University of Arizona and Visiting Professor, Centre for the Study of Public Policy at the University of Aberdeen. He has published widely on political behavior in the United States, Canada, and Europe.

NEIL MUNRO is a Senior Fellow in the Centre for the Study of Public Policy at the University of Aberdeen. He is coauthor with Richard Rose of *Elections Without Order: Russia's Challenge to Vladimir Putin* (Cambridge University Press, 2002).

Russia has reached its limit for political and socioeconomic upheavals, cataclysms, and radical reforms.

Vladimir Putin, millennium address, 2000

Russia transformed

Developing popular support for a new regime

Richard Rose, William Mishler, and Neil Munro

Centre for the Study of Public Policy, University of Aberdeen

CAMBRIDGE
UNIVERSITY PRESS

CAMBRIDGE UNIVERSITY PRESS
Cambridge, New York, Melbourne, Madrid, Cape Town, Singapore, São Paulo

Cambridge University Press
The Edinburgh Building, Cambridge CB2 2RU, UK

Published in the United States of America by Cambridge University Press, New York

www.cambridge.org
Information on this title: www.cambridge.org/9780521692410

First published 2006

Printed in the United Kingdom at the University Press, Cambridge

A catalogue record for this book is available from the British Library

ISBN-13   978-0-521-87175-4 hardback
ISBN-10   0-521-87175-1 hardback

ISBN-13   978-0-521-69241-0 paperback
ISBN-10   0-521-69241-5 paperback

Contents

Figures

Tables

Acknowledgments

A lot has happened since Mikhail Gorbachev started what was intended to be a renewal of the Soviet system and Boris Yeltsin led a campaign to disrupt it. The launch of the Russian Federation at the beginning of 1992 was a journey into the unknown. Experience since has made the consequences of this transformation clear to ordinary Russians as well as to political elites.

A lot was written about the Russian regime while it was new, not least by the present authors. However, the regime is no longer new. The time that has passed since its launch is now longer than the time required for post-Franco Spain to qualify as a democratic member of the European Union. It is also longer than the time between the Weimar Republic introducing democratic elections to Germany and its replacement by Hitler's Third Reich. The Russian Federation has not gone to either of these extremes, yet it has been transformed.

While the launch of a regime is an event, the development of popular support is a process that takes time to unfold. The purpose of this book is to chart the extent to which a no-longer-new regime can claim the positive support of its citizens or at least the resigned acceptance of those who regard it as a fact of political life that will not go away. The book asks: how has support developed? Is it due to economic success, which can be fickle; to political values, which need not be democratic; or to the passage of time, which is irreversible? The evidence used to answer these questions comes from a unique database, fourteen New Russia Barometer surveys that began in January 1992, the first month of the new regime; the most recent was conducted in January 2005.

In conducting the New Russia Barometer surveys, the authors have accumulated many debts. Tens of thousands of Russians have answered questions about how they have coped with transformation and what they think of the regime that has resulted from it. A special debt is owed to the staff of the Levada Center (formerly VCIOM, the All-Russian Center for Public Opinion), which has conducted the fieldwork for New Russia Barometer surveys with great professionalism, despite the difficulties created by the collapse of the Soviet Union and later by pressure from officials who tried unsuccessfully to undermine their independence. In an era of academic specialization, senior Russian scholars have been open to new approaches from the field of comparative politics.

The preparation of this book has been funded by a grant from the British Economic and Social Research Council (RES-000-23-0193) to study diverging paths of post-Communist regimes. The New Russia Barometer has also benefited from being part of the New Europe Barometer program of research, which since 1991 has conducted more than 100 surveys of mass response to transformation in sixteen post-Communist countries of Central and Eastern Europe and the former Soviet Union (see www.abdn.ac.uk/cspp). The Paul Lazarsfeld Society, Vienna, under the leadership of Dr. Heinz Kienzl, was the leading partner in the development of this program. Comparative data have been especially valuable in identifying under what circumstances and to what extent Russians have differed from people challenged by transformation from the Baltic to the Black Sea and west as well as east of Vienna.

Earlier New Russia and New Europe Barometer surveys have been supported by grants from scientific, governmental, and private foundations in Austria, Germany, Hungary, Sweden, and the United States as well as Britain; from the epidemiological research program of Sir Michael Marmot at the University College London Medical School; and from intergovernmental agencies including the World Bank, the European Commission, and UN agencies. At no point has any intergovernmental organization had any claim to influence the design or content of Barometer questionnaires and reports. That has remained the responsibility of the senior author of this book.

Portions of this book have been presented in academic seminars and public policy gatherings in Britain, the United States, Austria, Estonia, France, Germany, Hungary, Italy, Japan, Latvia, Lithuania, Slovenia, Sweden, Switzerland, and Taiwan, and published as "Resigned Acceptance of an Incomplete Democracy: Russia's Political Equilibrium," in *Post-Soviet Affairs*, 20, 3, 2004, 195–218. Anton Oleinik of Memorial University of Newfoundland made particularly cogent and useful remarks on an early draft of this manuscript, as did two anonymous reviewers of Cambridge University Press. The copyeditor, Karen Anderson Howes, did a splendid job of checking English-language expressions as well as Russian, and did so with great speed and clarity.

Introduction
Transformation and its aftermath

We are making such a large turn that it is beyond anyone's dreams. No other people has experienced what has happened to us.

Mikhail Gorbachev, April 15, 1991

I want to ask you for forgiveness because many of the hopes have not come true, because what we thought would be easy turned out to be painfully difficult. I ask you to forgive me for not fulfilling some hopes of those people who believed that we would be able to jump from the grey, stagnating totalitarian past into a bright, rich, and civilized future in one go. I myself believed in this. But it could not be done all at once.

Boris Yeltsin on retiring as president, December 31, 1999

Political transformation has long been a fact of life – and sometimes death. The First World War led to the collapse of the tsarist empire and of its neighbors, the Prussian, Austro-Hungarian, and Ottoman empires. This was followed by the creation of the Soviet Union as a Communist party-state and of fascist and Nazi regimes in Central and Eastern Europe. After the Second World War, democratic regimes were established in Western Europe, while Moscow installed Communist regimes behind an Iron Curtain that divided the continent.

In the past century, Russia has twice gone through a treble transformation of the state, the polity, and the economy. The first upheaval followed the 1917 Revolution that ended the tsarist empire. Lenin and his dedicated followers created a new state with new boundaries, the Union of Soviet Socialist Republics (USSR), and a Communist regime with the totalitarian goal of transforming the minds as well as the behavior of its subjects. Josef Stalin transformed a backward economy into an industrialized non-market economy, in which the commands of the Communist Party and the plans of bureaucrats decided what should be produced.

The second transformation began when Mikhail Gorbachev tried to reform the Soviet regime in the late 1980s. However, the unintended consequence of *glasnost* (openness) and *perestroika* (restructuring) was another treble transformation that Gorbachev aptly characterized as beyond any Russian's dreams or nightmares. At the end of 1991, the

1

Soviet Union dissolved into fifteen independent states. In place of a one-party regime with a totalitarian vocation, there is now a regime in which elections offer a variety of choices and people have freedoms previously denied them. A command economy in which people used connections to obtain goods that money couldn't buy in shops has been replaced by a market economy in which shops offer lots of goods for sale to those who have the money to buy them.

Transformation has challenged Russia's political elite to adapt to new political institutions or be consigned to the dust bin of history. There were neither precedents nor blueprints for what would happen. Boris Yeltsin became president with the optimistic belief that the country could "jump from the grey, stagnating totalitarian past into a bright, rich, and civilized future in one go." In reality, the Yeltsin administration proceeded by a painful trial-and-error process of responding to the great challenges facing the new regime. His successor, Vladimir Putin, reacted against the "upheavals and cataclysms" of the Yeltsin years and declared in a millennium address launching his period in office that the time had come to govern through what he called "the dictatorship of law."

Ordinary Russians too have been challenged by the intense and perva-sive effects of transformation. Since everyone was initially socialized to come to terms with the Soviet regime, the launch of the Russian Federa-tion was the start of a process of political re-learning on a scale that had not been seen in Europe since the fall of Nazi Germany in 1945 and the Soviet imposition of Communist regimes across half the continent. Eco-nomic transformation has altered the way in which you get food, whether you have a job, and how much or whether you are paid. Political trans-formation has made it possible *not* to take an interest in politics, since the Communist Party no longer has the power to compel youths and adults to pay lip service to the party line. Russians who do become involved in politics have had to work with the new regime by learning new skills, adapting skills learned in the Soviet era, or by combining the two.

In the aftermath of transformation, political elites and ordinary Russians have had to come to terms with each other. All leaders, whether democratic or authoritarian, require a combination of compliance and support from those they govern. Demands for compliance have been far fewer than in the previous regime. Instead of actively mobilizing the pop-ulation to advance Communist Party goals, up to a point the leaders of the new regime have accepted a degree of dissociation between gov-ernors and governed. This strategy confers new freedoms on ordinary people while leaving governors free to act as they wish. Demands for support have been limited too. Competitive elections have been "man-aged" in ways acceptable to the Kremlin (cf. McFaul, 2005). Instead of invoking democratic, socialist, or nationalist values as grounds for nor-mative support, governors have regarded it as sufficient for Russians to show resigned acceptance to the regime as a fact of life. In the words of a onetime Communist leader in Hungary, Janos Kadar, "He who is not against us is with us."

The first object of this book is to determine the extent to which Russians have developed support for the regime that has filled the void created by transformation. This is done by drawing on a unique source of evidence: fourteen New Russia Barometer nationwide surveys of public opinion from 1992 to 2005. It shows that Russians not only differ in their eval-uation of the current regime; they also disagree about what should or could replace it. Given these differences, the book's second object is to explain why some Russians support the new regime while others do not. Is it because they differ in age and education? In their political values or their assessment of the performance of government? Or is it because some people are winners while others are losers from the economic effects of transformation? Since opinions have fluctuated both up and down since 1992, the third object is to understand how the passage of time has altered attitudes. The dreams that people had at the start of transformation have been replaced by experience of its consequences. While many Russians find the new regime falls far short of their hopes and ideals, most who are not prepared to give it positive support are nonetheless resigned to accepting it as a lesser evil.

Transforming institutions and popular support

Transformation creates a fundamental discontinuity in the institutions of a society. Whereas an election can change the people and party in control of government while leaving its institutions intact, transformation changes the very structure of government. Transformation differs from political reform: it is not an alteration of institutions to make the political system work better; it is a disruption of institutions that replaces one political system with another.

Destruction and creation of regimes

In a sense all societies are in transition, for change is an inevitable part of political life. However, transformation is an abnormal condition of society, because it involves fundamental changes in its central institutions. Like war, it is an interruption in the everyday activities of a political society. Defeat in war does not necessarily transform a political regime. In the Second World War, the Netherlands and Norway were occupied by Nazi Germany for almost five years, but at the end of the war they restored their regime as it was before the war. However, the end of the war meant the fall of the Nazi regime and the creation of two German states, the democratic West German Federal Republic and the misnamed East German Democratic Republic.

Political transformation is most evident in the dissolution and creation of states. While at any given point in time the boundaries of states are fixed in international law, with the passage of time the boundaries of states expand or contract, new states emerge and some disappear from the map altogether. Ironically, Mikhail Gorbachev's attempt to restructure the Soviet Union led to the creation of more new states than at any time since the achievement of independence by African colonies. The collapse of the Soviet Union has resulted in the creation of new "unhistoric" independent states in Central Asia; historic nations such as Armenia became states; and nations such as Lithuania, Latvia, and Estonia, which had been independent states before 1939, regained independence.

Even if the boundaries of a state remain intact, the political regime – that is, the state's central institutions linking governors to governed – can be transformed. Whereas the boundaries of Latin American states, for example, have tended to be fixed for a century or longer, these states have experienced frequent changes of regime between civilian dictators, military rulers, and popularly elected governments. Among the member-states of the European Union, a big majority have had at least one change in political regime within the lifetime of some of their national leaders. Greece, Spain, and Portugal changed from undemocratic to democratic regimes in the 1970s; a bloodless 1958 military coup in France replaced the Fourth with the Fifth Republic; and Germany, Austria, Italy, and Finland changed regimes following defeat in the Second World War. By definition, all post-Communist states have had a regime change within the lifetime of a majority of their citizens, and a big majority have had changes in their territorial boundaries too.

An economic transformation can occur even without a fundamental change in the state or the regime. The transformation of Scandinavian countries from agrarian to industrial economies is an older illustration of this point, and Japan becoming a world economic power a more recent one. However, the Soviet Union was industrialized long before it collapsed. The Soviet legacy to the new regime was the need to transform a non-market economy into a market economy. Thus, when the Yeltsin administration sought to privatize state-owned industrial assets in the 1990s, it did so in the absence of a private sector.

The experience of Russians is extraordinary because transformation has occurred simultaneously and abruptly in three different dimensions of society – the state, the political regime, and the economy. It thus differs from a society in which transformation has been a process of evolution and each step has occurred at a different period in its history. For example, in England the supremacy of the rule of law and Parliament was established in the seventeenth century; the Industrial Revolution did not begin until the late eighteenth century; the development of a democratic regime based on universal suffrage was not completed until early in the twentieth century; and the dissolution of the British Empire came half a century after that.

Destruction and creation of popular support

If a new regime is to survive, it requires some form of support from its people. David Easton (1965: 159ff.), who initially developed the concept of political support, defined it in very general terms as, "A (the citizen) orienting himself favorably toward B (the regime)." This definition emphasizes that support is a state of mind. However, if it is to sustain the institutions of a regime, it must also lead to compliant behavior (see Rose, 1969).

The history of government demonstrates that the support of subjects can be maintained for a very long time by very different kinds of regimes. The pharaohs of ancient Egypt maintained a centralized system of autocratic rule for millennia, and the Roman empire lasted for centuries without modern means of telecommunication or coercion. The tsarist, Habsburg, and Prussian empires not only maintained their institutions but also expanded their territorial grasp for centuries before being disrupted by defeat in the First World War.

The less support a new regime has, the less effective it will be. Subjects who do not support the new regime are less likely to follow its laws and exhortations. They are also less likely to pay taxes, thus increasing the need for unpopular tax collectors or economically distorting taxes that cannot be evaded. Insofar as refusal to support the new regime reflects preference for an alternative regime, the new regime must invest substantial resources in political surveillance and intimidation of potential opponents and in propaganda designed to create support, or at least to produce passive acceptance.

Easton's definition of support is clinical rather than normative; there is no assumption that support can be given only to democratic regimes. The very detailed index of his 507-page study of political support lists only five references to democracy. This gives the term broad contemporary relevance, for many member-states of the United Nations today have regimes that are not democratic. Not only does history offer many examples of undemocratic regimes achieving substantial support, but also contemporary surveys show a substantial measure of support for regimes in countries that, at most, are only partly democratic (cf. Rose and Mishler, 2002).

Theories offer a variety of reasons why people might support their regime. Citizens can support a regime because it represents their political values, whether of democracy, ethnic communities, or Communism. Citizens may also support a regime because it "pays," that is, delivers economic benefits. In semi-democratic regimes, individuals may support the current regime as a lesser evil compared to other alternatives, for example, a foreign invader. In an authoritarian regime, subjects may be resigned to accepting that the regime will remain in place, whether they like it or not. Coercion is the ultimate inducement that the regime can offer, and fear of arrest or worse can lead individuals to show support publicly even if their private opinions are different.

In a regime that is older than its oldest citizens, political support is usually not in dispute, because everyone learns to support it through a continuous process of socialization that begins in childhood, as parents, school, and the media communicate the dominant political values and beliefs of a society. It extends into adulthood without interruption, reinforcing what was learned earlier. By the time a youth becomes an adult, he or she will regard the regime as the only form of government conceivable for their country.

Russia's transformation was a crash course in political re-learning; it changed people's lives as well as changing their system of government. Some changes were for the better and some for the worse, for example, the new regime immediately delivered freedom from a repressive party-state, but it also created treble-digit inflation and job insecurity. When transformation occurred, the median Russian was middle-aged and settled in his or her way of life. The Soviet regime was the only regime they had ever known. Transformation disrupted the collective norms and institutions by which individuals had learned to order their lives. Durkheim (1952) predicted that the consequence of such shocks would be anomie, that is, a loss of meaning in life leading, at the extreme, to suicide.

In the time that has passed since the Soviet Union disappeared at the end of 1991, Russians have had to alter their behavior or risk becoming marginalized in a post-transformation society. The disappearance of old institutions and the introduction of new ones has meant that concepts such as "freedom" and "market" are no longer abstractions, but realities that Russians experience in their everyday lives. Once it is realized that old institutions have disappeared and that new institutions show signs of persistence, people can adapt to what confronts them. Since the Russian Federation was launched, Russians have had time and opportunities to learn what their new system of governance is like. Instead of making judgments on the basis of hopes and fears, Russians can now draw on this experience to evaluate the aftermath of transformation.

Top-down and bottom-up approaches to transformation

Understanding transformation is both an intellectual and a practical task. Adam Smith wrote *The Wealth of Nations* in an intellectual attempt to make sense of the market economy; Smith generalized his theories of economic behavior from the bottom-up perspective of eighteenth-century merchants in the High Street around the corner from his lecture hall at the University of Glasgow. Karl Marx wrote a top-down account of the causes and consequences of the Industrial Revolution from a desk in the British Museum in London. The founders of the Soviet Union developed Marxism-Leninism as a doctrine to guide, or at least justify, their plans and actions to transform Russian society.

By the time the Soviet Union collapsed, social scientists had developed concepts and theories about every aspect of social life. The great majority of these theories were derived from Western, and above all Anglo-American, societies and had been tested in societies with established democracies and market systems. The emphasis was on explaining the stability of political and economic institutions. In the narrowly defined universe within which these theories were developed, the qualifying phrase – "all other conditions remaining equal" – was usually met. However, all other conditions were not equal in Communist regimes. The fall of the Berlin Wall has challenged Western social science theories to explain fundamental change as well as stability in regimes (cf. McFaul and Stoner-Weiss, 2004, 5ff.; Brady and Collier, 2004).

Transformation is a dynamic process, starting with the disappearance of the old order. There is then a period of turbulent change, followed by the institutionalization of a new regime. Thus, any theory purporting to account for what has happened in Russia cannot be based on a static analysis, such as a crossnational comparison of economic conditions in more or less democratic regimes. In order to account for the conditions leading up to transformation, the turbulence of the process, and its aftermath, theories must have regard to developments in historical time (Pierson, 2004). Moreover, attempts to predict Russia's future that ignore its present and recent past are utopian.

Top-down approaches to transformation

Because transforming changes have occurred in societies on multiple continents in the past two decades, this has encouraged some social scientists to view Russia's transformation in terms of general theories that are global in scope. Economic theories generalized from market economies, known colloquially as "the Washington consensus," were used by the International Monetary Fund and the World Bank to dispense advice and money to the Russian government. In the blunt words of Lawrence Summers (1991: 2), then chief economist at the World Bank, "Spread the truth – the laws of economics are like the laws of engineering. One set of laws works everywhere." When Summers became a senior Treasury official in the Clinton administration, he gained substantial influence in promoting this doctrine as United States government policy too. The billions of foreign aid that subsequently flowed into Russia from the West were a costly tuition fee to learn that the transformation of a non-market into a market economy is not the same as the transformation of an agricultural market economy into an industrial economy (Lopez-Claros and Zadornov, 2002; Wedel, 1998).

Insofar as Russia required fundamental economic change, this encouraged comparison with conventional developing countries. Shleifer and Treisman (2004) have used Latin American and Asian data about social and economic development to support their claim that Russia is a third-world country undergoing modernization. However, such a comparison ignores the historical fact that, when most third-world countries were primarily agricultural, the Soviet regime had transformed Russia into a society with large industries, cities, and high levels of education. While economically superior to other developing countries, Russia is inferior in political openness (Fish, 2005: 98ff.). The distinctiveness of Russia's economy before and after transformation has encouraged the self-mocking Russian boast, "We are not a third-world country but a fourth-world country."

Because Russia's political transformation has been contemporaneous with a global spread of democracy, this encouraged political scientists to analyze Russia as part of a global "third wave" of democratization (see Huntington, 1991) and even to see the Hegelian antithesis between democracy and Communism as resulting in the "end of history," that is, the triumph of democracy as the only ideology for governing a modern society (Fukuyama, 1992). This approach was particularly congenial to Western policymakers trying to understand a non-Communist Russia. It encouraged Western governments to provide funds for "democracy promotion" in Russia and other post-Soviet states. However, the assumptions of such efforts were not matched by realities on the ground (Carothers, 1999). A consequence of initially viewing Russia as a democracy is that it can now be examined as a "failed" democracy rather than as an example of Presidents Yeltsin and Putin having succeeded in maintaining a new regime by whatever means they thought effective (Fish, 2005).

Prior to the political collapse of the Soviet Union, scholars of Latin America and Southern Europe had developed a framework for analyzing regime changes as transitions from authoritarian rule (see, e.g., O'Donnell and Schmitter, 1986). This led some "transitologists" to recommend the application of Latin American models of regime change to post-Communist countries (see Schmitter and Karl, 1994; Bunce, 1995, 2003; Gans-Morse, 2004). In the abstract, such an approach could be justified. However, it ignored the concrete differences between "pre-modern" developing countries and a Soviet system that had been "anti-modern" (Rose, 1999). Unlike the Soviet Union, Latin American societies had not had totalitarian regimes that destroyed the institutions of civil society and markets. Confirming Russia's difference from Latin countries, a multicontinental comparative study of governance placed the Russian Federation in the bottom group, below countries such as India, Mongolia, and China (Hyden, Court, and Mease, 2004: chapter 2).

Because the Soviet Union created a Communist bloc of countries, its breakup has encouraged the comparative analysis of post-Communist regimes, in which Russia is simply one among more than two dozen cases. However, the paths of post-Communist countries have diverged. Eight are now democratic regimes and market economies belonging to the European Union, and two more are hoping to join shortly, while most of the Soviet republics that became independent with the breakup of the USSR have become undemocratic regimes. A comparison of post-Communist regimes from Turkmenistan and Kazakhstan to Hungary and the Czech Republic demonstrates differences rather than similarities in their trajectories. On most political criteria, the Russian Federation usually falls somewhere between the new EU member-states and Central Asian regimes (see chapter 2).

Scholars who specialize in Russian history are inclined to emphasize distinctive and even unique features of Russia's past and to argue that these tend to determine the path that the new regime will follow. Continuities between past and present are readily cited from tsarist and Soviet practice. However, the proposition – Russian history matters – raises the question: which history? Is it the history of the despotic reforms of Ivan the Terrible or of the successes and failures of nineteenth-century tsars? How relevant is the Soviet experience under Stalin as compared to that of Brezhnev or Gorbachev? Theories of persisting Russian values and norms imply that it will take generations for transformation to be rid of the legacy of the past and make the new regime effective.

Whatever the influence of the past, transformation also emphasizes the necessity to understand what is new. Kremlinology, that is, the intensive analysis of the actions and entourage of the head of government, emphasizes what is currently topical. It is equally applicable to a regime headed by an elected president, a Communist Party general secretary, or a tsar. Such accounts illuminate the intentions of leaders and the enormity of the challenges confronting them during and after transformation (see, e.g., Brown, 1996; Breslauer, 2002; Aron, 2000). However, a book entitled *Yeltsin's Russia* (Shevtsova, 1999) tells us more about Boris Yeltsin than it does about the 140 million Russians whose opinions the president was meant to represent. Books that bill themselves as about "Putin's Russia" imply that Vladimir Putin's departure from the Kremlin will produce a different Russian regime.

Policymakers from abroad favor Kremlinology because it implies that who you know is what matters. The temptation facing foreigners is to take from encounters with Russia's leaders what they would like to believe, because it is consistent with their own domestic political goals. For example, during the height of the Stalinist purges, the leading British Fabians, Beatrice and Sidney Webb (1937) returned from a trip to Russia with a glowing impression of what they lauded as a new and attractive civilization. In President Yeltsin's tumultuous time in office in the 1990s, President Clinton's policy toward Russia was more about backing Boris than about backing democracy (Marsden, 2005). Intergovernmental bankers can be impressed by personalities too. After a trip to Russia in the early period of transformation, the managing director of the International Monetary Fund, Michel Camdessus (IMF, 1994), told a press conference that he had faith that Russia's economic transformation was succeeding, citing "very strong personal assurances" given by Prime Minister Viktor Chernomyrdin and "especially impressive" religious leaders who assured him that "Russia's traditional spiritual values would enable the Russian people not only to cope with the difficulties of the transition process but also to make it more human."

This book is distinctive in focusing on the development of popular support during the decade and a half since the launch of the Russian Federation in 1992. It thus rejects the emphasis on "instant" history that characterizes journalistic Kremlinology. It also rejects the historicist view that knowledge of Russia in the sixteenth, seventeenth, eighteenth, nineteenth, or twentieth century before transformation is sufficient to understand popular support for the Russian regime today. Nor does it assume that the circumstances of transformation in 1991 are sufficient to understand its aftermath. Drawing on the New Russia Barometer survey, which started in January 1992, the first month of the Russian Federation, this book tracks the dynamics of popular attitudes over a decade and a half. It can thus test empirically the extent to which popular attitudes developed in the Soviet era have persisted or have been eroded by the passage of time. Moreover, the effects of political inertia, that is, the slow but steady pressure that the passage of time can exert on attitudes toward a new regime, can also be tested.

No government without subjects

A regime cannot persist without the willing or unwilling support and compliance of those subject to its authority. Without this, laws and *diktats* are empty pronouncements. In the eighteenth century, Grigory Potemkin, an agent of Tsarina Catherine the Great, was said to have constructed artificial villages showing her subjects enjoying a happy rustic life, so that when the empress toured newly conquered territories in the south she would believe that the land was wealthy and her subjects content. In Soviet times the Ministry of Economic Planning created statistical Potemkinvilles, figures that gave the appearance of a dynamic and successful economy.

Up to a point, the totalitarian aspiration of Communist rulers for a public show of total support was successful: public opinion was kept private. A character in a novel by Vladimir Dudintsev described people as having two persons in one body, the "visible" person doing and saying what the state commanded while the "hidden" person did and thought as he or she liked within a close circle of trusted family and friends. At the top of an hour-glass society, the Soviet elite managed the direction of the regime, while at the bottom their subjects sought to minimize contact with rulers (Shlapentokh, 1989; Rose, 1995c).

Since the collapse of the Soviet Union, there has been an explosion of research applying different methods to understanding how Russians have responded to transformation and its aftermath. Anthropological observation of a small group of people details the particularities of personal networks. However, it is misleading to generalize to a whole society from the study of a single village or a single block of flats. Rational choice theories offer an abstract theory of individuals maximizing welfare, but because they are general they fail to indicate what happens when individuals are challenged to maximize their welfare amidst the uncertainties of transformation and its aftermath. Official statistics offer data about the income of the average Russian, but say nothing about differences between Russians who are well above and well below average.

To understand what ordinary Russians think about transformation, we need unofficial as well as official data. This book applies normal social science methods to create a unique resource for studying the attitudes of ordinary Russians, the New Russia Barometer (NRB). Richard Rose created the NRB in order to collect empirical information about how ordinary Russians were responding to the unprecedented treble transformation of their society. Each Barometer survey interviews a representative nationwide sample of approximately 2,000 persons in cities from Murmansk to Vladivostok and in rural areas with a total population four times that of Moscow (see Appendix A; www.abdn.ac.uk/cspp).

Interviewing a representative sample of Russians shows how misleading it is to assume that what the Kremlin says determines what ordinary people think (see Mickiewicz, 2006) or to make blanket statements about what "all" Russians think. Politics is about the expression of conflicting opinions about government, and every survey shows that Russians are *not* of one mind politically. Instead of reporting holistic descriptions of a Russian "mentality" or "soul," NRB surveys have introduced a sense of proportion: surveys show that some Russians are of one opinion about the regime, while others hold the opposite view; they thus identify both majority and minority attitudes in the population.

Although concerned with public opinion, this book is not about what Russians want: it is about what Russians make of what they get. Many surveys have projected Anglo-American assumptions onto the population of Russia: for example, asking questions about satisfaction with the way democracy is working in Russia assumes that the regime is a democracy. The NRB avoids this mistake. It asks whether people support the current regime as it actually is. Since it also asks whether people think the current regime tends to be democratic or a dictatorship, it can show whether support is more likely to come from those who see the regime as a dictatorship or as a democracy.

Analyzing regime support

Because transformation is the start of a process of fundamental change, evidence from a decade ago is insufficient for understanding what is happening today. Equally, it is misleading to assume that what Russians think today is unaffected by what they have learned since the start of transformation. Because there have been fourteen NRB surveys since the start of the new regime, this book can analyze the dynamics of regime support.

Chapter 1 sets out the central thesis of this book: an understanding of development of regime support can be achieved only by taking the importance of time into account. In a regime in a steady-state equilibrium, the political commitments that people learn early in life can persist indefinitely, because the behavior of political elites and institutions follows a predictable path. However, sooner or later, elites will be challenged to introduce changes. The response can restore the status quo ante or introduce reforms that leave the regime intact but its institutions altered. By contrast, when a dynamic challenge leads to disruption and political transformation, both subjects and the political elite are forced to adapt. Initially, people do so on the basis of experience of the past or hopes and fears about the future. With the passage of time, individuals can evaluate the regime on the basis of its actual political and economic performance. The experience of Russians since 1992 has been a crash course in political re-learning.

To understand the dynamics of regime change requires a typology of regimes that elites can supply. In place of the teleological determinism of the consolidation-of-democracy literature, chapter 2 classifies regimes according to two criteria: whether the rule of law is respected and whether elites are accountable to the populace through free elections. This typology not only distinguishes between democratic and autocratic regimes but also between three types of autocratic regimes – constitutional, plebiscitarian, and despotic. Democratic regimes have developed differently: some have evolved slowly while others have had false starts. Post-Communist regimes have differed in their dynamics too. The Russian Federation has become a plebiscitarian autocracy holding elections without the rule of law. By contrast, new regimes in Central and Eastern Europe have become democratic members of the European Union, while in Central Asia post-Soviet regimes have become lawless, unaccountable despotisms.

Centuries of autocratic rule in Russia have involved a changing supply of regimes. Chapter 3 charts the process of change from tsarist despotism to the totalitarian despotism of Stalin's Soviet Union and the subsequent relaxation but not abandonment of a Communist Party dictatorship unconstrained by the rule of law. This history gave Russians lots of experience of coexisting with despotism. Mikhail Gorbachev's attempt to reform that regime ended in its disruption and the creation of the Russian Federation. The early years were necessarily turbulent as political elites tried to create new political and economic institutions and a new state. Since Vladimir Putin became president in 2000, the direction of government has been much more orderly and controlled, a process that has emphasized the autocratic rather than the plebiscitarian character of the regime.

Even though Soviet restrictions on freedom of speech kept public opinion private, Russians have always held political values. Chapter 4 draws on New Russia Barometer surveys from the early 1990s to provide a bottom-up view of Russian society at the start of transformation. Notwithstanding (or perhaps because of) lifelong indoctrination, most Russians were indifferent to or negative about Marxism-Leninism and about socialism. The values endorsed by a majority were freedom, *glasnost* (that is, openness), the unity of Russia, and Christianity. But amidst the turbulence of transformation, Russians also had immediate mundane concerns, such as queuing for hours to get bread and waiting weeks or months to get paid at work. Skills learned in Soviet times helped Russians to cope with the turmoil of transformation. It also taught Russians to be patient. Even if President Yeltsin believed it was possible to jump all at once from a grey totalitarian past into a bright and civilized future, most Russians did not.

Traditional theories of Russian political culture assumed that there was a consensus of opinion about basic political values, and the Soviet regime insisted that its subjects demonstrate total support for the regime. There were no public opinion surveys to challenge this assertion. Chapter 5 presents evidence from fourteen years of NRB surveys showing that Russians consistently *dis*agree when asked whether they approve of the current regime – and the percentage giving support goes up and down. There is a similar pattern of disagreement about the endorsement of alternative regimes such as dictatorship by a strong man or the return of the Communist system. The chapter sets out a series of hypotheses about why Russians differ: the influence of social structure, politics, the economy, and the passage of time. It also explains the innovative statistical measures that will be used to take into account how the passage of time can alter the extent of regime support.

Whether Marxist or not, sociologists explain political attitudes as a reflection of differences in social structure. There are disagreements about whether class, education, gender, religion, or other differences have the biggest impact on political outlooks. However, sociological theories agree in stressing that political support is less a result of characteristics of a regime than of characteristics of its subjects. Chapter 6 tests the extent to which social differences actually do account for how Russians evaluate the new regime and its alternatives. It finds that social structure has little influence.

In an established democracy, political performance and values can influence whether citizens vote for or against the government of the day while leaving support for the regime unaltered. By contrast, in a new regime, the evaluation of political performance can determine which regime an individual supports. Having lived under two different regimes enables Russians to evaluate the new regime as better than its predecessor or as a lesser or greater evil. Regime support can also reflect whether institutions are seen as trusted or corrupt, and approval or disapproval of the president. Chapter 7 finds that the influence of political values and performance is substantial, and sometimes changes with the experience gained through the passage of time.

The impact of the new regime on the economy has been great; it has also been erratic. Governors cannot deny responsibility for the costs of transformation, nor can they be stopped from claiming credit when the economy starts to boom. Generalizations about the influence of economic conditions need to take the ups and downs of the economy into account. It is also important to ascertain whether movements in the national economy count most, or whether individuals place more weight on the economic conditions of their own household. The New Russia Barometer's carefully designed set of economic indicators analyzed in chapter 8 show not only how much the economy matters for regime support but also which economic conditions, national or household, are most important.

One asset that any regime has is the fact that it is there: the longer a new regime manages to survive, the more pressure this exerts on subjects to accept it and to expect it to survive well into the future. The passage of time can also lead people to abandon support for alternative regimes if they think there is no hope of regime change coming about. The results produced by innovative statistical analysis show that the passage of time has created a political equilibrium in which many who disapprove of the economic and political performance of the regime are nonetheless resigned to accepting it.

The transformation of Russia is a reminder that popular support for a regime is inherently open to shocks. The final chapter asks: what *could* disrupt the political equilibrium that has emerged in the Russian Federation? Generational and social changes can have little impact on the equilibrium of support in the foreseeable future. Russians see their society as facing risks, such as an HIV-AIDS epidemic or a civilian nuclear accident. However, this would undermine political support only if the regime were blamed for a disaster. The immediate challenge to the regime's equilibrium of support is the term-limits rule that will require President Putin to pass control of government to a successor in 2008 or amend or bend the constitution. The response of ordinary people to the president's actions will show the extent to which Russians continue to support whatever regime the political elite supplies.

1   Time matters: the dynamics of regime support

Time is the dimension in which ideas and institutions and beliefs evolve.

Douglass North

No decade in the history of politics, religion, technology, painting, poetry and what not ever contains its own explanation. In order to understand the religious events from 1520 to 1530 or the political events from 1900 to 1910 you must survey a period of much wider span. Not to do so is the hallmark of dilettantism.

Joseph A. Schumpeter

While the moment when a new regime is proclaimed can be a televised event, establishing support for a new regime is a process. It takes time for subjects to learn about the strengths and weaknesses of the new regime and time to unlearn much that was taken for granted in the old regime. Reducing the complicated process by which people come to terms with a change in regimes to a single point in time is, as Schumpeter emphasizes, a sign of refusing to take a change of regimes seriously. It is a luxury that cannot be afforded by people who live through transformation and its aftermath.

To understand the dynamics of regimes, it is essential to recognize the difference between changes *within* a regime and changes *between* regimes. The former happens with considerable frequency; for example, elections offer regular opportunities for changing the persons or party in charge of government. The Communist Party of the Soviet Union managed a series of changes in leadership without disrupting the regime. However, a change of leaders from Khrushchev to Brezhnev is not the same as a change from Gorbachev to Yeltsin. Changes between regimes are far less frequent than changes within a regime. In Russia the monarchy that was overthrown in 1917 had been in place for centuries, and the Soviet Union lasted for three generations before it dissolved and the Russian Federation was created.

A political equilibrium reflects a balance between the institutions supplied by the political elite and the support given in response by its citizens.

As Peyton Young (1998) emphasizes, "Equilibrium can be understood only within a dynamic framework that explains how it comes about (if in fact it does)." If changes offset each other by pushing with equal force in opposite directions, a steady-state equilibrium is created. For example, an individual may be unhappy with the economic consequences of transformation but appreciate gains in freedom. Similarly, the dislike of a new regime by older Russians may be offset by support from the younger generation.

Because an equilibrium is the product of the interaction of a variety of influences, a change in any element can alter the level of aggregate support. It is therefore misleading to regard a steady-state equilibrium as stable, as is frequently done in characterizing long-established democratic regimes. Stability implies that a regime is static and any stimulus to change may be interpreted as a sign of pathological instability. Young (1998) criticizes the tendency of neoclassical economics to concentrate exclusively on "the way the world looks once the dust has settled." He argues:

We need to recognize that the dust never really does settle – it keeps moving about, buffeted by random currents of air. This persistent buffeting by random forces turns out to be an essential ingredient in describing how things look on average over long periods of time.

A steady-state political equilibrium exists when the net effect of disparate influences produces limited short-term fluctuations in political support, while leaving the average level of regime support much the same over a long period of time. A thermostat is a familiar device for maintaining a steady-state equilibrium. Since outdoor temperatures change within a 24-hour period and even more between winter and summer, a room can keep a constant temperature only if the thermostat frequently makes adjustments in the flow of heat or air conditioning.

The dynamics of regime support involve moving between periods of a steady-state equilibrium and periods in which that equilibrium is challenged, because the determinants of support change in ways that cause the level of support to deviate from its average level. In response, political leaders will try to restore the previous level of support. For example, if an unpopular policy appears to be eroding regime support, it can be abandoned. Alternatively, the pressures for change may be so strong that leaders will respond by reforming an institution of the regime in order to make it work better and thereby attract more support. For example, in Britain, the granting of the right to vote to women was a major reform of franchise laws, but it left the institutions of representative government intact. To maintain support over a long period of time, governors must make dynamic changes that alter but do not disrupt core institutions of the regime.

The greater the challenge to reform, the greater the risk of the disruption of a seemingly solid regime. Mikhail Gorbachev's structural reforms in the Soviet regime rapidly escalated into a struggle between advocates of alternative regimes. The introduction of multicandidate elections at the level of Soviet republics enabled Boris Yeltsin to mobilize popular support for radical change in the Russian Republic, and this tactic was matched by party leaders in other Soviet republics. In the Baltic republics, there were mass demonstrations supporting secession from the Soviet Union. The outcome was the destruction of the Soviet regime.

While the mass of the population cannot participate in the determination of the institutions of a new regime, ordinary people cannot be excluded from their implementation. A new regime confronts both its subjects and its leaders with many uncertainties; support cannot be taken for granted. Transformation forces individuals to re-learn political values and beliefs, and there can be a contradiction between what people had previously learned and what the new regime requires. A new regime that is unable to secure the support, or at least the resigned acceptance, of most of its population is vulnerable to disruption and disappearance before it can achieve a steady-state equilibrium.

The passage of time alters the conditions in which individuals decide whether to support a regime. The next section of this chapter examines support in a steady-state regime, in which the influences on support are persisting and fluctuate little. The second section considers dynamic challenges, in which political institutions are reformed without this disrupting the regime. If the reforms are a response to popular demand, popular support may strengthen. The concluding section focuses on the consequences of a transformation in regimes: not only must elites learn how to govern with new institutions, but also ordinary citizens must re-learn how to respond to political authority. This is the situation that has confronted Russians since 1992 – and Russians have differed in how they have responded.

Maintaining support within a steady-state regime

David Easton's (1965, 1975) model of political support postulates that a steady-state regime is in equilibrium because of a continuing feedback between inputs of popular support and the responses of the regime's governors. Each adapts to the demands and behavior of the other. Consistent with liberal democratic theories of government by "we, the people," Easton makes citizens the prime mover in this feedback process;

governors are responsible for delivering what people want. However, the model is equally applicable to a regime in which governors make demands on subjects, and subjects are expected to deliver what governors want. Russians have had more experience of being subjects than citizens. Therefore, in subsequent chapters, our focus is on how subjects of a regime respond to elite actions.

Following an established path

By definition, the path of a steady-state regime tends to be predictable because it depends on what went before. Theories of path dependence postulate that a regime's institutions will remain in a steady-state equilibrium because, "Once a country has started down a track, the costs of reversal are very high. There will be other choice points, but the entrenchments of certain institutional arrangements obstruct an easy reversal of the initial choice" (Levi, 1997: 28).

The logic of path dependence is that time matters: the longer a new regime can survive, the more difficult it will be for advocates of alternative regimes to mobilize support for disrupting it and introducing an alternative regime (see Pierson, 2004: chapter 1). Whatever happens early in the life of a new regime "locks in" institutions and interests that fix a path that both elites and subjects then follow, because of the political costs of subsequently making major alterations. The costs are higher still for those who would like to transform the regime for, as long as it retains the loyalty of the security services, those who plot its replacement can be subject to harassment, imprisonment, or exile.

Changes in the leadership of a steady-state regime occur without threatening political support. In a monarchy, succession is determined by strict laws of inheritance. In a contemporary democracy, a change in leadership is determined by an election held according to rules that voters accept. However dissatisfied with the result of the election, losers accept the outcome. Contentious successions, such as the exit of Richard Nixon from office and the court-determined confirmation of George W. Bush's election victory in 2000, can be cited as showing that "the system works," that is, fundamental disputes about who governs can be resolved within the framework of a steady-state regime.

Theories of path dependence are more applicable to established Anglo-American societies from which they are derived than to Central and East European countries that have repeatedly had regimes disrupted. For example, in an established regime, a theory of path dependence can explain why many people maintain a lifelong identification with the political party they first voted for. However, in post-Communist countries, electors cannot develop an identification with parties in an unsteady state, as political elites frequently break up and form new parties (see Rose and Munro, 2003: chapter 3).

A lifetime of learning starts early

Whether and why an individual supports a regime can be modeled as the outcome of a lifetime-learning process. The lifetime-learning model summarizes the effect on regime support of the accumulation of old and new experiences (Mishler and Rose, 2002; Rose, Mishler, and Haerpfer, 1998: 117ff., 194ff.; Rose and McAllister, 1990). Logically, the political values and norms that an individual learns first are more important because they establish criteria by which the subsequent performance of the regime is evaluated.

In a steady-state regime that does not change fundamentally during an individual's lifetime, the values learned early in life can be used to justify support in old age too. The focus of childhood socialization is not directly political; however, children learn what is normal in their society, including support for the regime. In Russia, the totalitarian aspirations of the regime placed intense pressures on parents not to challenge the party line when socializing their children. Expressing anti-regime values in front of children who might repeat what they heard was a risk. Children were taught at school to inform on enemies of the state; Pavlik Morozov, a boy who denounced his father for suspected anti-regime attitudes, was held up as a model of how Soviet youth should behave (Kelly, 2005).

Adults are directly aware of politics, as the political and economic performance of a regime provides feedback to individuals. In an established democracy, citizens can give feedback to the political elite by their votes in a free, competitive election. In a steady-state regime that is not democratic, subjects can give feedback to governors by showing support enthusiastically or sullenly, or shirking when asked to comply with the regime's demands.

Individuals can give unthinking support to a regime if they have been socialized to regard it as the only way in which the country could be governed. It is only half correct to say that these values are what citizens want government to do, for what people want is often what they have learned is normal in their society. Theories of political culture explain support for a steady-state regime as a consequence of the transmission of political values from one generation to the next over a century or more. While the values and norms learned early in life may subsequently be modified in accordance with changing circumstances, this will not alter the underlying consensus of support for the regime (Eckstein, 1988).

Different motives for supporting a regime

Normative theories of political support postulate that citizens are committed to a regime because it is legitimate, that is, the political elite governs in accordance with constitutional laws. A belief in the normative superiority of constitutional laws can lead individuals to comply with public policies that they think are wrong or against their interests. Normative motives are both an effective and an efficient way to maintain support for a steady-state regime, as long as governors act within the bounds of laws and popular expectations.

Rational choice theories postulate that people will support a regime if they calculate that it pays to do so. The payoff may be collective, as in the argument that a regime that maintains peace and a clean environment will gain support. The payoff may be psychological, in that people may regard their regime as a cause for national pride. The payoff may also be material: government policies can be credited with promoting economic growth and can finance a high level of pensions, health care, and education. In different periods, Soviet rulers appealed with each of these arguments. Even if subjects calculate that it does not pay to support the current regime, they may nonetheless give it resigned acceptance if they believe that there is no alternative.

A utilitarian calculus implies that a regime's steady state will be intermittently vulnerable to dynamic fluctuations, since the more frequently individuals recalculate whether it pays to support the regime the greater the chance that at some point they will decide it doesn't pay to do so and turn to disruptive behavior. This theory was often advanced by Western critics of moving rapidly to the market after the collapse of Communism, because doing so was likely to reduce benefits provided by the previous regime (see Przeworski, 1991).

The logic of rational choice can justify supporting an unsatisfactory regime when the alternative is perceived as a greater evil. Winston Churchill (1947) used this logic to defend democracy, with all its imperfections and faults, on the grounds that it had fewer shortcomings than all other forms of government that had ever been tried. The lesser-evil approach was very relevant in the Soviet Union when the Germany army invaded in 1941. Soviet subjects who did not support the Stalinist regime nonetheless fought to defend it when the alternative was Nazi rule.

Fear is the ultimate inducement that a regime can use to compel individuals to give a public show of support. If individuals calculate that if they do not show support for the regime they might lose their job, be imprisoned, or otherwise suffer, a regime does not need to make a continuing show of force in order to instill fear in its subjects. Intermittent and exemplary punishments demonstrate that sanctions for stepping out of line politically are at hand, and uncertainty about whether they will be invoked encourages caution among would-be political dissidents. While the use of terror in the Soviet Union was greatly reduced following the death of Stalin, this did not erase the knowledge of what could happen to those who did not show support for the regime.

The lifetime-learning model can explain why some individuals support a new regime while others do not. Whether an individual supports the current regime or an alternative depends on the priority given to different experiences and the extent to which they combine in ways that are mutually reinforcing or in conflict. In a statistical analysis, the combination of plus and minus signs is evidence of crosscutting political, economic, and social pressures. Since individuals differ in their values and experience, we should not expect every subject to respond alike to a new regime. If all the influences counterbalance one another, a steady state can remain steady indefinitely, as the Soviet regime was for decades after the death of Stalin. But indefinite maintenance of support is not a guarantee that it has reached the end of history.

Dynamic challenges

Sooner or later, an abrupt and often unexpected challenge punctuates a steady-state equilibrium (see Baumgartner and Jones, 1993: chapter 1). William Riker (1980: 443) has gone so far as to assert that "Disequilibrium, or the potential that the status quo be upset, is the characteristic feature of politics" (see also Dalton, 2004). However, this proposition is misleading insofar as it treats any and every potential challenge as threatening the disruption of a regime. Politicians share Riker's tendency to magnify greatly the fluctuations that occur even in a regime in a steady-state equilibrium. A rise of 2 percent in inflation or unemployment rates is a stimulus to alter economic policy, but not a sign of a crisis in support for a regime.

Alternative responses

Dynamic challenges are those so strong that they cannot be met by routine responses that keep support fluctuating in a normal way. Governors can respond with measures intended to achieve a restoration of the regime as it was before; they can offer reforms that are meant to alter the regime a bit while keeping support in a steady state; or the response can unintentionally lead to the disruption of the regime.

In an undemocratic regime, an elite that sees no cause for dissatisfaction with the status quo can react to public challenges by using coercion to restore a steady state in which subjects see they have no alternative but to go along with the powers that be. In East Germany, Poland, Hungary, and Czechoslovakia between 1953 and 1968, leaders of Communist systems successfully conserved their one-party states by forcefully suppressing anti-regime demonstrations.

In democratic regimes, the result of a challenge may be reform or a reversion to the status quo. In Britain the two-party system of competition between the Labour and Conservative parties was challenged in 1974 and after by much-increased popular support for the Liberals and the Social Democrats. The result has been the development of a three-party system, in which electoral competition is maintained, but not as before. By contrast, in the United States third-party presidential candidates have repeatedly won a significant number of votes, but Republicans and Democrats have responded in ways that have made such challenges singular events, and elections have reverted to what went before: two-party competition.

Political protests from subjects occasionally create pressures that threaten disruption if they are not met. In the United States, the 1954 anti-segregation decision of the United States Supreme Court was resisted by political leaders who wanted to maintain white supremacy in the Deep South. Black civil rights groups organized protests demanding implementation of the decision, and the white powerholders mobilized police and private intimidation in opposition. After hesitation, the White House and Congress passed the Voting Rights Act of 1965 guaranteeing Southern blacks the right to vote. The outcome was the dynamic reform of United States political institutions. Southern blacks who had been socialized to give resigned acceptance to a lilywhite regime quickly demonstrated their ability to contest elections, and white politicians had to re-learn how to seek votes under new rules.

Paradoxically, the longer a regime has maintained its existence, the greater are pressures for a dynamic change in the structure of the regime. The history of a centuries-old regime such as the English parliamentary system is a sequence of developments in which a steady-state regime is challenged to introduce structural reforms as a necessary condition of restoring support. It has maintained a monarchy and both an unelected and an elected chamber of parliament for many centuries, while altering how the country is governed. Reforms have gained support from emerging groups in society without losing traditional supporters.

The alternative to going back and forth between a steady-state regime and reform is a gross disequilibrium, when a regime's leaders do not respond constructively to challenges. The mobilization of tens of thousands of East Germans in demonstrations in early autumn 1989 is an example of a dynamic challenge going "over the top" and leading to transformation. Initially, the demonstrators demanded that the German Democratic Republic (GDR), a rigid one-party Communist regime, recognize the views of the people. While East German leaders were debating whether to appease or crush the demonstrators, demonstrators began demanding German reunification. Within weeks the dynamic had built up to the point that it had brought down the Berlin Wall and the GDR.

Political re-learning in a new regime

Disruption can come from multiple sources: intense conflict within the political elite; resigned acceptance unexpectedly turning to mass protest; pressures from foreign governments; or from the interaction of all of these. Whatever the sources, the result is a process of transformation that leads to a political void that only a new regime can fill. In a steady-state regime, there is a familiar path from the past to the present; however, disruption blows up the bridge that connects the two. Whatever nostalgia there may be for the past (see Munro, 2006), there is no going back to the regime as it was before.

Societies cannot live forever in a state of turbulence. The leaders of a new regime require some political support to be effective; otherwise, they risk lawlessness verging on anarchy. If a new regime cannot collect taxes, it may print money, as Russia did in the early 1990s, but this will create a new challenge to the regime. In an era of big government, subjects depend upon a new regime to continue providing such public services as water, rubbish collection, and electricity, and on welfare services such as education, health care, and social security. Failure to achieve order can make a new regime stillborn.

Elites search for a new path

The collapse of a regime is stark evidence that something was wrong with the way the country had been ruled. However, it does not mean that there is agreement about what was wrong. Even if there is agreement about faults of the old regime, this is insufficient to create a consensus in favor of what should replace it. Whatever choice is made, there is the risk that competition between alternatives will lead to the breakdown of the existing order.

To say that the leaders of a new regime choose between a democratic or autocratic system grossly overstates the freedom of choice of new leaders.

As Gerard Alexander (2002: 41) emphasizes, "The problematic element is not actors' basic preferences but their beliefs about regime alternatives," that is, about what is politically possible and what is politically impossible. In the unprecedented circumstances of the collapse of Communist regimes, there was much confusion about what was and what was not possible.

The first constraint is the legacy of the past. Even though founders of a new regime may want to reject it, they cannot undo what went before. Nor can they ignore the problems that their predecessors left behind. The legacy of the old regime is usually a mixed blessing. Established bureaucrats who can maintain major public services are an asset in meeting everyday responsibilities of the new regime, but a liability insofar as they obstruct institutional change. What is absent in a legacy can also be a problem. Russia lacked the "usable democratic past" that was an asset in building democracy in post-1945 Germany (Linz and Stepan, 1996: 452).

A distinctive feature of the Soviet legacy was a high level of corruption and a bureaucratic readiness to disregard the legal rights and entitlements of subjects. While the physical infrastructure of a modern economy remained, the economic infrastructure had been grossly distorted by the priorities imposed in the Soviet era. Because the economy had been governed by bureaucratic decisions rather than the market, initially factories could neither satisfy domestic demand nor manufacture goods for export. In addition, the new Russian regime had to repay substantial foreign debts incurred under Gorbachev. It took time, and a big boost in world oil prices, before the new regime could exploit Russia's legacy of natural and energy resources for political and economic advantage.

Whereas political elites in a regime in equilibrium can draw on past and current experience to predict the future, in the aftermath of transformation the only certain prediction is that the future will not be the same as the past. Because of a lack of experience in competitive elections, many of the political parties launched in the first elections in Russia and Eastern Europe quickly disappeared because of lack of popular support – and that included parties backed by President Yeltsin (Rose and Munro, 2003: chapter 5).

A second constraint is shortage of time and of people qualified to make choices about a new regime, because of the urgency of the need to fill the void in political authority. The suppression of opposition parties and the abruptness with which transformation came about meant that politicians were unprepared for transformation. Even where there were preparations for the reform of the one-party state, plans for a post-Communist regime could not be implemented until after it was clear that they would not be crushed once again by Soviet troops. Within the republics of the Soviet Union, only after Gorbachev was visibly losing control of the reform process and security services could elites begin to prepare for the breakup of the Soviet Union and the creation of a new regime.

Competitive elections were needed to blow away the old regime and give legitimacy to new leaders. However, an election could not be held until decisions were taken about the rules for conducting it and the powers that the election winners would have. Difficulties in securing agreement meant that elections were often held for a provisional government, postponing until later the problem of hammering out a constitution. In Czechoslovakia the upshot of its first free election was not a new constitution, but a confrontation between Czech and Slovak parties and the "velvet divorce" creating two new states.

In Russia the creation of the federation occurred with seeming ease but without agreement among elites. By virtue of being elected president of the Russian Republic in the final months of the Soviet Union, Boris Yeltsin remained president of the new regime. However, he confronted a Congress of People's Deputies that had been elected in multicandidate elections in 1990. The result was two years of struggle between the president and the Congress about where power rested in the new federation. The dispute was resolved only in a gun battle in which the president's troops defeated elected representatives barricaded in the Congress building.

Because a new regime is an unsteady state existing amidst great uncertainties, governors have no alternative but to make decisions. Every decision taken about a particular institution – for example, whether to have a presidential or a parliamentary regime or a system that mixes both – has a knock-on effect on other decisions. However, leaders of a new regime have no basis for predicting how choices made about institutions would interact with each other. An analysis of the choices facing Russia's leaders concluded that there were literally thousands of ways in which the institutions of a new regime could influence each other (Lynch, 2005: 173). In these circumstances, leaders could learn how to make the new regime survive only by acting, observing feedback, and learning from this process of trial and error.

In most post-Communist countries of Europe, politicians learned that making effective policies in a new regime is different from making speeches against the old one. For example, in three successive Polish elections the Solidarity protest leader Lech Walesa found his share of the popular vote falling from 75 percent to 48 percent and then to 1 percent. He was twice defeated by an ex-Communist apparatchik who was more adept at learning how to behave in the new regime. The process of learning from experience marked the end of what a Hungarian sociologist has called the "golden age of innocence and simplicity," because sustaining a new regime "is a much more difficult and complex task than [the new leaders] had imagined in the years and decades of despair and servitude" (Hankiss, 1990: 7).

Differential responses by subjects

The shock of transformation undermines old beliefs about what can be taken for granted. The introduction of a new regime as part of the treble transformation of the economy and the boundaries of the state forces people to think afresh about what government demands and whether they should support it. The decisions reached are likely to reflect political, economic, and social differences within society.

Differences in social structure, starting with age, can differentiate how people respond to a new regime. Older subjects have spent most of a long life giving positive or resigned support to the system they know best. By contrast, younger adults were socialized when uncertainties about the old regime were already evident, thus reducing attachment to what their elders took for granted. By the start of Vladimir Putin's second term, the youngest cohort of Russians had commenced political socialization in the new regime. The gains and pains of resocialization will vary depending on whether a person grew up in a home that benefited or suffered from the old system, for example, whether a parent was a party activist, a dissident, or just an ordinary subject. Differences in education should also influence regime support, since more-educated people should be better able to understand the challenges of transformation than less-educated people.

Political values and the evaluation of political performance also differentiate how citizens react to their new regime. The values that influence regime support can be democratic, Communist, or nationalist. In Central and Eastern Europe, nationalist values have favored new regimes that represent the rejection of Moscow's domination. However, in Russia the new regime is associated with the collapse of a Soviet ideal with which some Russians identified. Because every subject of a new regime has lived under at least one other political system, this experience enables people to evaluate the current regime as better, worse, or no different from the old regime. Individuals who share values can nonetheless differ in their political priorities. Russians who value freedom more than order should be more inclined to support a post-Communist regime, while those who give priority to order may reject the disorderliness inherent in a newly launched regime.

The transformation from a command to a market economy has forced Russians to re-learn everyday activities such as working and shopping. The costs of transformation, such as inflation and contraction of the economy, came before the benefits of economic growth and more consumer goods. At any given point in time, the distribution of costs and benefits is unequal between individuals. Even in the worst times of recession, some people make more money than others, and in boom times some are unemployed. In the course of time, the volatility of the economy can lead to individuals being both losers and winners, thus inducing changes in their support for the new regime.

The passage of time results in political re-learning, as experiences continuously accumulate. In time, subjects learn which of their initial expectations are met by the performance of the "real existing regime" under which they now live – and which are not. The longer a new regime persists, the more information subjects have about its political and economic performance. With the passage of time, the old regime and old ways of earning a living become more distant and less relevant. An individual who initially wanted the old regime to return can learn that this is unlikely to happen and become resigned to accepting the new regime. Through the feedback between elite initiatives and mass experience, attitudes and values supportive of the new system can gradually replace what was learned under the old one.

A new regime achieves an equilibrium of support when, as Juan Linz (1990: 156) puts it, both governors and governed accept it is "the only game in town." If this occurs, a new regime becomes path dependent – but the path is not the same as before and, because of the re-learning that individuals have experienced, motives for supporting it are unlikely to be the same.

2 The supply of regimes: democratic and autocratic

> Political systems pose a problem of choice: that choice presupposes a choice between better and worse, not between good and true or bad and false in the absolute sense.
>
> Giovanni Sartori

In hindsight, the choice of institutions for an established regime may appear inevitable, but when a new regime is being created it is anything but. The institutions of democracies take many different forms, and member-states of the United Nations demonstrate that there are many forms of undemocratic rule too. Moreover, political elites who bargain about what the new regime ought to be can disagree about what makes a political system better or worse. A despotic or plebiscitarian regime is no more a failed democracy than a democracy is a failed despotism. Each is a distinctive type.

The mass of citizens do not choose the regime that elites supply. Subjects are asked to accept or reject a bundle of institutions as a whole. If a referendum is held, there is no opportunity to pick and choose between the parts that constitute the new regime. The only choice is between voting for it or against it. Even if the ballot is held under conditions that are free and fair, the choice is hardly balanced if it is between endorsing institutions that have filled the void created by transformation or maintaining an uncertain and provisional authority.

To describe a new regime as in transition does not tell us where it is coming from or where it is heading. The introduction of competitive elections by new regimes on many continents has encouraged the analysis of transition as a process of democratization. Development has been seen as progress from the unsteady early phase of transformation to the institutionalization of necessary features of governance and ultimately the consolidation of a steady-state democratic regime. However, this model fails to capture the different directions in which new regimes have been going (Diamond, 1999; Carothers, 1999).

A decade and a half after the collapse of the Soviet Union, it is no longer sufficient to describe successor regimes as post-Communist. While factually correct, such a statement raises the question: what kinds of regimes now govern these states? Given their diverse political histories and circumstances, how similar or different are they from each other – and from Western ideas of a democratic political system?

The regimes that have filled the void created by the collapse of Communism differ greatly. The personalistic dictatorship of Turkmenistan has nothing in common with the multiparty government of Estonia except that both were created as successor states of the Soviet Union. Regimes of Central and Eastern Europe have been endorsed as democratic by the European Union, while post-Soviet regimes in countries such as Belarus and Uzbekistan have received international recognition as undemocratic. To understand the dynamics of two dozen different post-Communist regimes, of which Russia is but one example, we must examine how they differ from each other as well as how similar or different they are from Western ideas of democratic government.

The first task in comparing regimes is to distinguish between undemocratic types as well as between democratic and undemocratic regimes. The next section sets out two defining attributes: whether political elites are accountable to the rule of law and whether the mass of the population can participate in the choice of governors. These distinctions are used to create a fourfold typology of regimes. A majority of regimes in the world today are either plebiscitarian or despotic autocracies rather than being democratic. The third section contrasts different ways of developing democratic regimes in Europe with the paths of post-Soviet regimes.

Defining regimes in two dimensions

Since a political equilibrium involves a relationship between governors and governed, it is appropriate to define regimes by characteristics of both groups. Conventionally, regimes are classified by the extent to which the mass of the population can participate in elections. It is also important to differentiate regimes by the extent to which the actions of political elites are bound by the rule of law, for a lawless regime can manipulate elections in ways that are neither free nor fair, and it can act arbitrarily if it is not accountable to the courts.

Rule of law: binding or weak

The rule of law is central in creating and maintaining accountability. If governors disregard constitutional constraints or act outside the law, in a rule-of-law regime the courts can hold governors accountable. This is a necessary condition for a modern state, because laws bind bureaucrats delivering public services to carry out decisions taken by policymakers. As long as bureaucrats follow the law, there is accountability within government. If public officials dispense public services according to their personal discretion, governors are not in control of government. In many parts of the world, including successor states of the Soviet Union, the accountability to the law of bureaucrats and national leaders cannot be taken for granted.

The rule of law is also a necessary condition for citizens to hold governors accountable through free and fair elections. If election laws are interpreted to favor the government of the day, or if opposition candidates are intimidated and votes fraudulently totaled, the winners of an election will be chosen by governors rather than by the electorate. Only if winners of an election accept the constraints of the law will losers be protected from the abuse of governmental power. Even if elections are competitive, voting one set of governors out of office in a corrupt regime and replacing them with equally corrupt successors will produce no more than a rotation of rascals.

Governance according to the rule of law developed in Europe centuries before regimes claimed to be democratic (Cohen, 1985; Dyson, 1980; Finer, 1997: 71ff.). A state in which officials act in accordance with the rule of law is a *Rechtsstaat*. Courts can strike down actions of governors that violate the law. Actions of governors are predictable because they are in accordance with established rules. Individuals know what their rights are and what they are not; so too do those who enforce laws. The eighteenth-century Prussian regime pioneered the *Rechtsstaat*, that is, administration according to the law. While these governors were not accountable to a mass electorate, they were accountable to the courts. The practice of Russia's tsars was different.

Regimes differ in the extent to which governors are accountable to the rule of law or arbitrarily ignore restrictions on their actions. However, political science has flourished most in societies in which the rule of law existed before universal suffrage. Thus, the rule of law is usually taken for granted rather than stipulated as a necessary condition of a democratic regime. Definitions of democracy concentrate on the extent of popular participation, electoral competition, and freedom of expression (see Munck and Verkuilen, 2002). However, the rule of law cannot be taken for granted in many countries, including post-Communist regimes. Holding elections in a regime in which the rule of law is frequently breached is an exercise in "democratization backwards" (Rose and Shin, 2001).

More or less participation

Participation in elections can be restricted to a select few. When most people are excluded from the right to vote, they are subjects of a regime rather than citizens. Citizens have a right to participate in the choice of government but subjects do not. Both subjects and citizens are expected to support whatever regime political elites supply.

In the nineteenth century, European regimes denied the right to vote to the majority of both men and women. In England, for example, most men did not become eligible to vote until 1884, and universal suffrage on equal terms for men and women was not achieved until 1928. In the United States, racial restrictions were not effectively outlawed until 1965. Moreover, representatives were often elected to parliaments that had no power to hold the government of the day accountable, as was the case in pre-1914 Germany, or to parliaments in which non-elected members, such as the House of Lords in England, had substantial power (Seymour and Frary, 1918; Rokkan, 1970).

Initially, regimes established in Central and Eastern Europe following the First World War held competitive elections in which most adults were eligible to vote. Elections tended to produce a great multiplicity of parties, reflecting the turbulence of new regimes and the multiethnic composition of many societies. Even when there was a broadly based franchise, the absence of a secret ballot meant that rural tenants could be intimidated by their landlords, as happened in Hungary (Sternberger and Vogel, 1969). By the mid-1930s, in every country in the region except Czechoslovakia, elections were suspended or were unfairly manipulated by the government. Immediately after the end of the Second World War, multiparty elections were held in many Central and East European countries. However, they led to coalition governments. Backed by the presence of Soviet troops, Communist parties quickly seized control and created party-states with unfree elections (Furtak, 1990).

In Russia, a Constituent Assembly was elected by universal suffrage immediately after the 1917 revolution. Bolshevik candidates won about a quarter of the votes, but Red Guards soon used physical force to take over the assembly on their behalf (Radkey, 1950). Marxist-Leninist doctrine was ambivalent about elections (Pravda, 1978). Communist practice favored the mass mobilization of the population but rejected the idea that voters should have a choice. Thus, at polling stations, an individual had the alternative of dropping an unmarked ballot in a box, which was a sign of endorsing the official Communist candidate or calling attention to himself or herself by marking a ballot in opposition to the party's choice. Very few did the latter. Party officials responsible for turnout routinely falsified vote counts, assuming that everyone on the electoral register had voted for the party (cf. Brunner, 1990).

Differentiating regimes that elites supply

Conventionally, political scientists define some regimes by what they are, democratic, and others by what they are not, undemocratic. This one-dimensional approach fails to give any positive information about regimes that are not democratic; all are lumped together in a residual category (for an example, see Przeworski, et al., 1996). Such treatment of a majority of the world's past and present regimes imposes a false uniformity on systems of government as different as those of King George III of England, Stalin's Soviet Union, and contemporary Haiti. While a one-dimensional scale may facilitate statistical analysis, it is inadequate for dynamic analysis, because it fails to account for differences in the legacies that new regimes receive from their predecessors (cf. Linz, 2000; Brooker, 2000). It also fails to identify different directions in which new regimes can develop. While regimes can differ in being relatively steady or subject to a degree of challenge, they differ even more in whether they are democratic or autocratic.

Alternative forms of regimes

Defining regimes in terms of the rule of law and electoral participation produces a two-dimensional classification. Regimes can be characterized as autocratic or accountable, according to the extent to which governors are constrained by constitutional rules or claim power to act without regard to lawful constraints. Regimes can be characterized as democratic or oligarchic depending on whether all adults or only a few can participate in elections. Regimes may both adhere to the rule of law and offer free elections; they may have one of these characteristics but not the other; or neither. Combining these two sets of attributes identifies four different ideal-type regimes: accountable democracies, constitutional oligarchies, plebiscitarian autocracies and despotic autocracies (Figure 2.1).

In a *despotic autocracy*, power is exercised arbitrarily at the will of the few, and little attention is given to legitimating that power through unfair or unfree elections. Decisions by rulers can override any provision of the constitution, and the judicial system does not constrain governors. The scope of a despot's willfulness can be extended through household guards, for example, the *oprichniki* of Ivan the Terrible. Administrators who serve a despotic regime are not bureaucrats, but officials with substantial discretion to exploit the powers of their office to enrich themselves and create

Figure 2.1 *ALTERNATIVE FORMS OF REGIME*

PARTICIPATION	RULE OF LAW	
	Arbitrary	Binding
Restricted	Despotic autocracy	Constitutional oligarchy
Universal suffrage	Plebiscitarian autocracy	Accountable democracy

a network of political clients. The absence of rule-bound behavior creates insecurity among those who benefit from serving the despot, since their position can be revoked at the will of a ruler suspicious that his (it is rarely her) underlings are threatening the despot's position. Insecurity, suspicion, and plots are all familiar features of Russian history.

As long as the scope of a despot's arbitrary power was limited to face-to-face communication with courtiers and trustworthy administrators, the impact on subjects was limited. The twentieth century saw the creation of totalitarian regimes that went beyond traditional despotism, because demands on subjects were unlimited (Linz, 2000). Despotic regimes recognize some areas of social life as outside the concern of the state; a totalitarian regime wants to control the totality of the lives of its subjects. A totalitarian regime is organized, systematic, and pervasive in its efforts to mobilize subjects to act as it commands. It creates a party to exercise top-down control of civil society institutions such as universities, churches, the media, business, and trade unions and uses modern technology to spread its ideology and "crowd out" the idea that there is any alternative to the powers that be. In the Soviet Union, the Communist Party was the central mobilizational weapon; in Hitler's Germany it was the Nazi Party. Both regimes created internal security services to spy on their subjects and coerce those deemed enemies of the regime. The Soviet regime shows that a despotic regime can maintain a steady-state equilibrium for more than a generation; the totalitarian regime of North Korea, established in 1948, is older than two-thirds of the regimes governing member-states of the European Union.

In a *plebiscitarian autocracy*, there are elections with mass participation and a degree of competition, but governors are not accountable to the rule of law. Nor are governors accountable to the electorate, for a lawless regime can organize elections that are unfree and unfair. In the cynical words of a character in a play by Bertholt Brecht, if too many votes are cast against it, "the government can dissolve the people and elect another."

The French Revolution's idea of government by the will of the people led both Napoleon I and Napoleon III to hold plebiscites in which questions formulated by the emperors were the subject of a popular vote – and the ballots were administered so that the emperor's will was sure to be endorsed (Morel, 1996: 68ff.). Plebiscitarian autocracies are today familiar in Latin American countries, where they are sometimes labeled delegative democracies, since the winner of an election claims the right to act without regard to constitutional constraints (O'Donnell, 1994). In Argentina, for example, Juan Perón used popular election as president to establish personal rather than lawful rule. After Carlos Menem was elected with the personalistic slogan *siganme* (follow me), he led a government that was corrupt and murderously repressive. A plebiscitarian regime can persist indefinitely, it may be a staging post toward a despotic regime, or on occasion the votes of the plebs defeat the candidates of the government (Schedler, 2006), as in the so-called Orange Revolution in Ukraine in 2004.

In a *constitutional oligarchy*, the actions of governors are not constrained by elections, but they are constrained by the rule of law. Courts have sufficient independence to void actions of governors inconsistent with the law and to protect subjects if the regime resorts to unlawful intimidation. Although the behavior of the regime may not be popular, it is predictable. For example, laws and regulations about censorship and freedom of association set out what people are free to do as well as what they are not free to do. Laws confer a degree of autonomy on civil society institutions such as universities, business corporations, and the media. There can be an assembly of oligarchs, consisting of the nobility, rich landowners, religious leaders, and/or representatives of an unrepresentative electorate. It can criticize or obstruct government measures and may even hold the government accountable.

In Britain and Scandinavia, democracies have evolved from early nineteenth-century constitutional oligarchies. Pre-1914 Germany was a constitutional oligarchy too, but did not survive defeat in the First World War. The short-lived Weimar Republic was replaced by a despotic regime under Adolf Hitler because it could not balance pressures from anti-democratic forces of the right and left. In the contemporary world, Singapore is an example of a constitutional regime that combines adherence to the rule of law with restrictions on accountability to its subjects.

In an *accountable democracy*, governors not only are chosen through elections in which the mass of the population can vote, but also are accountable to the rule of law. This definition of democracy emphasizes free and fair elections, consistent with Joseph Schumpeter's (1952:

271ff.) classic definition of democracy as a system in which political elites supply parties that voters can choose between. It adds the requirement that leaders are accountable not only to the electorate but also to the courts.

Making the rule of law a defining characteristic of democracy avoids what Terry Lynn Karl (2000: 95) has called "the fallacy of electoralism," which "privileges elections over all other dimensions of democracy." It is recognized that all elections are not the same. Elections in which the winning party or presidential candidate receives 99 percent of the vote are not competitive, and elections in which voters are intimidated and the regime's officials fraudulently manipulate the counting of ballots are not fair (cf. Hermet, Rouquié, and Rose, 1978; Boda, 2005). Countries that hold unfree or unfair elections are not defective democracies, but plebiscitarian autocracies.

Most regimes autocratic

The existence of multiple types of regimes makes it misleading to discuss the dynamics of post-Communist transformation in terms of a common origin, let alone a common goal, whether democracy or autocracy. Political transformation can lead toward or away from a regime with free elections and constrained by the rule of law. It can also result in the substitution of one despotism for another, or a plebiscitarian regime can become despotic when its elite no longer wants to risk holding multiparty elections. The Middle East offers striking examples of regime change without democratization. Posusney (2004: 135) characterizes the region as having a "stubbornly undemocratic" history of "resilient authoritarianism."

To determine the number of regimes in each category of the typology in Figure 2.1 requires measures of free and fair elections and of the rule of law. A global evaluation of elections is provided by an international non-governmental organization (NGO), Freedom House (www.freedomhouse.org). While 64 percent of regimes hold elections with competing candidates and all adults eligible to participate, dozens of countries impose restrictions on civil liberties and political rights that make their ballots unfree, unfair, or both. Taking this into account reduces to less than half the proportion of the world's regimes that today offer meaningful participation in elections.

Transparency International (TI) is an international NGO that has pioneered an index focused on the extent to which officials conform to the rule of law or are corrupt when administering public policies. Its Perception of Corruption Index (PCI) is compiled from expert assessments of bribery and favoritism in government contracts worth millions and of the extraction of small sums to get things done locally. Since there is a strong correlation between a high level of corruption in government and political repression, especially in the most corrupt countries, the PCI can be used as a proxy indicator for adherence to the rule of law.

Corruption is evaluated on a scale ranging from 1 for a regime that is totally corrupt to 10 for a regime completely untainted by corruption (www.transparency.org). In principle, every regime could be deemed law-abiding; however, this is not the case. There are big variations in the degree to which the regimes included in the PCI are honest or corrupt. Since the European Union requires its members to adhere to the rule of law, it offers a benchmark for labeling regimes as relatively honest or relatively corrupt. Among EU member-states, Poland ranks lowest, with a rating of 3.4, just above the median country in the overall global rating. Its rating is used here to divide regimes into those tending to respect the rule of law and those that are most corrupt.

Together, despotic and plebiscitarian autocracies constitute a majority of regimes in the world today and have more than half the world's population. These regimes differ between personalistic dictatorships, party-states, and military rule but they have in common a lack of respect for the rule of law. Regimes that respect the rule of law as well as holding free elections are a minority in the world today (Figure 2.2).

Despotic autocracies, 26 percent of the total, are unconstrained by the rule of law as well as avoiding free elections. This type of regime can be found on most continents, ranging from Saudi Arabia to Angola, Pakistan, China, and Haiti. Soviet successor states such as Tajikistan and Turkmenistan are aptly characterized as despotisms too.

More than a quarter of regimes are plebiscitarian autocracies, which hold competitive elections but in which the rule of law is often not observed. This category includes such countries as Indonesia and the Philippines, where control of the government can change hands but there is also a high level of corruption. Post-Soviet regimes such as Ukraine have been in this category, because election outcomes have not overcome persisting departures from the rule of law.

Only 8 percent of regimes are today constitutional oligarchies, in which public officials act in accordance with national laws, but these national laws do not make the government accountable to the electorate. Singapore is the best-known example, for its rulers boast of "good" (that is, honest) government and its TI rating is higher than that of the United States and most European Union member-states. However, Singapore's leaders reject democratic government as an Anglo-American idea inconsistent with Singapore's definition of Asian values (cf. Zakaria, 1994). Hong Kong is another Asian regime that is rated as more honest

Figure 2.2 *GLOBAL OVERVIEW OF REGIME TYPES*

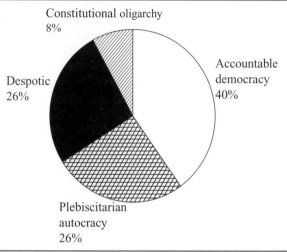

Constitutional oligarchy
8%

Accountable
democracy
40%

Despotic
26%

Plebiscitarian
autocracy
26%

Source: A total of 157 countries rated by both Freedom House (FH),
Freedom in the World 2006, www.freedomhouse.org, and Transparency
International (TI), *Perception of Corruption Index 2005*,
www.transparency.org/cpi/2005/cpi2005_infocus.html.

Accountable democracy: FH score 1 to 4 and TI score of 3.4 or higher;
constitutional oligarchy: FH score of 4.5 to 7 and TI score of 3.4 or higher;
plebiscitarian autocracy: FH score of 1 to 4 and TI score below 3.4;
despotism: FH score of 4.5 to 7 and TI score below 3.4.

than the United States, but its government is accountable to a Communist government in Beijing rather than to the Hong Kong electorate.

Among the 40 percent of regimes that are democratic today, those that
have achieved this state by slow evolution over a century or more are
in a minority. Most democratic regimes have become so in the past two
decades. In addition to new regimes in Central and Eastern Europe, new
democracies can be found in Africa, Asia, and Latin America.

Contrasting dynamics of regimes

While leaders of every new regime want to develop popular support,
this goal has been pursued in very different ways. Differences between
regimes today reflect contrasting dynamics. The oldest democracies have

gradually evolved from constitutional oligarchies. By contrast, some countries made a false start: an early attempt at democratization was abandoned in favor of autocratic rule before a subsequent attempt was successful. In addition, democratic regimes have recently emerged in some countries with little or no democratic history. The dynamics of post-Communist regimes are even more differentiated: some have taken the opportunity to become accountable democracies while others have become new plebiscitarian or despotic autocracies.

Democratization with or without false starts

The oldest democratic regimes have had an evolutionary rather than a revolutionary development. The starting point for Britain, Scandinavian countries, and the Netherlands was a steady-state constitutional autocracy in which the regime followed the rule of law, but the law greatly restricted the right to vote. The government was accountable not to a popular parliament but to a monarch or an unrepresentative assembly (see e.g. Rustow, 1955; Daalder, 1995). Challenges over a long period from the urban middle class and then from an emerging working class gradually led to an expansion of the franchise and the seamless modification of a constitutional oligarchy into a regime in which the government accepted both the rule of law and accountability to a mass electorate.

The success of North European countries in avoiding the costs of political disruption and regime transformation has made them textbook examples of democratization. However, because it took centuries for these regimes to evolve into democracies, the examples are irrelevant in a world in which transformations occur abruptly and political elites are challenged to prepare a new regime in a few months. Furthermore, the slow evolution of the earliest democracies is not characteristic of most of today's regimes.

Most European countries that are now accountable democracies have arrived at this position after false starts, veering between constitutional oligarchy, accountable democracy, and despotic or plebiscitarian autocracy. Autocratic regimes such as Prussia institutionalized rule-of-law practices in the nineteenth century. The franchise was then extended; Austria as well as Germany gave the majority of males the right to vote before Sweden did (Bartolini, 2000: 120). The breakup of empires after the First World War was followed by the creation of new regimes nominally committed to the rule of law and popular elections. However, by the early 1930s, new democracies had collapsed and were replaced by despotic autocracies (see Linz and Stepan, 1978).

The transformations wrought by the Second World War gave some European countries a second chance to become accountable democracies. Military defeat voided the Nazi and fascist regimes of Germany, Austria, and Italy, as well as the Vichy regime in France. Each country created a new regime with leaders who had entered politics during the country's democratic period in the 1920s or before 1914, when their country was a constitutional oligarchy. The leaders drew on prior experience with the rule of law and added accountability to a mass electorate. In 1945 the founders of the Second Austrian Republic even reinstated the democratic 1920 constitution of the First Austrian Republic. Within two decades, Germany and Austria had arrived at a steady-state equilibrium (see Weil, 1987). Major challenges have arisen since, such as German reunification, extremist violence, corruption, and mafia scandals in Italy. Each regime has responded to these challenges and maintained support. France is unique in that it did so by making a peaceful regime change from a democratic but inefficient Fourth Republic to a more effective and still democratic Gaullist Fifth Republic.

In the 1970s, three Mediterranean countries – Spain, Portugal, and Greece – that had seen new democracies collapse after false starts between the wars each made a second and more successful attempt at democratization. After the Franco regime gained power in Spain by overthrowing a democratic republic in a bloody civil war, it gradually evolved into a constitutional oligarchy in which Spaniards were unable to vote but the rule of law was established. Franco's death was followed by the transformation of that regime into an accountable democracy. The Portuguese constitutional oligarchy was transformed by a military coup and negotiations that quickly led to free elections. Greece experienced more cycling between regimes. The end of occupation by Nazi Germany was followed by a civil war, and a colonels' coup in 1967 introduced a military dictatorship. The Greek military then peacefully transferred power to a democratic regime in 1974.

While their origins have differed, as have their contemporary challenges, these regimes have maintained popular support by shifting between a steady state and periods of reform. In some countries, challenges have gone well beyond the normal scope of electoral competition. In Northern Ireland and in the Basque region, armed groups have sought to disrupt the British and Spanish regimes, and new types of terrorist attacks have occurred since 2001. These developments are a reminder that a steady-state regime, however long it has lasted, is not permanently free from challenges.

The return to Europe

Prior to 1914, Central and East European lands were an integral part of a European system of multinational empires. Lands that were governed as part of the Habsburg or German empires – what is now the Czech Republic, Hungary, Slovakia, Slovenia, and much of Poland – thus had the experience of a constitutional oligarchy. Bulgaria, Romania, and southern parts of what was once Yugoslavia were subject to a despotic Ottoman autocracy. Between the wars, new independent states were launched throughout the regime. Some initially had democratic regimes but, except for Czechoslovakia, they did not last long.

From the perspective of Central and Eastern Europe, Communist regimes were an alien imposition. When it became clear in 1989 that Soviet troops would no longer use force to repress demands for change, subjects no longer had to pretend to support their regime, and elites came under overwhelming pressure to introduce new regimes. The election of parliaments by proportional representation has resulted in government by a coalition of parties that bargain with and restrain each other. Elected presidents have acted as counselors and sometimes constraints on parliamentary leaders, rather than turning into dictators (see Taras, 1997). Ex-Communists have accepted the new system and opportunistically formed parties that have competed for office by offering voters what they want, sometimes with success.

From the Baltic to the Black Sea, new regimes have held free and fair elections that have repeatedly turned the government of the day out of office without threatening to disrupt the regime. Elections have also shown how little popular support there is for parties that challenge the regime. In most Central and East European countries, anti-regime parties have usually failed to win seats in the parliament. Anti-democratic parties have polled smaller shares of the vote than Le Pen's National Front in France or Jörg Haider's Freedom Party of Austria.

Leaders of new regimes set as their goal the "return to Europe," a phrase symbolizing the rejection of Soviet-imposed institutions and practices and the hope of establishing democratic regimes. The Europe that post-Communist regimes have sought to join is not the same as before (Rose, 1996b: chapters 1–3). The creation of the European Union has offered regimes the opportunity to become integrated in continent-wide institutions. The EU's criteria for membership emphasize political and civil liberties, market institutions, and the rule of law (Jacoby, 2004; Vachudova, 2005). In May 2004, eight countries – the Czech Republic, Estonia, Hungary, Latvia, Lithuania, Poland, Slovakia, and Slovenia –

Table 2.1 *Modern and anti-modern states compared*

	Modern	Anti-modern
Processes	Laws and rules applied	Rules bent, broken
	Transparent	Controlled or opaque
Decision-making	Rational	Fanciful calculation
signals	Prices, public opinion	Ideology
Outcomes	Efficient administration	Inefficient
	Effective	More or less effective

Source: Derived from Rose, 1999.

became members of the European Union. Their regimes are now no longer in transition away from Communism; they now have the status of new European democracies.

Post-Soviet regimes: an anti-modern legacy

The successor states of the Soviet Union had very different origins from Central and East European countries.[1] The Soviet Union originated from a tsarist empire that was a despotism rather than a constitutional oligarchy. The Soviet legacy to successor regimes was that of an anti-modern state. A modern state rules by laws and transparent processes that enable leaders to respond to feedback from subjects and thereby provide efficient and effective administration (see Weber, 1948). The logic of political and economic development on many continents has not necessarily involved democratization; it has been a process of modernization, that is, the introduction and gradual institutionalization of the rule of law and bureaucratic administration. By contrast, the Soviet Union rejected this path: Marxist-Leninist ideology provided the rationale for being consciously and aggressively different from the Weberian ideal-type modern state (Table 2.1).

Socialist "legality" was used to justify the arbitrary power of the Communist Party (Sachs and Pistor, 1997). Laws were bent or broken in pursuit of goals endorsed by the party. The situation was summed up by the Russian saying: "The law is like a door in the middle of the field; you can walk through it if you want, but you don't have to." The selective

---

[1] Although Estonia, Latvia, and Lithuania were republics of the Soviet Union, this was a consequence of conquest and annexation during the Second World War. Henceforth, in this book they are described as part of Central and Eastern Europe, as is appropriate to their histories and their membership of the European Union today.

enforcement of law intimidated potential critics into an outward show of support for the regime. Officials could waive enforcement of rules and allocate favors to benefit political supporters or in return for bribes.

Instead of transparency in public administration, Soviet censors controlled the flow of information, and much that happened was reported partially or not at all. For example, the disastrous nuclear explosion at the Chernobyl power station in 1986 was not publicly admitted until more than two weeks after it happened, and the full text of Nikita Khrushchev's 1956 speech denouncing Stalin was not published in the Soviet Union until 1989.

For all the discussion of cybernetics by Soviet technocrats, the system did not allow for the feedback of information between governors and governed. Elections mobilized a show of popular support for the party-state, but did not reflect what people were thinking or what they wanted. Commanders of the planned economy dictated what goods and services the economy produced without regard to consumer demand. This non-market economy created a parallel "uncivil" economy that was inefficient, corrupt, and opaque (Rose, 1993).

The regime's problem was not a shortage of information but a surplus of dis-information, since economic and electoral data gave misleading accounts of what people actually wanted. This led to fanciful rather than rational decision-making for, without knowledge of the consequences of commands, Soviet governors believed they were succeeding when the opposite was the case. When the Soviet Union broke up, leaders of successor regimes faced a challenge that has been described as "rebuilding the ship of state at sea" (Elster, Offe, and Preuss, 1998). A more accurate description would be: "building a modern ship of state at sea" (Rose, 1999).

Given the Soviet legacy, it is hardly surprising that all twelve post-Soviet regimes are rated in the bottom half of the Transparency International Perception of Corruption Index. The only difference is the extent of corruption. On a 10-point scale, Turkmenistan is rated at 1.8, the same position as Haiti and below Nigeria. The oil-rich regimes of Azerbaijan and Uzbekistan have ratings below Sierra Leone and Albania. Corruption in the Russian Federation is judged bad by absolute and by relative standards, 2.4. In Armenia, Azerbaijan, Georgia, Moldova, and Tajikistan, the regime's claim to the monopoly of force has been challenged by armed forces from neighboring countries and in Russia by insurrection in Chechnya. Where there is armed conflict, the rule of law tends to be intermittent. Amnesty International (www.amnesty.org) annually reports extra-legal violations of human rights in most countries of the Commonwealth of Independent States.

All post-Soviet regimes have held elections of a sort, but often these are plebiscites held to demonstrate that the regime can mobilize support by using its resources to produce the result it wants (cf. Wilson, 2005; Fish, 2005: chapter 3). For example, Turkmenistan followed the Soviet practice of electing the *turkmenbashi* (president) with 99.5 percent of the vote in 1992. A plebiscite subsequently extended his term with the endorsement of 99.99 percent of the vote; he was then made leader for life in 1999. In Uzbekistan, Islam Karimov was elected president in 1991, his term was extended by a plebiscite in 1997, and he was reelected in 2000 with 91.9 percent of the reported vote. In Belarus, Aleksandr Lukashenka initially won a competitive election. In a 1996 referendum, 70 percent of the reported vote endorsed a new constitution giving extensive powers to the president. Following the appearance of overwhelming endorsement in a 2006 election, Lukashenka confirmed the despotic character of the regime by arresting opponents.

The extent to which an election is competitive is indicated by the share of vote won by the government candidate. In post-Soviet regimes, non-competitive elections are the norm. In five countries, the winning candidate in the latest presidential election was credited with more than 90 percent of the first-round vote, and in four others, including Russia, the winner secured at least 71 percent of the officially reported vote (Table 2.2). Only in Ukraine and Moldova did the leading candidate or party win less than half the first-round vote, the normal result in a multiparty democracy.

The Office for Democratic Institutions and Human Rights (ODIHR) of the OSCE (Organization for Security and Co-operation in Europe) is ready to send observers to evaluate the extent to which elections are free and fair (Boda, 2005). However, before it does so, the regime must be prepared to accept OSCE observers on terms that enable them to move freely and meet all parties. The most autocratic regimes refuse to accept observers on any terms or lay down restrictions that cause the OSCE to refuse to send observers. Leaders of the post-Soviet countries have criticized foreign-observer teams, and President Putin has declared that the Russian regime is the only institution qualified to evaluate Russian elections.

The OSCE did not send observer missions to the latest national election in three post-Soviet regimes, Turkmenistan, Tajikistan, and Uzbekistan, because the regime's conditions in each case would have limited their free-dom. In most CIS countries where observers have been sent, the OSCE qualifies the results by using such terms as "free but unfair" (for example, television pays very little attention to opposition candidates) or "undue government influence" (for example, opposition candidates are harassed

Table 2.2 *Conduct of elections in post-Soviet states*

		Presidential election	
	OSCE assessment	%	Year
Unfree or unfair			
Turkmenistan	Avoided	99.5	1992
Tajikistan	Avoided	97.0	1999
Georgia	Competitive but unfair	96.3	2004
Uzbekistan	Avoided	91.9	2000
Kazahkstan	Undue govt. influence	91.0	2005
Kyrgyz Republic	Competitive but unfair	88.8	2005
Belarus	Undue govt. influence	82.6	2006
Azerbaijan	Undue govt. influence	76.8	2003
RUSSIA	Competitive but unfair	71.3	2004
Disorderly but competitive			
Armenia	Undue govt. influence	67.5	2003
Ukraine	Competitive and fair	41.1	2004
Moldova	Competitive and fair	46.1*	2005

*Vote for largest party in parliament; president elected by parliament

Source: OSCE election reports of Office for Democratic Institutions and Human Rights, www.osce.org/odihr-elections/eom.html; country results from a variety of national sources.

or vote totals are falsified). While the existence of undue influence or unfair practices may not change the outcome of an election – for example, Vladimir Putin was a certain winner of the 2004 Russian presidential election – it does show that the regime does not respect the rule of law.

Labeling post-Soviet states in Central Asia as *despotisms* reflects the readiness of regimes such as Kazakhstan, Tajikistan, Turkmenistan, and Uzbekistan to govern corruptly and use arbitrary actions and even force to intimidate critics. Administrative means produce election results that appear to show popular support but are neither free nor fair. Whereas unfair elections are only occasional, there is steady pressure on subjects to give resigned acceptance to the powers that be.

Because the rule of law is weak in all post-Soviet countries, no CIS regime can be described as a democracy or a constitutional oligarchy. Yet these countries differ in the extent to which elections offer the opportunity to protest and to which subjects enjoy some political and civil rights. Ukraine provides the most striking example of a *plebiscitarian autocracy*. Notwithstanding a high level of corruption and intimidation of political opponents, opponents of the "party of power" have consistently won a significant share of the vote, and in the winter of 2004/5 a series of competitive elections culminated in the victory of the opposition candidate for president. While Moldova has had a high level of corruption, opposition parties have been able to contest elections and, if only because political elites are not united, there has been a degree of electoral competition. In Georgia, too, corruption has been tempered by electoral competition and popular demonstrations forcing a president elected by fraudulent means in 2003 to cede power to an opposition leader elected with an overwhelming majority (cf. Table 2.2).

The use of generic labels to characterize particular regimes cannot accommodate the nuances that give a regime its distinctive character. Since the start of the Russian Federation in 1992, analysts have shifted from characterizing it by a simple label, such as "democratizing," to describing it as a hybrid, even if there is no agreement about whether the dominant elements are democratic or autocratic (cf. Diamond, 2002). In this book, the Russian Federation is characterized as a plebiscitarian autocracy. Elections give it a claim to be plebiscitarian, while limited regard for the rule of law makes it an unaccountable autocracy.

Different kinds of steady states

The British economist Lord Keynes grouped equilibriums under two headings – optimistic and pessimistic. Optimists have viewed the transformation of regimes as leading to democracy. By contrast, pessimists have seen it as consolidating autocratic regimes. The regimes created in the wake of the collapse of Communism have developed in diverging directions: some have become accountable democracies, while others have become autocracies.

Central and East European regimes are now converging with other countries of Europe through membership in the European Union, a league of twenty-five countries committed to free elections and the rule of law. Throughout the EU, governors are accountable to their citizens through free elections. Thus, Freedom House rates both post-Communist and long-established democracies at the same level (see Figure 2.3). The eight new enlargement countries of the European Union conform to Joseph Schumpeter's definition of democracy: citizens can use their votes to turn the government of the day out of office. The defeat of governing parties in free and fair elections is more frequent than in older member-states of the EU.

Corruption in EU states is primarily concerned with using public office for private profit; it is not politically motivated as is vote fraud. Italy and Greece, like Poland and Latvia, demonstrate that corruption in public administration can coexist with electoral accountability. Even more important, corruption among EU countries is not paralleled by the

Figure 2.3 *DIFFERENTIATING REGIMES ACROSS EUROPE*

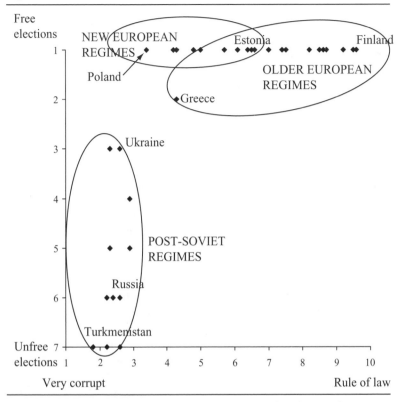

Source: Thirty-seven European countries rated on freedom by Freedom House, *Freedom in the World 2006*, www.freedomhouse.org; and on rule of law by Transparency International, *Corruption Perceptions Index 2005*, www.transparency.org/cpi/2005/cpi2005_infocus.html.

existence of a political police that infringes the liberties of citizens by arbitrarily arresting critics, censoring newspapers, or closing down civil society organizations. However, there is not yet convergence in avoiding corruption, for the level of corruption ranges widely within both old and new European Union member-states. Among long-established EU members, Finland has a PCI rating of 9.6, while Greece has the lowest rating, 4.3. However, the legacy of Communist rule has resulted in widespread corruption that detracts from the rule of law (see Wedel, 1986; Clark and Wildavsky, 1990; Miller, Grodeland, and Koshechkina, 2001). Six enlargement countries meet the minimum standard for EU eligibility set by Greece; only Poland and Latvia rate worse than Greece. However, corruption is more widespread in enlargement countries; the mean for the group is 4.8 compared to 7.7 for older EU regimes.

The extent of political convergence among EU members is partial (Figure 2.3). All demonstrate a commitment to electoral accountability, and governors do not abuse the law to intimidate their critics or win elections fraudulently. However, there is a substantial amount of corruption in many EU member-states and the dispersion in official behavior is found among established member-states as well as among enlargement countries.

Post-Soviet regimes differ in kind from those Central and East European post-Communist regimes that are now in the European Union (Figure 2.3). None has regularly held free and fair elections. The Freedom House index differentiates post-Soviet regimes as either "partly free" or "unfree." In the former group, it is possible for a plebiscite intended to support the government to produce the "wrong" result, as happened in Ukraine in the winter of 2004. Among despotic autocracies, the ruling power makes sure that the vote count is what it wants, regardless of what the electorate wants (see Table 2.2).

All the Soviet successor regimes appear very corrupt in an international perspective (Figure 2.3). The median post-Soviet regime is in the bottom quarter of Transparency International's global ranking. Much corruption in the post-Soviet bloc involves violations of the rule of law for personal gain. However, violations of the law for private profit coexist with violations of the rule of law for political ends, for example, using the security services to intimidate or jail political opponents and suppress criticism. The Putin administration has used the selective enforcement of laws to take over independent media outlets and jail wealthy critics on the grounds that they have violated tax laws. The tendency of post-Soviet regimes in Figure 2.3 to cluster and not to overlap with old and new regimes in Europe indicates substantial similarities between plebiscitarian and despotic regimes: the leaders of both types of regimes can act arbitrarily if they choose.

Classifying regimes at a single point in time does not characterize their dynamics. The older regimes of Europe have become accountable democracies by very different paths. Their recent histories show that challenges can be met with dynamic changes that maintain popular support. Despotic post-Soviet regimes differ in kind, but they can also be steady-state regimes. However, popular support may not be voluntarily given due to normative commitment; it can be the product of a low-level equilibrium trap in which subjects give up hope of an alternative and become resigned to accepting what the political elite supplies (Rose, Mishler, and Haerpfer, 1998: 14).

3 A changing supply of Russian regimes

> Although the past has been overthrown, it has not been overcome.
>
> V. I. Lenin, 1923

> Merely experimenting with abstract models and schemes taken from foreign textbooks cannot assure that our country will achieve genuine renewal without any excessive costs. The mechanical copying of other nations' experience will not guarantee success either.
>
> Vladimir Putin, millennium address, 2000

While the regimes supplied by the tsars and by the Communist Party of the Soviet Union differed radically in their goals, both were outside the mainstream of European political development. Thus, Vladimir Putin was correct in emphasizing that what is viewed as *normalno* by the country's political elites is not what is normal in democratic regimes of Europe or in the United States.

Under the influence of Mongol invaders and Byzantine civilization, the tsarist regime originated as a despotic autocracy resembling an Asian empire rather than a European feudal state (Hosking, 2001: chapter 1). The nineteenth-century industrialization of Europe produced a reaction from Slavophile writers, who stressed Russia's uniqueness. Western travelers saw Russia as alien to Europe too (see Wolff, 1994; Hedlund, 1999: chapter 4). While European regimes came and went, the Russian tsars successfully maintained their regime through cycles of steady-state and dynamic equilibrium for more than three centuries before being overthrown in 1917.

Although Lenin was familiar at first hand with European constitutional autocracies and democracies, the Soviet Union was founded as a challenge to European regimes. In pursuit of the goal of Communism, it rejected the bureaucratic rule-of-law norms of Max Weber, the classic liberalism of John Stuart Mill, and the social democratic reliance on collective institutions of civil society. The developmental goals of the Soviet

Union – industrialization, urbanization, and education – made it appear to be modernizing. Communists proclaimed Soviet industrialization as proof of the superiority of a non-market economy, but critics saw it as a "pseudo-modern" state (Winiecki, 1988), and Martin Malia (Z, 1990: 298ff.) described the contrast between Soviet ideology and reality as creating a "surreal" system. Yet the Soviet regime persisted for almost three-quarters of a century.

Writers on Russian society have emphasized continuities in the despotic regimes that elites have supplied. For example, George Kennan, a leading US State Department official and scholar, advised a young diplomat going to Moscow in 1981, "Don't worry about any studies of what has happened since 1917 and the Russian Revolution. Go get yourself a couple of good nineteenth-century memoirs" (quoted in Ryavec, 2003: 54), and political scientist Stephen White (1979: ix) invoked political culture to argue that there were "important elements of continuity between the pre- and post-revolutionary systems." A functionalist argument for continuity is given by Wesson (1986: xii): "Continuity rests not so much on tradition and inherited political culture as on the fact that Russians have faced the same major political problems since 1917 as before: namely, to hold together and rule the huge multinational realm in the face of forces of modernity and to modernize economically and militarily without modernizing politically."

There was never any pretence that the regimes supplied by tsars and by commissars were a response to popular demands. The role of the Russian masses was to accept whatever elites supplied, whether it was justified by an appeal to the values of Holy Russia, Marxist-Leninism, or Soviet patriotism. While the tsarist and Communist regimes now belong to history, each has left a legacy, not only in the institutions that elites control but also in the minds of subjects who have had to learn and then re-learn what is "normal" in two different regimes.

The absence of public opinion surveys in earlier times is no reason not to reflect on the popular support, positive or resigned, that enabled past regimes to persist for so long. The first section of this chapter describes how despotic regimes claimed support, and the second shows how Russians learned to cooperate and sometimes evade the intrusive demands of a totalitarian Soviet regime. The creation of the Russian Federation has required intensive re-learning by Russia's political elites. Boris Yeltsin learned how to survive, no easy achievement in the aftermath of transformation. Vladimir Putin has sought to "normalize" the regime's claims for popular support by strengthening the autocratic element in Russia's plebiscitarian autocracy.

An alternation of despotisms

For long periods the history of government in Russia has been an account of cycles between periods of steady-state despotism punctuated by dynamic challenges that were met with repression or reform, or a mixture of the two. The continuity of tsarist rule through the centuries was comparable with that of the Habsburg emperors. Notwithstanding the Soviet regime's emphasis on the cult of the leader, it lasted much longer than the regimes of Napoleon and Hitler, and during its lifetime France had three regimes and Germany four.

Russian history belies the assumption that regime transformation leads to democratization directly or indirectly. Neither the court of the tsar nor the Central Committee of the Communist Party of the Soviet Union (CPSU) claimed support based on free elections. Yet the persistence of each regime required active or passive support from its subjects. The tsarist regime sought this by invoking traditional and religious norms and relied on a heavy-handed security service to intimidate and punish those who challenged it. The CPSU sought support by proclaiming an end to class exploitation, industrializing the economy, and promoting science. It used the state security services to intimidate or punish those who did not give overt evidence of supporting the party line.

Deference to the tsar

For more than 350 years, Russia was governed by a despotic regime that arbitrarily coerced nominal elites as well as the rural masses. It was formally established in 1547 by Ivan the Terrible, who repudiated the power of nobles to restrain royal authority, thus removing institutions of accountability found in European feudal systems. After the fall of Orthodox Constantinople to Ottoman invaders, the regime claimed to be the defender of the true Christian faith. In words of a monastic apologist, "All the empires of Christendom are united in thine, the two Romes have fallen and the third exists and there will not be a fourth" (quoted in Neumann, 1996: 7; see also Duncan, 2000). The tsar's regime was patrimonial. He "considered his domain to be his private property rather than a community with sovereign rights and interests," and he and his personal staff exercised absolute authority over laws, property, and security forces (Weber, 1947: 347ff.; Remington, 2006: 122ff.).

The regime established by Ivan the Terrible was subsequently challenged by assassinations and war – but it survived by a process of dynamic adaptation. For example, Peter the Great, who ruled from 1696 to 1725, moved the seat of government from the Asiatic fortress of Moscow's

Kremlin to the Baltic Sea, creating St. Petersburg on territory conquered from Sweden. Peter emphasized that the West offered many examples for emulation ranging from science to the adoption of Western dress in place of dress appropriate to Eastern courts. However, the methods that Peter employed in attempting to Westernize Russia were those of a traditional Russian despot.

After participating on the winning side in the Napoleonic wars, Tsar Alexander I joined in the Holy Alliance with the Habsburg and Prussian monarchs to maintain the existing social and political order against challenges stimulated by the French Revolution. Notwithstanding the emancipation of 22 million Russian serfs in 1861, the great majority of the country's population remained rural and isolated. Concurrently, the industrialization of much of Europe made Russia relatively more backward economically (Gerschenkron, 1962).

The expansion of the tsar's territories into Central Asia and the late nineteenth-century development of railroads and telecommunications increased the importance of the imperial administration, but it failed to create a rule-of-law bureaucracy (Ryavec, 2003: chapter 1). Laws repeated the doctrine that subjects were obligated by "God himself" to obey the tsar's commands (White, 1979: 27). Popular demonstrations following defeat in the Russo-Japanese War in 1905 were initially met with gunfire by palace guards and then by elections to the Duma (parliament) by procedures that were hardly democratic (Emmons, 1983). Within two years, concessions to the Duma were effectively annulled.

When the First World War broke out in 1914, the tsarist empire became a battleground – and much territory was lost to German troops. In February 1917, demonstrations by workers in Petrograd (its name Russified from the Germanic St. Petersburg) led the military garrison and the Duma to defy the tsar and side with the demonstrators. Tsar Nicholas II abdicated and a broadly representative Provisional Government was established under Alexander Kerensky. In late October 1917, Bolsheviks stormed the former tsar's Winter Palace in Petrograd and arrested Provisional Government ministers. A Soviet government was established under Vladimir Lenin. Tsar Nicholas and his family were shot in July 1918, thus marking the literal death of the tsar's personalistic despotism.

The Soviet Union: totalitarian mobilization in a party-state

The Union of Soviet Socialist Republics (USSR) was established in 1922, after a period marked by the loss of territory to newly independent states in Eastern Europe, such as Poland, and a civil war between anti-Bolshevik "White" troops and their Western allies, and the "Red" Bolshevik regime.

The new regime was a one-party state, for the key political position was not that of president or prime minister but general secretary of the Communist Party. Josef Stalin held this office from 1922 to 1953.

The new regime sought to transform a politically, economically, and militarily weak state into an ideal Communist society (Jowitt, 1992). Its vision was literally totalitarian, recognizing no distinction between state and society; everything was made a matter of political concern from agriculture to alcoholism to art. The means of achievement was the mobilization of the entire population and the refashioning of their nature to create a new Soviet man.[1] An ideal new Soviet man

obediently complies with commands emanating from authorities; he seeks to frustrate the actions of those who break the customary norms of behavior; he fully supports his leadership; he possesses a standardized and ideologized consciousness; he feels responsible for his country as a whole; he is ready to sacrifice himself and to sacrifice others. (A. Zinoviev, quoted in Heller, 1988: 47)

The mobilization of support for the new regime involved ideological indoctrination, fear, and terror. The party used Marxist-Leninist ideology to justify to semi-literate Russians disoriented by transformation the necessity of harsh measures being taken to transform Russian society. The ideology also promised a better life at an unspecified future date. The flexibility of Marxist principles meant that their application to concrete problems could be discussed and interpreted in ways justifying abrupt reversals of policy. However, the party confined debate to private meetings of party councils; the doctrine of democratic centralism meant that, once the party line on an issue was promulgated, discussion was ended and intense pressures were exerted to mobilize support.

The Communist Party used extreme methods to indoctrinate Russians socialized under the tsar to support the new regime. Fear and terror were used to make sure that people who had doubts about the party line nonetheless publicly supported it to avoid the suspicion that they were enemies of the state. When the forced collectivization of agricultural land, known as the Revolution from Above, met with the resistance of peasants in the early 1930s, Stalin ordered land confiscated and peasants sent to labor camps or executed. In the famine that followed, an estimated 5 to 8 million people died (Wädekin, 1994: 399).

Within the Communist Party, Stalin maintained support through repeated purges of suspected rivals. Show trials of leading Communists were held and confessions were extracted prior to execution. By the end

[1] In the usage of the time, the phrase was deemed to include women. The Soviet regime recognized women as having the same obligation and right to work as men. However, women were rarely found in the decision-making institutions of the Communist Party.

of the 1930s, less than half those occupying leading party positions at the start of the purges had survived. Arrest on suspicion was tantamount to a sentence of guilt. The motto of the state security police was said to be "Give us the man and we will find the crime" (see Yakovlev, 2002). Millions were deported to the gulag (system of labor camps), and millions died there (Solzhenitsyn, 1974; Conquest, 1990). The terror cowed subjects to support what they were told to, whatever their private opinions. For example, the widow of a purged senior Communist cut out her husband's face from their family photograph album to signal to the secret police who searched her apartment regularly that she would do whatever the party wanted in order to save her daughter from the gulag (King, 1997: 7).

The events of 1939–41 dramatically illustrated the speed and scale with which loyal Communists were expected to reverse their views. In August 1939, a pact between Stalin and Hitler turned the party's ideological enemy into a partner in the military occupation of Poland and the Baltic states, and made Allied opposition to Germany an "imperialist war" which good Communists were meant to oppose. Less than two years later, the German invasion of the Soviet Union turned the war into an "anti-fascist" crusade. In mobilizing support for military defense, the Communist Party invoked patriotic rhetoric, and the brutality of the German advance was effective in making the Soviet cause the lesser evil.

The Communist Party established an elaborate repertoire of institutions routinely socializing new generations to support the Soviet regime. Schoolchildren were taught to inform on suspected enemies of the state, including their parents. Marxist-Leninist doctrines permeated everything from the teaching of literature to biology. Even if the lessons taught were not accepted, incessant exposure to the party line and multiple barriers to contacts with foreigners and foreign ideas left Russians with no understanding of alternative types of regimes. The ability to repeat the Marxist-Leninist catechism was a necessary condition of educational success, and enrollment in Communist youth organizations was compulsory.

Indoctrination continued at the place of work. By the 1970s, official statistics recorded 3,700,000 work place *agitatory* encouraging "correct" political discussions and exhorting workers to meet their factory's monthly production targets. There were 1,800,000 *politinformatory* promoting the party line through group discussions in which the comments of each participant were monitored. An additional 300,000 lecturers presented a more sophisticated version of the party line to managerial and professional groups. Party schools with more than 20 million participants each year awarded certificates in Marxist-Leninist studies which were useful for career advancement (White, 1979: 75ff.).

The radio, the party press, publishing houses, theater, cinema, and television were controlled to propagate the party line. Official texts were read carefully so people would know the politically correct thing to say at a given moment. The more sophisticated also read statements between the lines in an effort to understand what was going on behind the ideological facade. Writers and artists who did not conform to official standards of socialist realism were threatened with prison or with having their work banned. Composers such as Dmitri Shostakovich gave obeisance to the party line on music.

With one fulltime proponent of the party line for every sixteen households in the Soviet Union, Communist ideology was pervasive. Officials in senior positions in all walks of life were expected to give lip service to Communist values, whether or not individuals believed what they were told. The breadth and intensity of the party's ideological mobilization was sufficient to crowd out the formation and, even more, the dissemination of views different from the party line.

Post-totalitarian adaptation

The strength of Communist Party organization enabled the regime to survive the death of Josef Stalin in 1953. The aim of Stalin's successors was to maintain the leading role of the Communist Party of the Soviet Union by reforming Stalinist institutions. In a secret speech to the 20th Congress of the Communist Party in 1956, Nikita Khrushchev, Stalin's successor, denounced him for crimes and proposed actions to reduce terror and strengthen support for the regime.

Given the extreme nature of its totalitarian aspirations, any adaptation of the Communist regime could only be in a post-totalitarian direction. By the benchmark of Stalinism, Nikita Khrushchev's peaceful retirement in 1964 – rather than his being imprisoned or shot – was a sign of "liberalization." In addition, some Western Sovietologists interpreted rising levels of education and living standards as indications that sooner or later the Soviet Union would become normal by Western standards (cf. Parsons, 1967: 492, 518; Hough, 1977).

Leonid Brezhnev, Khrushchev's successor as party secretary, had joined the Communist Party in 1931 and risen through the ranks to a high position under Stalin. After the challenges of preceding years, Brezhnev was content to preside over a steady-state regime that was normal by Soviet standards. Just as Bismarck had promoted social welfare to create mass support for the constitutional autocracy of imperial Germany a century earlier, the National Economic Plan began to provide consumer goods with the intent of "buying" support, or at least political quiescence, from its subjects. The policy was aptly described as "welfare system authoritarianism" (Breslauer, 1978; cf. Cook, 1993). However, the costs of ending shortages of consumer goods while simultaneously funding increased spending for the military-industrial sector were difficult for the command economy.

By the standards of Soviet normality, under Leonid Brezhnev the regime was in a steady state. The Communist Party retained its leading role in directing its institutions. Ideological indoctrination was maintained, even though the apparatchiks responsible were no longer idealists but opportunists. As Henry Kissinger (1994: 519) described high-level Soviet officials whom he met during the Brezhnev years, they had a "passionate belief in the system to which they owed their careers." The insulation of political leaders from feedback encouraged complacency and inaction. A party that had set out to transform society had become an organization incapable of reforming itself (see Roeder, 1993).

The Soviet regime under Brezhnev remained a despotic autocracy, for there was no rule of law. While under Stalin the security services labeled those it hunted as ideological enemies of the state, under Brezhnev those accused of undermining the regime were more likely to be labeled corrupt. The regime's security police continued to administer "controls affecting every aspect of Soviet citizens' daily lives: individuals could not move, take a vacation, travel abroad, register their cars, or obtain a driver's license without authorization from the police" (Shelley, 1996: xv–xvi). The idea of holding an election with choice was anathema to the Communist Party, which wanted to retain its position as the sole as well as leading party. A scholarly book about the scope for choice in undemocratic elections found more evidence of electoral competition in Kenya, Cameroon, and Syria than in the Soviet Union under Brezhnev (Hermet, Rouquié, and Rose, 1978).

Mass response: coexisting with despotism

A democracy or a constitutional autocracy leaves citizens free to make many decisions about what they do. By contrast, the Soviet regime's efforts at totalitarian mobilization were pervasive, covering leisure time, education, and work as well as affairs of state. While individuals were not meant to have any choice about supporting the regime's demands, the inability of any regime to achieve total control of society meant the goal could not be completely achieved. For Communist leaders, this was a sign of failure to create the new Soviet man; for ordinary Russians, it was a measure of freedom to lead your life as you wished rather than as they told you to do. The outcome of this tension was an uneasy coexistence between governors and subjects.

In the absence of feedback to advise leaders of the extent to which they were actually succeeding in their aims, information was channeled through party apparatchiks, who had many incentives to report what leaders wanted to hear. Party officials manufactured evidence of popular support such as election results, showing that everyone turned out to vote and voted correctly, that is, supported the Communist Party. Economic statistics were expected to show that targets in the National Economic Plan had been met. In the absence of a free flow of information, it was easy for Soviet officials to produce "satisfying" statistics. To describe such data as "lies" is to misunderstand the nature of the regime; they were numbers that could be used to create a show of support for it.

For the mass of Russians, coexistence provided a space in which people could lead lives free of the intrusive monitoring of the regime. People of a dissident inclination could pass the time in studying astronomy or Renaissance musicology. The mass of the population could minimize the time and energy devoted to public shows of regime support and maximize the time spent on private pursuits, whether playing with their children, listening to nineteenth-century music, or growing food at their *dacha*, activities that brought everyday satisfactions to Russians and avoided conflicts with the powers that be. In the words of Archie Brown (2004), post-totalitarian changes meant that Soviet citizens could "retreat into their private lives and be reasonably sure they would not be arrested because of anonymous denunciations or the political police's need to fill a quota."

Up to a point, coexistence could operate through the mechanisms of an hour-glass society, in which political elites interacted intensively at the top about matters of party interest, such as the policy of the Soviet Union toward capitalist countries, and the mass of the public interacted intensively at the bottom about matters of household interest, such as how to get consumer goods that were perpetually in short supply. Horizontal ties were absorbing. They offered immediate benefits such as promotion for party apparatchiks and for ordinary regll relief from the drabness of the official version of Soviet life.

However, there were times when the two halves of the hour-glass had to cooperate, for example, when hospital treatment was needed by a family member. Ordinary individuals learned to work the political system to get what they wanted through connections (*blat*) that involved friends or friends of friends doing favors, or exchanges that could involve payment in kind (a chicken in return for the supply of under-the-counter goods) or even payment in cash (Ledeneva, 1998).

Pervasive control of civil society institutions by the party-state made it virtually impossible for individuals dissatisfied with the regime to cooperate in organizing protests. The pervasive network of the security services meant that people who held dissident opinions could express them only to one or two trusted friends. Individuals could write letters to the editor complaining about particular cases of maladministration or unfairness – as long as they did not describe them as symptoms of faults in the Soviet regime (Shlapentokh, 2001: 129). A typical form of non-cooperation was shirking at work. As long as the factory manager produced reports stating that production norms had been met, workers did not need to bother with the quality or even the quantity of goods produced. As long as lip service was paid to Communist ideology, any mental reservations were irrelevant. In the post-totalitarian Soviet Union, as long as individuals gave a public show of support, the regime was indifferent to their private opinions. However, for individual dissidents, the effect was profoundly demoralizing. The dissident poet, Nadezhda Mandelstam, described "fear and its derivations: the heinous awareness of shame, restrictions and full helplessness" as "stronger than love and jealousy, stronger than anything which is human" (quoted in Shlapentokh, 2001: 251n; cf. Clark and Wildavsky, 1990).

Ideological indoctrination was successful in achieving popular endorsement of some political values propagated by the regime. The Soviet Interview Project surveyed Russians, primarily Jews, who had emigrated from the Soviet Union in the late 1970s and were thus less likely to be pro-Soviet (cf. Millar, 1987: chapter 1). It found that emigres endorsed the Soviet regime's ownership of heavy industry and provision of education and health services. The American organizers of the Soviet Interview Project mistakenly interpreted the endorsement of collectivist welfare values as evidence of "regime support" (Silver, 1987: 109ff.), when in fact these values were not distinctively Communist but common to social democratic and Christian democratic parties across Western Europe. Distinctively Communist practices, such as the collectivization of agriculture and the system of internal passports that restricted free movement between cities, were heavily rejected by emigres.

The great mass of the population came to cooperate with the regime without the fervency of true believers in Marxist-Leninist ideology or the frustrations of dissidents. The German invasion of the Soviet Union in 1941 gave a patriotic impetus to mobilization in support of the regime. Rising living standards after the Second World War did not bring the Soviet Union to the level of capitalist Europe, but it was an improvement on living standards in the decades when industrialization at any price was the priority of the regime. The dangers of political involvement in

Stalin's time, when purges were often targeted at those who were politically active, encouraged people to become politically indifferent. People whose indifference to political mobilization had led to their castigation as "Philistines" in Stalin's time were reclassified as innocuous in Brezhnev's era (Shlapentokh, 2001: 138).

Instead of the regime adapting to its citizens, as in a democratizing polity, Soviet subjects adapted to the regime.[2] Even among those who had emigrated in the early 1970s, more than four-fifths did not voice hostility to the system as a whole. Furthermore, very few reported engaging in political activities inconsistent with Soviet norms (Bahry, 1987: 65; Silver, 1987: 114). From the perspective of Communist leaders wanting to maintain a steady state of support for the regime, this was sufficient.

From reform to transformation and a new equilibrium?

An unexpected generational change occurred in 1985 when Mikhail Gorbachev assumed the general secretaryship of the Communist Party following the deaths of Leonid Brezhnev and his two elderly successors. Gorbachev came to office believing in the need to introduce dynamic reforms. However, instead of reforms moving the regime to a new equilibrium, Gorbachev's actions disrupted the Soviet Union, leaving a legacy of lawless autocracy. To mobilize a show of support, the leaders of the new Russian Federation have invoked plebiscites.

Reforms induce disruption

Perestroika (restructuring) was intended to stimulate a stagnating Soviet economy. Whereas in the mixed economy of West European states politicians could change the mix of state and market, in the Soviet Union marginal adjustments were not possible because the state's total command of the economy meant there was no market sector. Introducing market mechanisms meant abandoning Soviet-style socialism.

Glasnost (openness) was intended to open up discussion among Communists about how to resolve the country's problems. Because the Communist Party was divided about Gorbachev's reforms, it was no longer a reliable institution for mobilizing support. At the 1988 Party Congress, Gorbachev promoted the introduction of multicandidate elections within

---

[2] For studies using fragmentary documentary sources from the 1930s, see Davies, 1997, and Fitzpatrick, 1999. For evaluations of sources from the post-transformation period, see the materials cited and discussed by Shlapentokh, 1989 and 2001 (especially chapter 10 and notes), and interviews with emigres conducted by Inkeles and Bauer, 1959, and Millar, 1987.

a one-party regime, with the intent of mobilizing support for his reform proposals. Because multiple candidates appeared on the ballot, voters had a choice between backing traditional Communists who opposed reforms and radical members of the party who demanded greater changes than Gorbachev was prepared to offer.

The first semi-competitive elections in Soviet history were held for the Congress of People's Deputies in March 1989. The results showed that the apparatchiks who told people what to think had failed to understand what the people actually thought. Instead of official candidates being endorsed by 99.9 percent of the electorate, some were defeated or failed to win at least half the votes of the registered electorate. Moreover, Boris Yeltsin, whom Gorbachev had removed from a prominent position in the party because of his populist demands, won a Congress seat with 89 percent of the vote in a Moscow district. Three more elections followed: none went according to Gorbachev's plan (White, Rose, and McAllister, 1997: chapter 2).

In response to opposition within the party, Gorbachev decided to make the presidency a powerful elected institution, thus replacing Politburo legitimacy with popular legitimacy. In default of an equally well-known opponent, at this time Gorbachev could have stood for popular election and expected to win. However, he avoided seeking popular election. Instead, he became president in March 1990 after being endorsed by the Soviet Congress of People's Deputies. The ballot revealed Gorbachev's limited support within the Communist leadership. Although unopposed, he was supported by only 59 percent of Congress delegates (Brown, 1996: 198ff.).

The shift from dynamic challenge to disruption gathered momentum. By allowing elections in the fifteen Soviet republics, Gorbachev enabled Yeltsin and other party functionaries to claim popular support and control government offices independently of the Kremlin. In 1990, the newly elected Supreme Soviet of the Russian Republic chose Boris Yeltsin as its chair. Yeltsin used the occasion of an all-union referendum in March 1991 to create the post of president of the Russian Republic, which was still part of the Soviet Union. In June 1991, he was elected to that post with 57.3 percent of the vote, compared to 16.8 percent for Gorbachev's former prime minister, Nikolai Ryzhkov, and fewer votes still for four other candidates.

Traditional Communists sought to reassert the party's monopoly of power in a highly centralized Soviet Union by launching a putsch to oust Gorbachev in August 1991. The army and the security services remained neutral and the putsch failed within a week. Leaders of republican-level institutions reacted to this aggressive attempt to restore the old political equilibrium by accelerating pressures to disrupt it. On December 8, 1991, the leaders of the republics of Russia, Ukraine, and Belarus signed a declaration of independence marking the end of the Soviet Union; nine days later Gorbachev accepted this declaration. On December 25, 1991, an independent state, the Russian Federation, came into existence and a treble transformation began.

Surviving: the Yeltsin achievement

Boris Yeltsin was a charismatic leader in the strict Weberian sense of the term: his populist attacks on the Gorbachev reforms were central in disrupting the Soviet regime. In response to the attempted Communist coup in August 1991, Yeltsin became a plebiscitarian tribune, standing at a symbolic barricade in front of the White House, the home of Russia's popularly elected assembly, to denounce the Communist putsch. In a grudging tribute to Yeltsin's role in disrupting his reform agenda, Mikhail Gorbachev subsequently remarked, "I should have sent him as an ambassador to some banana republic" (www.cdi.org/russia/johnson/5395.html; cf. Breslauer, 2002; Brown, 2004).

Initially, institutions of the new regime were a legacy from the Soviet era. Boris Yeltsin owed his position as head of the Russian Federation to election as president of the Russian Soviet Federal Socialist Republic of the Soviet Union. The legislature was the Congress of People's Deputies of the old Russian republic. The new regime's courts were staffed by judges appointed in Soviet times and trained in interpreting the law to favor the party-state. In the Soviet regime, all the institutions were subordinate to the Communist Party of the Soviet Union. However, the failed putsch resulted in that party being declared illegal.

In the absence of a new constitution, the first years of the regime were marked by a struggle for supremacy between politicians controlling different institutions. Boris Yeltsin used popular referendums to give support to his claim for supremacy. However, the framing of questions and the timing of ballots were plebiscitarian. They also showed how unsteady was the state of the new regime. In the April 1993 referendum, the question put was: "Do you have confidence in the president of the Russian Federation, B. N. Yeltsin?" In reply, 59 percent of votes showed confidence in Yeltsin. The forced-choice nature of the question obscured the shallowness of his personal support. In a New Russia Barometer survey in June 1993, only 4 percent expressed a lot of confidence in Yeltsin, while 30 percent expressed some confidence. By contrast, 40 percent said that they did not have much confidence and 27 percent expressed no confidence at all.

Along with the economic turmoil of transformation, there was a continuing conflict between the Kremlin, which favored a presidential constitution, and the Congress, which favored a parliamentary system. Personal rivalries exacerbated the dispute. On September 21, 1993, President Yeltsin broke the deadlock by dissolving Congress and calling a December election. The Congress responded by impeaching Yeltsin and naming Vice-President Aleksandr Rutskoi as his successor. Yeltsin ordered troops to blockade the White House, where the parliament met. Congress members barricaded themselves inside. On October 3, Congress supporters lifted the blockade and marched on the state television station but were repulsed. The next day, troops loyal to Yeltsin bombarded the White House. After more than 100 people were killed, the deputies and their supporters surrendered.

After winning the battle with the Congress, Yeltsin quickly produced a presidentialist constitution, and it was put to a popular vote for approval on December 12, 1993. Official results confirmed the Constitution, but the endorsement was weak. The turnout was just over half the registered electorate, the minimum required by law for the endorsement to be valid. Of the reported vote, 56.6 percent approved the Constitution. The large minority that voted against what Yeltsin proposed showed that plebiscites were open to the expression of opposition to a degree unheard of in Soviet times. Opponents charged that the results were obtained by Soviet-style manipulation (Sakwa, 2002: 54ff.; Wilson, 2005: 75f). Michael McFaul (2001: 17) described the new regime's Constitution as "imposed."

While the constitutional referendum gave President Yeltsin the formal authority he sought, it was not evidence of popular confidence. Only 22 percent of voters favored the Constitution *and* believed it would produce a lawful and democratic state (Figure 3.1). Most people who voted for the Constitution did not believe it would create a lawful and democratic state. This negative view was even more widespread among those voting against the Constitution (Figure 3.1).

The election of the Duma, the new representative chamber of parliament in December 1992, showed most Russians using their new freedom to register apathy or antipathy to the government. Russia's Choice, the pro-government party of Yegor Gaidar, won only 14.5 percent of the proportional representation vote. The rabidly nationalist Liberal Democratic Party of Vladimir Zhirinovsky came first with 21.4 percent of the vote, and the Communist Party of the Russian Federation came third with 11.6 percent (Rose and Munro, 2003: chapter 16).

In the presidential ballot of June 1996, the leading candidates, Boris Yeltsin and a Communist Party apparatchik, Gennady Zyuganov, offered a choice between regimes. While Yeltsin defended the treble

Figure 3.1 *PESSIMISTIC VIEW OF THE RUSSIAN CONSTITUTION*

Q. What was your vote on the Russian Constitution?
Q. Will the new constitution ensure a lawful and democratic Russian state?

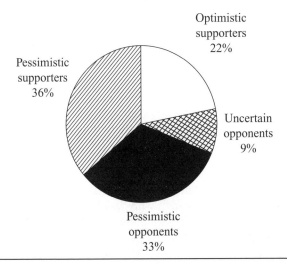

Source: New Russia Barometer III (1994). *Optimistic supporters*: approved
constitution and said it would ensure a lawful and democratic state;
pessimistic supporters: approved constitution but did not think it would
ensure lawful state; *uncertain opponents*: disapproved constitution and did
not know if it would ensure lawful state; *pessimistic opponents*: disapproved
constitution and did not think it would make for a lawful state.

transformation, Zyuganov attacked what had happened since the unrav-
eling of the Soviet party-state after the "golden days" of Leonid Brezhnev.
The first-round ballot gave Yeltsin just over one-third of the popular vote;
Zyuganov just under one-third; and one-third went to other candidates
or against all. In the second-round runoff, in which only two names were
on the ballot, Yeltsin won with 53.8 percent of the vote (Table 3.1).

The 1993 Constitution granted broad authority to the president, but
Boris Yeltsin's style of leadership was better suited to disrupting the
old regime than to creating a steady-state new regime. In the terms
of the Fabian socialist, Beatrice Webb, who divided politicians into a's
(anarchists) and b's (bureaucrats), Yeltsin was an "a." In keeping with
the tradition of earlier Russian leaders, Yeltsin has been described as
governing in the personalistic "neopatrimonial" manner of a primitive
dictator; "nothing happened in the pyramid of power until the president
did something" (Lynch, 2005: 153; cf. Aron, 2000). A striking example

Table 3.1 *Presidential elections 1996–2004*

Rounds	Elections			
	1996		2000	2004
	1st	2nd	1st	1st
	%	%	%	%
Incumbent: Yeltsin/Putin	35.3	53.8	52.9	71.3
Communist runnerup	32.0	40.3	29.2	13.7
Others	32.7	0.0	18.9	15.0
Against all	1.6	4.8	1.9	3.4
Turnout	69.7	68.8	68.6	64.3

Source: Rose and Munro, 2003: 281–282f.; Central Electoral Commission, 2004.

of neopatrimonialism was the scheme that helped finance Yeltsin's 1996 election campaign. Businessmen who had made money during transformation loaned money for the campaign in return for an option to purchase valuable state assets for a small fraction of their value – if Yeltsin won (Klebnikov, 2000; Freeland, 2000). He did, and they became billionaires. The erratic use of presidential prerogatives was increased by Yeltsin's drinking bouts and periodic ill health. Surprise interventions included the sacking of one Russian prime minister who had proven unpopular, Yegor Gaidar, and another, Evgeny Primakov, when his popularity appeared a threat to Yeltsin.

The ultimate challenge of a charismatic leader is whether the regime outlives his time in office. Stalin and de Gaulle successfully met that test; Hitler and Mussolini did not. As the end of President Yeltsin's second term approached, the question of succession became immediately pressing. One alternative canvassed – suspending the constitutional rule limiting the president to two terms – would have identified the regime personally with Yeltsin and made its disruption more likely whenever he left office. A second alternative – allowing a free-for-all competition in the presidential election of 2000 – risked the powers of the presidency coming into the hands of a political opponent who could punish Yeltsin and his family for actions that had enriched them.

The challenge was met by measures that were abnormal but not unconstitutional. In August 1999, Yeltsin named the little-known Vladimir Putin as prime minister. A month later bombs destroyed blocks of flats in Moscow and southern Russia, and the second Chechen war began. Shortly thereafter, Vladimir Putin's popularity began to take off. On the last day of 1999, Boris Yeltsin resigned, making Putin acting president.

In accordance with election law, the presidential contest scheduled for the following summer was moved forward to March 2000. This led to Putin's election as president with an absolute majority of the vote in the first round. Putin decreed an official amnesty protecting the Yeltsin family from legal action because of corruption or other abuses of official powers (Rose and Munro, 2002: chapter 4). Boris Yeltsin thus passed a test that many charismatic leaders failed: the regime he created remained in place. But so did many of its problems (Smith, 1999; Huskey, 2001).

Changing leaders and steadying the state

On becoming president, Vladimir Putin declared his objective was to replace the uncertainties and turbulence of the Yeltsin administration with greater order, by increasing the power of the state and decreasing "the degradation of state and public institutions" (Putin, 2005: 1). To increase the power of the state, Putin endorsed "the dictatorship of law." When questioned about democracy during a meeting with President Bush, Putin replied:

Democracy should not be accompanied by the collapse of the state and the impoverishment of its people. I'm sure that democracy is not anarchy and laissez faire. (quoted in Watson, 2005)

The identification of deficiencies in institutions was shared by many Western experts. However, their prescriptions have differed. In the words of an Organisation for Economic Co-operation and Development expert, "Russia does not need a strong state; it needs a state different in kind to that which it inherited from the Soviet Union" (Tompson, 2004: 115; cf. Holmes, 2003).

Reflecting his political origins in the bureaucracy of the state security service, the KGB, Vladimir Putin has given priority to strengthening the autocratic rather than the plebiscitarian element of the Russian regime. An early action was to "repatriate" to the Kremlin powers that Boris Yeltsin had granted regional governors in order to win their support. Although the regime remains nominally federal, the reforms have strengthened the *vertikal*, that is, the capacity of Moscow to control regional governors. In his first term, Putin established seven federal districts or super-regions to "supervise" the eighty-nine regions; five of the seven district heads were generals. Governors and chairs of regional legislature were then removed from the upper tier of the Duma, the Federation Council, thus losing their immunity from prosecution. Tax laws were changed so that more tax revenue came to central government and less went to the regions (Petrov and Slider, 2005). In his second term,

Putin has gained the power to appoint all governors, thus making them dependent on the Kremlin for their office.

Consistent with his socialization as "a pure and utterly successful product of Soviet education" (Putin, 2000: 41), the president has reduced the scope for organizations to act independently of the regime. On the economic front, Putin has repatriated properties of selected oligarchs, that is, Russian business tycoons who made billions of dollars through the privatization of natural resources during the Yeltsin presidency and who subsequently, in Putin's eyes, "*failed the loyalty test*" (Brown, 2001b: 48; italics in the original), that is, promoted public criticism of his administration through their media interests. In Putin's first term, Boris Berezovsky, a tycoon with oil interests who also owned majority stakes in ORT television and TV6, fled abroad to avoid prosecution; groups close to the Kremlin took over his media assets. Then Vladimir Gusinsky, owner of Media-Most and NTV, which broadcast a satirical political puppet show, was arrested and threatened with criminal prosecution on tax charges. On surrendering his media interests, he was allowed to flee abroad. In his second term, Putin moved against Aleksandr Khodorkovsky, owner of Yukos, one of the world's major oil producers. Khodorkovsky was convicted and jailed in 2005 on charges of fraud, theft, and tax evasion. Yukos was driven into bankruptcy by Russian courts and then sold off to an obscure company that met the Kremlin's loyalty test (Tompson, 2004).

Since the Soviet regime did not permit independent institutions of civil society to exist, they were non-existent or weak when the Russian Federation was launched. A study of political parties in the early 1990s was aptly entitled *Democracy from Scratch* (Fish, 1995; see also Lukin, 2000). Since NGOs are by definition independent of the state, the Putin administration has sought to restrict their autonomy. In November 2001, it promoted a civic forum to discuss ways in which NGOs could be mobilized in support of public policy (Remington, 2006: 168–169). Individual journalists perceived by the Kremlin as unfriendly have been intimidated by threats and pressures on their employers (Fish, 2005: 67ff.).

Attacks on selected media tycoons have made it difficult for NGOs critical of the regime to find domestic financial support (cf. Alfred Evans, Henry, and Sundstrom, 2006). To reduce the scope for "interference" in Russian affairs by foreign funders of Russian NGOs, a law restricting such financial support was enacted in 2006. It would allow authorities to terminate funding by such organizations as George Soros's Open Society Institute and the Ford Foundation.

While competitive elections have continued to be held, their top-down management has increasingly turned them into plebiscites. In the election in 2000, there were eleven different candidates on the ballot representing communist, liberal, and nationalist groups and nominal independents. However, the candidates were not competing on level terms. As the acting president, Vladimir Putin was seeking confirmation in office; the other ten were challengers. The administrative resources of the presidency were mobilized to make the ballot appear to be an endorsement of a trustworthy leader – and the administrative resources of the Kremlin are far greater and less constrained than in established democracies (Wilson, 2005). The fragmentation of competition enabled Putin to win a landslide victory with 52.9 percent of the vote; almost half the vote was split between ten other candidates.

Notwithstanding the shortage of time, prior to the Duma election in December 1999, the Kremlin created Unity as a party to support Putin; it came a very close second to the Communist Party with 23.3 percent of the vote. In the new Duma, there was ample time for the Kremlin to use its patronage to coopt the support of Duma members, especially nominal independents, and to change the electoral law. It organized a party to provide legislative support, United Russia, a merger of Unity and its major centrist competitor, Fatherland. The creation of a large party representing the Kremlin isolated the Communists and pro-market liberals at the extremes (Remington, 2006). A new law on political parties was designed to reduce their number by increasing the barriers for parties to qualify for the ballot. While most political scientists endorse a party system in which larger and fewer parties compete for votes, in Russia, "The attempt to freeze the system is occurring at a time which is particularly beneficial for the Putin presidency" (Bacon, 2004: 49).

At the 2003 Duma election, United Russia won almost half the seats in the Duma and the remainder were split among three parties and independents. By the time the Duma was organized, the attraction of patronage from the Kremlin gave United Russia a two-thirds' majority, sufficient to amend the constitution. Whereas previously the chairmanship of Duma committees had been shared between parties, United Russia claimed the chairmanship of all committees. United Russia's general secretary, Valery Bogomolov, declared, "The Duma's place is not for political discussion but technical issues" (quoted in Jack, 2004). Raising to 7 percent the minimum share of the vote required to win proportional representation seats has made it more difficult for opposition parties to win seats, and the elimination of single-member districts has made it virtually impossible for independent politicians to win seats in the Duma (see chapter 10).

The presidential election of 2004 demonstrated how a nominally competitive election can effectively be a plebiscite. Neither the Communist Party nor the Liberal Democratic Party bothered to nominate its leader: the Communists nominated a former Agrarian Party member, and Vladimir Zhirinovsky nominated one of his former bodyguards. One candidate, Sergei Mironov, speaker of the upper house of parliament, endorsed Putin and compared his own role with that of a contender for the heavyweight boxing crown: by appearing on the ballot, he gave Putin a chance to show his knockout strength (Franchetti, 2004). The two candidates that could claim independence from the Kremlin – Irina Khakamada and Sergei Glazyev – together polled only 7.9 percent of the vote. OSCE observers declared that, while the unfair conduct of the election boosted Putin's share of the vote to 71.3 percent, his popularity was sufficient to secure him a majority of votes without such a boost (see Colton, 2005).

A decade and a half after the foundation of the Russian Federation, Vladimir Putin appears to have established an elite equilibrium: those seeking office or influence accept it as "the only regime in town." Elite support for the regime is, however, only half of what is needed to establish a steady-state regime. It also requires the willing or at least resigned acceptance of the Russian people.

4   Uncertainties of transformation: a view from the bottom

> I survived.
>
> Abbé Sieyès, when asked what he did during the French Revolution

Regimes are assessed from the top down by constitutional lawyers, by journalists, and by ambitious political elites. In the Soviet era the top-down approach to politics was of overwhelming importance. In the new regime, attention continues to be concentrated on the world of politics within the *koltsevaya doroga*, the ring road of Moscow. The Kremlin puts pressure on the media to spin stories to its liking. Television programmers want pictures showing the president in motion or of a celebrity commentator against a Moscow backdrop. Print journalists can report a wider view of life, but favor what is immediate and what is exceptional rather than the "ordinariness" of everyday life.

However, it is politically as well as methodologically misleading to infer mass opinion from the statements of political elites. Even though in international law the government may legitimately claim to speak for the whole population, every election shows that the electorate is divided. Social science offers a way to capture differences of opinion through a sample survey representative of the population nationwide. A carefully designed questionnaire can capture political attitudes toward transformation and relate them to differences in the social and economic circumstances of respondents. If questions are repeated in a number of surveys over the years, this will differentiate between firmly held values that change little in response to events, and opinions that show a trend or fluctuate over time.

The unrelenting efforts that the Communist regime made to mobilize its subjects reflected the need of governors for the passive support of those at the bottom of society. However, ordinary Russians did not welcome the intrusion of government into their ordinary lives. During the uncertainties of the Gorbachev reforms, those at the bottom of the political order were passive spectators of the struggle within the Soviet elite. Only after reforms introduced competitive elections did Russians express their rejection of the powers that be. Unlike East Germany, there were no big street demonstrations for or against the Soviet regime. Unlike Yugoslavia, the breakup of the Soviet Union did not precipitate a major war between CIS countries. But transformation did disrupt the non-market economy on which Russians had relied for their daily sustenance. The immediate question facing ordinary Russians was not "How should the country be governed?"; it was "How can our household get its daily bread and potatoes?"

Before *glasnost*, the Communist regime sought to keep public opinion out of politics: the party knew what people ought to think, and whatever line it pronounced was obediently repeated by subjects. *Glasnost* made it possible for social scientists to conduct surveys of public opinion. The next section describes how the New Russia Barometer (NRB) was developed in the final months of the Soviet Union to record how the Russian population was reacting to transformation. The second section reports political values of Russians at the beginning of a political voyage toward an unknown destination in a ship of state of uncertain seaworthiness. Since the immediate concern of Russians was to cope with material challenges, the third section reports strategies that households used to find food for each day's meals and to get by throughout the year. In addition, Russians had to come to terms with new institutions. Contrary to the expectations of many Westerners, Russians responded to political transformation with patience rather than frustration and protest.

From controlled to free inquiry

The totalitarian vocation of the Soviet regime meant, as dissident Nadezhda Mandelstam wrote, "No group has the right to its own opinion" (quoted in Wyman, 1997: 3). For ideological reasons, the Soviet regime could not admit popular dissatisfaction. Yet it also maintained an elaborate domestic security apparatus, implying that some subjects held anti-regime opinions that should be suppressed.

Opening up Pandora's box

The first social science surveys of Russians were conducted outside Russia. The Second World War resulted in a substantial displacement of Russians, and many thousands ended up in Western nations. They were interviewed in a massive project sponsored by the United States government (see Inkeles and Bauer, 1959). The decision of the Brezhnev administration to allow Jews to emigrate was followed up by large-scale surveys of Russian-born immigrants to the United States and Israel

(Millar, 1987; Ofer and Vinokur, 1992). Influences on political, social, and economic attitudes familiar in Western societies, such as age and occupational class, were found to create differences among emigrants too.

Within the Soviet Union, sociology was abstract, philosophical, and ideological. Because empirical research could produce knowledge independent from the party line, it was discouraged and controlled. Russian social scientists who wanted to maintain their professional positions applied self-censorship. Those who published what the party disapproved of were deprived of their posts. The desire of the party-state to understand the world of work and younger citizens did permit some small-scale surveys. Boris Grushin pioneered surveys in Taganrog. However, his work caused a reaction against empirical research. Between 1967 and 1981, Grushin had four manuscripts about public opinion turned down by Soviet publishing houses (Shlapentokh, 1987).

The opening up of society and the introduction of competitive elections made the political elite conscious of the need to understand how people at the base of society were reacting to unprecedented changes at the top. The rapidity with which opinions appeared to be changing in response to Gorbachev's initiatives placed a premium on obtaining information quickly. A sample survey of public opinion can be conducted quickly and report results within a week of the last interview. Moreover, survey interviews can ask more questions than an official census, and can ask topical or politically sensitive questions that official censuses avoid.

In 1988, the All-Union Center for Public Opinion Research (VCIOM) was created under the sponsorship of the State Labor Committee and the All-Union Trade Union Council. Its director was Tatyana Zaslavskaya, and Grushin and Yury Levada, who became director in 1992, were also involved. Official sponsorship provided the funding required to meet the capital costs of establishing a nationwide infrastructure of interviewers and computer links with VCIOM's Moscow headquarters. Respondents who had heard criticisms of government voiced on state television became aware that it was not dangerous to voice opinions critical of government. Before Mikhail Gorbachev left office, all kinds of surveys of public opinion were undertaken and published.

The New Russia Barometer

In response to the fall of Communist regimes after the fall of the Berlin Wall in November 1989, Richard Rose began developing a survey questionnaire to study the response of ordinary people to the transformation of their societies. The first survey went in the field in Bulgaria and

Czechoslovakia in spring 1991, and in autumn 1991 the multinational New Democracies Barometer was launched in collaboration with the Paul Lazarsfeld Society, Vienna, to monitor public opinion across Central and Eastern Europe (see www.abdn.ac.uk/cspp).[1]

In May 1991, Rose met Peter Aven, then a junior research fellow at the International Institute for Systems Analysis in Vienna and the following year a minister in the Yegor Gaidar government. With characteristic Russian forcefulness, Aven urged Rose to do a survey in Russia. A conference in Cambridge in July 1991 gave an opportunity for extensive discussions with Russian social scientists about what should and could be done to learn more about what ordinary Russians were thinking. Discussions were suspended by the abortive coup and then resumed in November 1991 in Moscow, where the first New Russia Barometer questionnaire was prepared. The snow was falling, and the Soviet Union was falling too. The initial New Russia Barometer survey went in the field in January 1992, the first month of the Russian Federation.

The New Russia Barometer has sought to apply normal political science methods in abnormal circumstances. When a country is undergoing a treble transformation, novel questions are required. Whereas Western surveys deal with competition between political parties for votes, the New Russia Barometer asks about competition between regimes for popular support, since the fundamental choice is not who governs but what kind of political system a country is to have. Instead of assuming that Russia's rulers have been trying to build a Western-style democratic regime, the NRB asks Russians to say what they think of the regime that actually governs them. Most Western surveys in Russia use a destination model, that is, asking questions about democratic and market norms in order to measure how near or far Russians are from endorsing Western values; they usually ignore the Soviet legacy. The New Russia Barometer is concerned with how people evaluate their past experience, as well as their present views and hopes and fears for the future.

The bottom-up construction of the NRB questionnaire has the same theoretical basis as classic American public opinion studies, "the point of view of the actor," that is, the world as it appears to people being interviewed (Campbell, et al., 1960: 27). Asking about topics and abstractions that Russians neither know nor care about invites the creation of answers that are ephemeral "non-attitudes" (Converse, 1964). The NRB surveys recognize that people will give the most meaningful answers to questions

[1] The results of NRB surveys can readily be compared with more than 100 New Europe Barometer surveys covering sixteen post-Communist countries, including all eight new member-states of the European Union, Balkan countries, and other CIS countries such as Ukraine, Belarus, and Moldova (see www.abdn.ac.uk/cspp; Rose, Mishler, and Haerpfer, 1998; Rose, 2005).

that refer to their own experiences and that of people they know. Therefore, the first section of each NRB questionnaire concentrates on activities that at the time of transformation were anything but routine, such as getting paid if in work, and growing food on a household plot. Before the term became fashionable, the NRB asked batteries of questions about informal and formal social capital (for the full English-language text of all questionnaires, see www.abdn.ac.uk/cspp/quest-index.shtml).

From the beginning, NRB surveys have been conducted in collaboration with the leading Russian not-for-profit survey institute, founded as VCIOM, which carries out a diverse range of surveys. Its director, Professor Yury Levada, had been deprived of his chair at Moscow State University in 1972 for lecturing on Talcott Parsons. In 2003, the Putin government used a characteristic legal technicality to take control of VCIOM and appoint a director dependent on the government. Its professional staff reorganized their work as the Levada Center, and the same people continue to conduct NRB surveys (www.levada.ru). To avoid confusion with the organization now under the control of the government, NRB surveys are consistently referred to as conducted by the Levada Center.

New Russia Barometer surveys are nationwide samples of the population of the Russian Federation from Murmansk to Vladivostok. The breakup of the Soviet Union radically simplified the task of interviewing, reducing the population from a multiethnic conglomeration of peoples in fifteen very diverse republics to that of the Russian Federation, in which four-fifths of the population are Russian. Because it is a nationwide survey, five-sixths of NRB respondents do *not* live in Moscow.[2] NRB surveys normally interview 1,600 to 2,000 people. The large sample size reduces sampling error to a few percentage points.

Russia's history of restrictions on freedom of expression implies that people will not voice their "real" opinions when interviewed. Insofar as this is the case, answers to political questions should be uniform, and uniformly positive. However, this is not the case. Instead of everyone giving the same answer, as happened in Soviet elections, NRB respondents consistently divide in their political opinions and, as subsequent chapters will show, a majority often report negative views of the regime, of the president of Russia, or of both. Nor have Russians taken refuge by answering "don't know" to questions critical of the regime. Because the NRB survey focuses on familiar topics, don't knows are relatively few.

---

[2] Because of problems of sampling when the Soviet Union broke up, the first NRB sample in January–February 1992 was of the 73 percent of the Russian population living in urban areas. All subsequent NRB surveys have covered both the rural and urban population. Systematic comparison of urban and rural respondents has found little difference in political attitudes, and in multivariate statistical analyses place of residence has little or no significant influence on political opinions.

Table 4.1 *New Russia Barometer surveys since 1992*

	Date	N respondents	Context
I	1992 26 Jan.–25 Feb.	2,106	Start of Russian Federation
II	1993 26 June–22 July	1,975	Inflation high; no constitution
III	1994 15 March–9 April	3,535	After first Duma election
IV	1995 31 March–19 April	1,998	Relatively uneventful
V	1996a 12–31 January	2,426	Between elections
VI	1996b 25 July–2 August	1,599	After presidential election
VII	1998 6 March–13 April	2,002	Just before ruble devaluation
VIII	2000a 13–29 January	2,003	Between elections
IX	2000b 14–18 April	1,600	After Putin's first election
X	2001 17 June–3 July	2,000	Relatively uneventful
XI	2003a 12–26 June	1,601	End of Putin's first term
XII	2003b 12–22 December	1,601	After Duma election
XIII	2004 18–23 March	1,602	After Putin's reelection
XIV	2005 3–23 January	2,107	Relatively uneventful
	Total respondents	28,155	

For example, when asked about the extent of corruption among Russian government officials, only 2 percent reply don't know. When the 2005 NRB survey asked whether respondents thought people in their community were afraid to say what they think to foreigners, 75 percent said they were not afraid to voice their views. Only 5 percent thought people were definitely afraid and 20 percent thought this somewhat likely. The minority of Russians who indicated some fear in speaking out did not answer key political questions differently (Rose, 2006a).

While transforming events may be concentrated into a short period of time, it takes years for their consequences to emerge. In 1992, political opinions were based on hopes and fears for the future; today, they can be based on a decade and a half of experience of how the new regime actually works. To understand under what circumstances and to what extent the new regime has developed popular support requires asking the same questions repeatedly over a decade or longer in order to see how much or how little Russians change their political evaluations in response to the ups and downs of the economy, changes in presidents, and the passage of time.

The New Russia Barometer provides trend indicators about support for the regime and its alternatives from the time the first round went in the field in January 1992 to January 2005, the latest survey analyzed in this book (Table 4.1). With the passage of time, researchers as well as Russians have learned from experience. Thus, the Barometer has added questions to evaluate fresh developments and as analysis of previous surveys has called attention to points meriting more consideration. Because of competition for space on the questionnaire, some indicators are omitted from some NRB rounds in order to explore fresh points (see Appendix A for details). Between 1992 and 2005, a total of fourteen New Russia Barometer surveys were conducted. Some surveys have been fielded shortly before or after an election and some when conditions appeared *normalno*, a word that refers to different circumstances than the English idea of what is normal. Of this total, seven NRB surveys were fielded when Boris Yeltsin was president and seven since Vladimir Putin became president.[3]

Values amidst uncertainty

Transformation radically alters the conventional definition of politics as the art of the possible. The 1917 Russian Revolution made what was formerly unimaginable seem possible, and so did the collapse of the Soviet Union. What Russians could now hope for was no longer limited to what the Communist Party would allow.

For the great majority of Russians, the new regime was an unknown phenomenon. Few had knowledge of foreign countries to employ as a source of guidance or evaluation. The first NRB survey found that only 5 percent had a friend or relative living in the West, and the vast majority had never traveled outside the Soviet bloc. The Communist Party carefully controlled what could be learned about capitalist societies that Marxist theory predicted were bound to collapse. A saying about the two principal newspapers of the Soviet Union – *Pravda* (Russian for truth) and *Izvestiya* (Russian for news) – was: "In the news there is no truth, and the truth is not in the news."

Enduring values

The collapse of the Soviet Union made it possible for Russians to articulate, in public, privately held opinions. Since the first New Russia Barometer survey went in the field a few weeks after the new regime was launched, the replies given reflect what Russians believed after a lifetime of exposure to Soviet doctrines. Given the vacuum in institutions, the NRB questionnaire concentrated on asking people to evaluate eight

---

[3] December elections for the Duma and for the presidency a few months later have resulted in two surveys in some years and none in a subsequent year. Where two surveys are held in the same year, they are distinguished by the addition of an a or b to the year.

Table 4.2 *Values at the start of transformation*

Q. We often hear the following words. What feelings do they evoke?			
	Positive (%)	Difficult to answer (%)	Negative (%)
Freedom	78	17	4
One and indivisible Russia	75	20	5
Christianity	73	24	3
Glasnost	63	21	16
Capitalism	25	46	28
Socialism	24	42	33
Perestroika	21	33	45
Marxism-Leninism	16	46	37

Source: New Russia Barometer I (1992).

political symbols relevant to different Russian regimes – tsarist, Soviet, and prospective (Table 4.2).

Slavophiles and their latter-day Soviet followers argued that political freedom was inconsistent with or irrelevant to Russian values and institutions. The first NRB survey showed the speciousness of that argument. The most frequently endorsed value was freedom (*svoboda*): 78 percent of Russians felt positive about freedom, and only 4 percent were negative. Furthermore, even though openness (*glasnost*) was part of the failed package of Gorbachev reforms, Russians could differentiate its meaning from its source. Openness was endorsed by 63 percent of Russians, and only 16 percent were negative.

A lifetime of indoctrination into Marxist-Leninist ideology generated indifference and even dislike. Only 16 percent of Russians felt positive about Marxism-Leninism compared to 37 percent negative; a plurality were indifferent. Classroom indoctrination made every Russian adult aware of differences between economic systems: socialism was what people ought to want and capitalism was bad for society. However, a plurality of Russians expressed indifference to both types of economic symbols. Among those with opinions, 24 percent showed positive attachment to socialism, with which every Russian was familiar in its "real, existing" form, while 33 percent were negative. Similarly, capitalism was positively endorsed by 25 percent, 28 percent were negative, and the largest group had no opinion. Only 7 percent of Russians reflected the traditional party line, being positive about Marxism-Leninism and socialism and negative about capitalism. By contrast, 12 percent took the diametrically opposite position, being positive about capitalism and negative about socialism and Marxism-Leninism.

Whereas Gorbachev's tolerance of freedom of discussion was widely welcomed, his effort to reform the Soviet socialist system (*perestroika*) had little support among the mass of Russians. Only one-fifth were positive about it and a plurality were negative. In the final years of the Soviet Union, Boris Yeltsin had exploited this sentiment by arguing that Gorbachev's reforms were not going far enough. However, after the experience of the post-socialist transformation of their society, public opinion reacted in favor of the unreformed Communist system (Figure 7.2).

Communist campaigning against religion and the promotion of a materialist approach to life did not create negative views of Christianity; it was counterproductive. Even though few Russians are church-goers (see chapter 6), almost three-quarters reported feeling positive about Christianity, more than four times the percentage feeling positive about Marxism-Leninism. Hardly anyone was negative about Christianity.

The nationalist slogan – "one and indivisible Russia" (*edinaya i nedelimaya Rossiya*) – was denounced as counterrevolutionary by Stalin and Trotsky. However, it was positively endorsed by three-quarters of Russians in 1992. This does not reflect a yearning for life under the tsar; instead, it appears to be a reflection of national pride. Early in the process of transformation, the NRB found that 71 percent felt proud of being Russian, compared to only 16 percent having no opinion and 12 percent lacking pride.

Pride in Russia is national rather than a reflection of the imperial position of Russians in the Soviet Union. The first NRB survey asked "What would you like this country to be?," and offered five different choices. Only 19 percent said they would like to see the Soviet Union continue as it was; an additional 22 percent endorsed a reformed Soviet Union with strong republics. The largest group, 39 percent, favored a united, independent Russia with a strong government in Moscow or with significant powers devolved to Russia's regions. The median group, 19 percent, favored a Commonwealth of Independent States with Russia an active partner.

At the beginning of transformation, a big majority wanted the new regime to follow a distinctive Russian path rather than try to emulate European countries. When the third NRB survey asked whether the country should develop like West European countries or according to "our own" traditions, only 22 percent endorsed following a European path, compared to 78 percent wanting the regime to develop according to national traditions. While Boris Yeltsin and Vladimir Putin governed differently, neither sought to emulate West European methods of governance.

Given the experience of the Soviet past, in which both freedom and order were lacking, a positive appreciation of both values is understandable. In a democratic regime, freedom and order are necessarily joined.

However, the immediate consequence of Russia's transformation was more freedom and less order. When the first NRB survey asked about the consequences of the Gorbachev reforms, 70 percent said that it had given people the opportunity to say what they thought, but 75 percent also considered that the new regime was failing to maintain order in society. This does not imply that Russians would sacrifice freedom for order, but that they valued both (see Carnaghan, 2001).

Coping strategies

Soviet ideology was profoundly and pervasively collectivist: the party-state's control of society's resources was justified on the grounds that it should and could look after the welfare of all Soviet subjects. In order to establish the extent to which Russians were committed to collectivist values, the first New Russia Barometer survey included a battery of questions asking people to choose between the state taking responsibility for welfare and individuals doing so.

After the experience of how the Soviet regime looked after the welfare of individuals under "real existing socialism," a majority of Russians consistently rejected collectivist in favor of individualist values (Figure 4.1). Income equality was rejected by seven-eighths of respondents in favor of individual effort determining what people earned. Furthermore, two-thirds thought that enterprises would be better run by market-oriented entrepreneurs than under state ownership. Notwithstanding the insecurities induced by transformation, almost three-fifths preferred a job that paid more money, even if it risked unemployment, rather than a secure job that paid less. Almost half did endorse the state being responsible for benefits such as education and health care, a normal feature of a European welfare state.

The legacy of the Soviet Union was a population dominated by those who were prepared to look after themselves. In response to the four questions reported in Figure 4.1, one-quarter of Russians chose the individualist option all four times, and an additional 32 percent endorsed the individualist option three times. By contrast, only 4 percent consistently endorsed the collectivist alternative for all four questions, and 14 percent endorsed that alternative three times. While this does not mean that Russians were bursting to become businessmen and -women, it does show that people were not prepared to trust the Soviet state to look after their needs, an attitude that continued in the new regime.

Russians were challenged to look after themselves by the treble transformation of society. It was a textbook example of collective shock that Emile Durkheim (1952: 252) characterized as producing widespread anomie,

Figure 4.1 *ENDORSEMENT OF INDIVIDUAL RESPONSIBILITY*

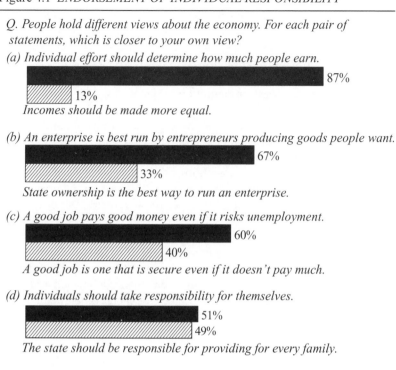

Q. People hold different views about the economy. For each pair of statements, which is closer to your own view?

(a) Individual effort should determine how much people earn.

87%

13%

Incomes should be made more equal.

(b) An enterprise is best run by entrepreneurs producing goods people want.

67%

33%

State ownership is the best way to run an enterprise.

(c) A good job pays good money even if it risks unemployment.

60%

40%

A good job is one that is secure even if it doesn't pay much.

(d) Individuals should take responsibility for themselves.

51%

49%

The state should be responsible for providing for every family.

0%   20%   40%   60%   80%   100%

Source: New Russia Barometer I (1992).

a lack of social norms to live by. In his classic study of *Suicide*, Durkheim argued that the disruption of collective norms was likely to create "intolerable suffering," even to the point of self-destruction. New Russia Barometer surveys have found that Durkheim grossly overstated the negative effects of societal transformation on individuals. Instead of feeling a sense of helplessness, the median Russian feels he or she has some control over his or her life and more Russians feel a sense of control over their lives than feel helpless (Rose, 2003).

Coping through the household economy

While waiting to learn about the regime political elites would supply, Russians had to get on with the everyday business of living. However, the pervasive effects of transformation meant that Russians could not carry on everyday activities as before. Short-term economic costs were visible in shops, where goods were in short supply or prices rose weekly or daily with inflation, while the prospect of material benefits was distant. In pursuing daily needs for food and household staples, Russians adapted strategies developed in days of the command economy. Concurrently, the patience developed in Soviet times enabled Russians to live with uncertainties that went far beyond the Western definition of deferred gratification.

In the command economy, shortages of goods were chronic problems. Even if people had privileged access to some shortage goods or could use connections to get goods under the counter, virtually every household had to rely on shops for some everyday necessities. Unlike a market economy, there was no certainty that shops would have what people needed. Searching for shops where goods were available was so routinized that many families had a designated shopper or shared the task of queuing according to the circumstance of family members.

The breakdown of the command economy intensified shortages, since shops could no longer rely on normal sources of supply, and consumers could no longer rely on customary connections. In January 1992, half of Russian adults spent at least two hours a day queuing for food and other necessities (Figure 4.2). Russians who did not spend time queuing were

Figure 4.2 *QUEUING FOR HOURS THE NORM*

Q. About how much time do you spend each day standing in queues or searching for what you need in shops?

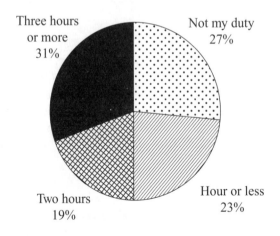

Three hours or more 31%

Not my duty 27%

Two hours 19%

Hour or less 23%

Source: New Russia Barometer I (1992).

not well-connected or rich but members of a family in which another person searched and queued, such as an office worker who could leave the office in the morning and return in the afternoon without losing any pay. Half of Russians aged sixty or over reported spending at least three hours a day searching for goods or queuing, thus becoming non-waged workers in Russian-style retail distribution.

In a market economy, queuing is not necessary because a sufficient quantity of goods is produced to fill the shelves of shops. The move to the market was quickly reflected in individual experience. By the time of the second New Russia Barometer in 1993, the amount of time the median person spent queuing was no more than an hour a day. In 1994, more than two-thirds of Russians said their households no longer needed to spend even an hour a day queuing. The question was then dropped from NRB surveys, since a shortage of goods in shops had been replaced by a shortage of money to buy goods on display.

In addition to queuing, in Soviet times most Russian households supplemented foodstuffs they found in shops with food they grew on small vegetable plots or at their *dacha*. When the Russian Federation was launched, more than two-thirds of households had a plot of ground where they could grow food, including 54 percent of urban residents. In addition, many had relatives or friends with land to grow food. The plots that urban-dwellers cultivated were not those of rural relatives; they were normally a bus-ride or suburban train-ride away. Having home-produced sources of staple foods insulated Russians from the worst effects of inflation and helped avoid destitution (Rose and Tikhomirov, 1993).

When the formal institutions of Soviet society collapsed, a majority of Russians had social capital that they could use. It had been developed in Soviet times in order to get things done by hook or by crook, as appropriate to the situation. Sometimes it took "pre-modern" forms, such as relying on family and friends for household repairs or transport, and sometimes "anti-modern" forms, such as relying on connections or bribes to supply housing or a university place to persons not entitled to these benefits. Social capital was more often used to exploit the regime for a family's benefit than to support it for the collective good (cf. Rose, 2000b; Putnam, 1993; Rose and Weller, 2003).

During the first year of the new regime, the effects of economic transformation caused the majority of Russians problems, but they were difficulties that households could overcome. When the NRB asked if households had gone without food, clothing, or heating in the past year because of a shortage of goods or money, only 2 percent could be described as threatened with destitution, because they often went without all three necessities, and 17 percent went without two necessities. However, 17 percent had all three necessities throughout the year and 45 percent always had two. The median Russian reported sometimes going without food or needed clothes but, thanks to the centralized and subsidized system of heating Soviet-era homes, never going without heating. Households were resilient when confronted by the disruptions of transformation, from time to time tightening their belts or mending clothes and then returning to their normal standard of living (cf. Rose, 1995a).

The negative impact of transformation was reduced because the official economy was not the only economy on which Russians relied. Most Russian households had a portfolio of economies combining official wages, cash received in the unofficial economy, and social economies in which household members did things for themselves and exchanged services with friends and relatives without any money changing hands. The first NRB survey found that only a third of Russians relied solely on their official job or pension; a year later only one-quarter were vulnerable because of relying solely on the official economy (Rose, 1993). Reliance on a portfolio of economies, unofficial as well as official, enabled most Russians to cope with the effects of economic transformation without approaching destitution.

Coping politically: patience not protest

In a major comparative study entitled *Why Men Rebel*, Ted Gurr (1970) theorized that, if a new regime is unable to meet expectations of its subjects, this makes individuals frustrated, and frustration will encourage popular protests that can lead to the disruption of the regime. In advancing this argument, Gurr drew on a large body of psychological research demonstrating a correlation between frustration and aggressive behavior by individuals.

However, generalizations based on clinical psychology ignore the repressive constraints that a regime can impose on individuals, forcing people to contain their frustration. In the Soviet Union, repression could lead to alcoholism whereas aggression could lead to the gulag. The repressive power of the Soviet regime was demonstrated by the fact that the collectivization of agriculture, which forcibly transformed the lives of millions of peasants, did not create a rebellious anti-regime movement in the countryside. Nikolai Shmelev explains this as due to peasants "lacking political organization and confidence in their own power" when confronted by agents of a regime prepared to kill to enforce their demands (quoted in Shlapentokh, 2001: 146).

Gurr's model of frustration leading to aggression ignores the importance of patience (Rose, 1997). While a frustrated child can immediately express himself or herself by striking out at a parent, a frustrated subject cannot spontaneously take actions that would challenge a regime. To organize a rebellion against a national government takes time and patience. Bolshevik opponents of the tsar were patient; the 1917 Russian Revolution was the result of a generation of activities by organizers who did not know whether they would live to see the day when their hopes might be realized. In the Soviet era, the party-state's emphasis on the time required to build Communism taught its subjects to be patient. The brutal means used to turn a rural into an industrial society were described as costs that had to be paid to arrive at a classless society some day. No indication was given as to when this goal would be achieved. Whether or not a Russian believed that the costs of transformation would bring benefits, in a repressive political system there was little alternative to waiting patiently.

The transformation of the bureaucratic command economy into a market economy imposed more than half a dozen years of costs, involving double- and treble-digit rates of inflation annually and the contraction rather than growth of the official economy. This did not cause great frustration, because there were low expectations of whether or when the new regime would deliver benefits. Russians showed the hallmark of patience: a readiness to live with uncertainty for an indefinite period (Figure 4.3). When the second NRB survey asked Russians how long it would be before they would be content with their standard of living, 50 percent did not know when or whether they would ever become satisfied. One-quarter thought that they would never be satisfied, and one-fifth thought it would take anything from a year to ten years to become content.

The absence of aggressive responses to transformation was not due to a lack of interest in politics. Transformation gave a novel stimulus to the political awareness promoted by the mobilization efforts of the Soviet regime. When the first New Russia Barometer asked whether people were interested in political affairs, five-sixths said they were. Four-fifths followed the news on television, three-fifths read about politics in the newspapers, and more than half discussed politics with friends. The median Russian followed the news in at least two different ways. The key word was "follow," for Russian subjects had been socialized to wait patiently to see what the regime supplied.

Russians preferred to follow politics from a distance rather than become actively involved in protest activities. When the first New Russia Barometer asked about mass political demonstrations, there was an overwhelming belief that protests would occur: 93 percent thought there would be protest demonstrations about inflation, 81 percent expected protests about the political situation, and 76 percent protests about unemployment (Figure 4.4). Altogether, 67 percent thought protests likely on all

Figure 4.3 *UNCERTAINTY MET WITH PATIENCE*

Q. How long will it be before you have reached a standard of living with which you are content?

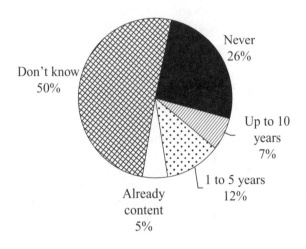

Source: New Russia Barometer II (1993).

three counts, 21 percent on two counts, 8 percent on one count, and only 4 percent thought there would not be any protests.

However, the majority of Russians wanted to stay home rather than participate in demonstrations; less than one-quarter said they would definitely demonstrate against inflation, one-sixth would demonstrate against unemployment, and barely one-tenth would definitely participate in political demonstrations. In the early days of the new regime, there was no way of knowing whether the security services would respond to protests with violence and mass arrests. The mass disinclination to protest was borne out by events. In the early years of the new regime, when its support was most uncertain, no nationwide protests were organized. Even when political confrontation between the People's Congress and the Kremlin was at its height in Moscow in early autumn 1993, those who went into the street to protest were a tiny and deviant proportion of the city's population. Muscovites, like Russians in other cities, preferred to go into the street to join queues for shortage goods and to watch political confrontations on television.

Figure 4.4 *RUSSIAN VIEW OF PROTEST: LEAVE ME OUT*

Q. Do you consider it likely that in 1992 there will be mass demonstrations and protests: about inflation? About the political situation in Russia? About unemployment?
Q. If mass demonstrations occur, will you take part?

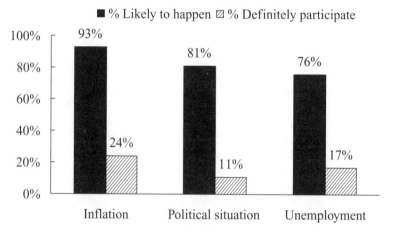

Source: New Russia Barometer I (1992).

An additional reason for abstaining from protest was the belief that it would be of little use. While a big majority of NRB respondents felt free to say what they thought, the government was also seen as free to do whatever it wanted. At the start of transformation, 78 percent thought that ordinary people had little or no influence on government. Nor was there an expectation that the new regime would be more responsive to protests. When asked to forecast how much influence on government ordinary people were likely to have in five years, 62 percent were negative about the prospects of future influence.

Up to a point, patience gave elites time to develop a new regime by a process of trial and error. However, once the consequences of elite actions became clear, ordinary Russians were confronted with the stark choice of whether or not to support the new regime that elites had supplied.

5 Changing levels of regime support

> We must distinguish between government all wise, all just, all powerful,
> and government as it actually is.
>
> Alfred Marshall, *Principles of Economics*

In every political regime, there is competition between people and ideas. In an established democratic system, elections resolve the question: who governs? The competition for ideas includes differences between those who advocate marginal reforms and people satisfied with government "as it actually is." Support for the existing regime and the rejection of alternatives are taken for granted; demands for reform are intended to improve rather than replace a regime.

In a new regime, there can be competition for support between regimes, since everyone knows from experience that there is more than one way that their country can be governed. Political competition is not only about improving the existing regime but also about replacing the current regime by one or more alternatives. To achieve a political equilibrium, the new regime must build positive support for itself, or at least demonstrate either that it is preferable to any alternative regime, or that it is the only regime that is politically possible.

The level of political support at any given point of time is less important than how that support is changing – and in what direction. Insofar as a new regime has little or no reserve from habits of the past, losing support from one year to the next invites ambitious politicians to come forward with an alternative regime and mobilize support to replace it. As long as a new regime is gaining popular support, this discourages those who initially had doubts or preferred an alternative from endorsing regime change and gradually can lead to a steady-state equilibrium. Before either outcome is arrived at, support can veer up and down, leaving a new regime in an unsteady state indefinitely.

Since regimes can alter abruptly while the population does not, transformation raises questions about the extent to which public opinion changes when institutions change. If the values and beliefs of the public are fixed in youth and early adulthood, as theories of political culture and socialization postulate, a change of regimes will create a gap between what new rulers supply and what most subjects regard as normal and desirable, thus making it difficult to achieve support for the new regime. On the other hand, if elites create a new regime in accordance with public opinion, a high level of support can be promptly forthcoming. This has happened in East European countries, where a Moscow-imposed regime was replaced by a national regime accountable to a national electorate. However, in Russia the collapse of the Soviet Union was an unwelcome shock.

The purpose of this chapter is to track the changing level of popular support for the new Russian regime and potential competitors, and then to set out hypotheses about why Russians differ in their views – and why their divisions change with the passage of time. Whether support is relatively high or low, each survey finds Russians divided into three groups: those with a positive view of the regime, those who are negative, and a neutral group. Over a decade and a half, there have been substantial alterations in the percentage of respondents in each group. Popular attitudes toward alternative regimes are more complicated because there are multiple alternatives. Four are examined: getting rid of parliament, becoming a dictatorship, a return to Communism, or letting the army rule. An individual who is very much against the current system can endorse multiple alternatives, but those who favor a single alternative disagree about which alternative ought to be adopted. The dispersal of support between alternatives has meant there is no majority for any one, and a plurality reject all alternative regimes. Four testable hypotheses about the causes of these differences are set out in the third section: socialization and culture matter; the performance of political institutions matters; economics matters; and the passage of time matters. The chapter concludes with an explanation of the statistical methods used to test to what extent and under what circumstances the evidence endorses each hypothesis.

Variable support for the regime as it is

Because support is a generic concept, there is a multiplicity of ways in which questions can be formulated, reflecting differences between theoretical contexts as well as between national contexts. To understand the full implications of political support, it is necessary to have an indication of how strong or weak are the views of those who support and those who reject the regime, and not just a simple percentage figure showing how many are positive about it. Since there is no consensus among political scientists about how much support is enough, trend data is essential to know whether support is increasing or falling. NRB surveys provide empirical evidence about all these points.

Measuring support

Theories of democracy focus on abstract ideals that can be applied to many types of relationship. However, endorsement of the democratic ideal is not the same as the evaluation of a system of government as it actually is. In an established democratic system, replies to the question "Generally speaking, are you satisfied with the way that democracy is working in this country?" can identify dissatisfied democrats who would like to see reforms introduced while continuing to support the regime. However, in an autocratic regime, such a question rests on a false premise, that the regime is democratic, when this is not the case (Canache, Mondak, and Seligson, 2001). When the claims of a regime to be democratic are contested, as in the plebiscitarian autocracy of Russia, it is necessary to measure support independently of endorsement of democracy as an ideal (for further discussion, see Rose, Mishler, and Haerpfer, 1998: chapter 5).

The New Russia Barometer takes a realistic approach: it asks for an evaluation of the regime that political elites have actually supplied; this does not assume that the regime is democratic or autocratic. A realist question makes it possible to ascertain the extent to which there is support for regimes that are plebiscitarian autocracies, constitutional autocracies, or even despotisms. The approach is especially suited to monitoring trends in countries in which the character of the regime is changing as well as contested, and this has been the case in Russia since 1992. Survey evidence shows that it is not necessary for a regime to be democratic to achieve a significant level of popular support (Rose and Mishler, 2002).

While support is a word that is easy to understand in colloquial conversation, the difference between the regime as a set of durable institutions and the government of the day is not so easy to distinguish. However, political transformation gives concrete significance to differences between types of government, since it involves a very public change between two regimes. The New Russia Barometer measure makes use of this fact. It first asks respondents to evaluate the pre-*perestroika* regime, the first regime under which these adults lived, before asking about the current regime.

Q. Here is a scale for ranking how the political system works. The top, plus 100, is the best, and the bottom, minus 100, is the worst. Where on this scale would you put:
(a) The political system before perestroika?

(b) Our current system of governing?
(c) The system of governing we will have in five years?

The current regime is defined ostensively, that is, by pointing at what is there; it thus avoids the use of a label that can be disputed, such as calling the system democratic. Ostensive definition also avoids linking a system of government that has been around for centuries to transient personalities, as is done in American references to the Bush administration or British references to the Blair government. The question also avoids confusing institutions of the regime with its outputs, as happens in a question asking about satisfaction with the performance of government, which can be interpreted as referring to how well the government of the day is managing the economy, a topic that is dealt with in a separate and parallel set of questions (see chapter 8).

In a new regime, the critical issue is whether there is support for the regime as a whole, since there can be competition to replace it. In a new regime, people must accept or reject the regime as it is, a package supplied by elite politics. Like most political packages, the institutions of a new regime are a mixture of attractive and unattractive parts. Evaluating it is like voting in a referendum: a person can only endorse or reject what is actually on offer without alteration, or abstain.

The NRB treats the regime holistically, because transformation is about a pervasive change in central institutions of the state and in their relationship. It is difficult to raise this issue in an established democratic regime in which the great majority of people cannot conceive of being governed any other way than "the American way" or "the British way." Instead, surveys ask about support for particular institutions, such as the courts, or the legislature, or about office-holders such as the president or prime minister. Signs of dissatisfaction or distrust are sometimes "overinterpreted" as indicating a threat to the regime. In fact, such statements indicate no more and no less than a desire to reform institutions or change leaders (see Dalton, 2004: vii, 6ff.).

Unlike Dahl's distinction between democracy and polyarchy, which focuses on the best and the second-best, the NRB scale gives equal weight to negative and positive alternatives. The scale is intentionally long to capture the intensity of respondents' feelings; people can express 100 percent approval or 100 percent loathing. The length of the scale thus captures important differences of degree between those who are lukewarm and those who are very enthusiastic in support for a regime. It also differentiates between those who are somewhat critical and those who are 100 percent against the current regime. The midpoint for evaluating the regime, 0, is the psychological as well as the arithmetic midpoint. An individual

Figure 5.1 *TREND IN SUPPORT FOR NEW REGIME*

Q. Here is a scale for ranking how our system of government works. The top, plus 100, is the best; the bottom, minus 100, the worst. Where on this scale would you put our current system of governing?

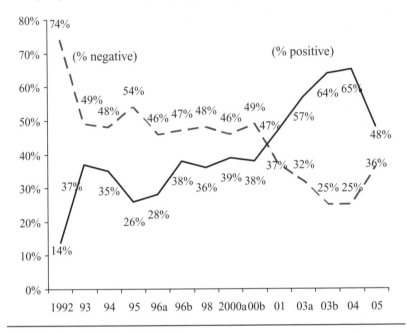

Source: New Russia Barometer surveys.

can choose it if he or she has a neutral attitude or no opinion about the regime.

Variations within and across years

When the first New Russia Barometer went in the field, the Russian Federation was four weeks old. While the old regime was gone, the new regime was a blank. The new regime started off with a big majority of Russians disliking it; 74 percent gave it a rating between −1 and −100, while only 14 percent showed positive support and 12 percent had no opinion (Figure 5.1). Statistically, this implied that the new regime's support could only rise, as it had a low base. However, politically it implied that the new regime was vulnerable to collapse.

Across the years, Russians have continuously been divided about support for the regime, and the aggregate level of support has fluctuated.

After a year, Russians had had at least a little experience, and the median Russian was neutral, falling between the 37 percent supporting the new regime and 49 percent negative. After annual fluctuations, another low point was reached in 1995, when only 26 percent gave positive support to the regime. By 2001, a plurality of Russians were positive about the new regime, and after the presidential election of 2004 a high point was reached when 65 percent were positive. However, a year later support had fallen to 48 percent.

The mean rating given the regime provides a second way of tracking aggregate support. With the passage of time, the central tendency of Russian public opinion has moved from being negative to neutral. In 1992, the mean rating of the regime was −38. It then began to rise, that is, to become less negative (Figure 5.2). It was not until the eleventh NRB survey in 2003 that the mean rating of the regime became slightly positive. Even though 64 percent were positive about the regime in 2003, the tendency was to give it lukewarm endorsement: the average rating of the regime was only +14 on a scale that ran as high as +100. However, by 2005 the mean level of support had fallen back to 0, the exact midpoint of the scale.

Even though the mean rating of the regime tends to hover around the neutral midpoint, this does not mean that most Russians are neutral about it. Instead, it reflects the tendency of those Russians voicing positive support to be counterbalanced by Russians who are negative about the regime. The extent to which Russians are dispersed in their evaluation is summarized statistically by the standard deviation; two-thirds of all replies will normally be within one standard deviation in each direction from the mean. The bigger the standard deviation, the wider the dispersion of regime evaluations. The vertical bars in Figure 5.2 show the standard deviation.

In every NRB survey, there has been a wide dispersion of Russian opinion; the standard deviation has been as high as fifty-two points and never lower than forty-one points. In the first NRB survey, when public opinion about the regime was most negative, two-thirds of Russians gave responses within the range −79 to +3. In the twelfth NRB survey, when the level of support was highest for the current regime, two-thirds were in the range between +61 and −34. When the mean was exactly 0 and the standard deviation +/−45, this indicated that one-sixth of Russians gave the regime a rating higher than +45 and one-sixth gave it a rating lower than −45.

While Russians consistently differ about support for the new regime, there is not polarization between extreme supporters and extreme opponents. In the first NRB survey, when the greatest proportion of Russians were negative about the new regime, only 5 percent gave it the worst

Figure 5.2 *WIDE DISPERSION IN SUPPORT FOR NEW REGIME*

Q. Here is a scale for ranking how our system of government works. The top, plus 100, is the best; the bottom, minus 100, the worst. Where on the scale would you put our current system?

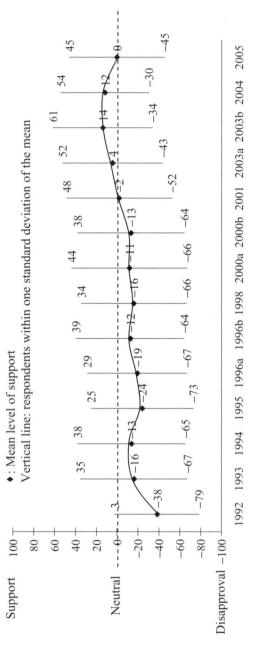

◆ : Mean level of support
Vertical line: respondents within one standard deviation of the mean

Source: New Russia Barometer surveys.

possible score of –100, and in 2004, when support was highest, less than 1 percent gave it the highest possible rating. The distribution of evaluations is bell-shaped, that is, the largest proportion of Russians tend to be close to the year's mean and since the mean is closer to the neutral midpoint than to an extreme point on the scale, they can be described as moderately positive or moderately negative about the regime.

Statements that Russians support or reject the new regime are misleading: in nine NRB surveys, the median respondent has been neutral. There have only been two years in which an absolute majority of NRB respondents have been negative about the regime and three years in which a majority have been positive. However, neutral subjects are consistently the smallest of the three blocs of opinion.

A notable proportion of Russians have been "floating" supporters or opponents of the regime, sometimes endorsing it, sometimes being negative, and sometimes voicing neutral opinions. The aggregate replies illustrate this. For example, when the percentage of Russians feeling positive rose from 14 to 37 percent between 1992 and 1993, this implied that a majority of those registering support had been neutral or negative the year before. The shift from 74 percent being negative about the regime in 1992 to 65 percent being positive in 2003 indicates that more than half of those who had earlier been negative subsequently switched their views.[1]

An important political consequence of "floating" supporters is that the percentage of Russians who have at some time endorsed the regime is substantially larger than the percentage doing so at any one point in time. Thus, people who do not support a regime in one particular survey are not necessarily implacable opponents of the regime; sometimes they may favor the regime, sometimes oppose it, and sometimes be neutral. Individuals who are intermittently positive and negative are more likely to show resigned acceptance than to challenge it. Many supporters of alternative regimes float too, and people who waver back and forth in their views of a dictatorship are less likely to invest the time and effort needed to overthrow the current regime than those who consistently prefer regime change.

The dispersion of opinion about the new regime is best summed up verbally by the statement "some Russians support it while others don't"; and for many individuals it is a question of saying "sometimes I support the regime and sometimes I don't." Thus, instead of generalizing about

[1] The calculations about floating support are net estimates, based on the assumption that every changer moves in the same direction, thus treating net and gross change as the same. Panel studies that reinterview the same individuals about voting behavior find that Russians register a significant amount of movement in countervailing directions, thus making gross change greater than net change (e.g., Colton, 2000: chapter 4).

what all Russians think, we need to understand why Russians differ in whether they support the current regime at any point in time – and what makes Russians change their mind from time to time.

Dispersed support for alternative regimes

A political equilibrium depends not only on support for the current regime but also on rejection of alternatives: the more inclined people are to reject alternative regimes, the more convincing is the current regime's claim to be "the only regime in town." The simplest place for people to look for alternatives is to the past. In the case of Russia, every adult has experienced a Communist regime and, although far distant in time, the tsarist regime has also been a historical fact. The contemporary world also offers alternatives, such as General Pinochet's use of the military to establish an anti-Communist regime in Chile or the resort to civilian dictatorships in Eastern Europe between the wars. In its first two years, the New Russia Barometer concentrated on collecting evaluations of the Soviet regime and the new regime. Beginning in 1994, it also began asking about preferences for a variety of alternative regimes. Rejecting the current regime is no evidence that Russians agree about what they would like to replace it.

Some support for varied alternatives

The strongest expression of a desire to disrupt the status quo is the view that anything is better than the current regime. Therefore, the New Russia Barometer asks if people would approve the suspension of parliament and elections, the institutions that make Russia a plebiscitarian autocracy. Since parties and parliament are distrusted by more than four-fifths of Russians (chapter 7), it would be logical if a big majority wanted to sweep away these distrusted institutions. However, this is not the case. A clear majority, 58 percent, have disapproved of doing away with representative institutions, and 6 percent have no opinion (Figure 5.3). At no time have a majority of Russians endorsed getting rid of elections and parliament.

Since Russians have lived most of their lives in a Communist party-state, people can speak from experience when asked whether they would like the system restored. Unlike Central and East European countries, where Communist apparatchiks adapted to party competition by abandoning the former regime, the Communist Party of Russia does not denounce the old regime. Moreover, it has consistently finished first or second in elections of the Duma and the president. When the NRB first asked if people would like to see the old regime restored, 23 percent

Figure 5.3 *ENDORSEMENT OF ALTERNATIVE REGIMES*

Q. There are different opinions about how to run the state. To what extent do you think it would be better to:

(a) Suspend parliament and elections.

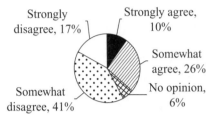

(b) Restore the Communist system.

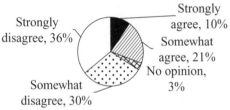

(c) Tough dictatorship is the only way out of the current situation.

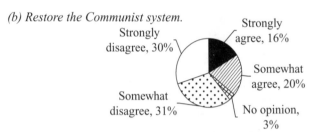

(d) The army should govern the country.

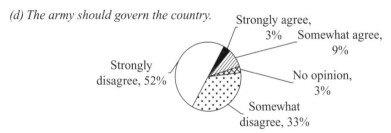

Source: New Russia Barometer surveys.

replied that they would like it back, 16 percent said don't know, and 62 percent were negative. Since then, the number of those favoring a return to Communist rule has risen, while the vote for the Communist Party has declined. Overall, 36 percent have said they would like to see the Communist regime restored; however, most in this category are not strongly committed. Those definitely against a return to a Communist regime outnumber those definitely in favor (Figure 5.3).

In all regimes a degree of leadership is necessary to give direction to government, and politicians such as John F. Kennedy, Margaret Thatcher, and Vladimir Putin have sought votes by promising strong leadership. In a society with a history of despotism, the distinction between a strong leader and a dictator is critical (Rose and Mishler, 1996). Hence, the NRB asks people if they would like a tough dictatorship. In every year an absolute majority have rejected turning to a tough dictatorship, but a substantial minority have been in favor. Over the whole period, almost one-third have endorsed a tough dictatorship while two-thirds have rejected it, and those strongly against a dictatorship outnumber those strongly in favor by a margin of more than three to one (Figure 5.3). While the proportion endorsing a dictatorship is substantial, the political effect is discounted, since it would be difficult to get agreement among the political elite or among the general public about who the dictator ought to be.

Military rule is a familiar form of autocratic government in many parts of the world. Latin America, the Middle East, and Africa are full of examples of a general seizing power in a bloodless or bloody coup. Between the two world wars, military figures were politically prominent in Eastern Europe too. However, in Communist regimes, the military was subject to a very high degree of political control. Party watchdogs (*zampoliti*) were placed in the command structure of the military and Stalin executed generals he suspected of being insufficiently loyal. The regime's desire to keep the military out of politics is shared by the Russian people (Figure 5.3). Those favoring military rule average 12 percent and have never been higher than 15 percent.

At times the New Russia Barometer has asked about additional forms of rule, starting with the longest-lasting regime in Russian history, that of the tsar. While the execution of the tsar's family has ruled out a restoration of the monarchy, it remains the only historical alternative to a Communist regime, and some historians have argued that centuries of tsarist rule acculturated Russians to accept a despotic autocrat. When the fourth to the tenth New Russia Barometers asked if people would like a return to the tsar, an average of 90 percent rejected the idea. Since it is now viewed as part of the distant past, the question was dropped.[2]

---

[2] By contrast, in Bulgaria and Romania, where monarchies were politically salient up to the end of the Second World War, up to one-fifth endorsed a return to a monarchy in

Figure 5.4 *TRENDS IN ENDORSING ALTERNATIVE REGIMES*

(% respondents approving)

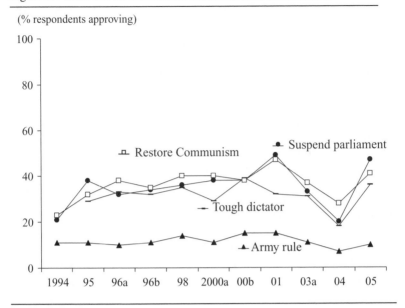

Source: New Russia Barometer surveys.

Fluctuations in support for alternative regimes are notable, but smaller in scale than the ups and downs in support for the current regime (Figure 5.4). Across more than a decade, support for a dictatorship has ranged between 18 and 36 percent; for returning to a Communist regime between 23 and 47 percent; and for the suspension of parliament and elections between 21 and 49 percent. The least fluctuation is in the endorsement of army rule; the proportion rejecting it is consistently very high, more than five-sixths of Russians.

Competition divides support for alternative regimes

While at any given moment a country can only have one regime, there is no restriction on the variety of alternative regimes that can compete for support. As the example of Weimar Germany demonstrates, a democratic regime can simultaneously find that it is competing for support with Communist, nationalist, and Nazi alternatives.

The political vacuum left by the collapse of the Communist party-state created an opening for competition between alternative regimes. Thus, a

New Europe Barometer surveys in the mid-1990s. In the 2001 Bulgarian parliamentary election, the party led by the nominal heir to the throne, King Simeon II, won 42 percent of the vote; it won 22 percent in 2005.

Communist regime is not the only alternative that at one time or another has attracted endorsement by more than two-fifths of Russians: a tough dictatorship can do so too, and the idea of getting rid of parliament and elections is similarly appealing (see Figure 5.4). While the aggregate number of endorsements is large, anti-regime elites cannot easily cooperate to give force to these numbers. Even if all opponents of the regime agreed to the abolition of parliament and elections, there would be no agreement among them as to whether the Communist Party should again establish a party-state or which person was tough enough to be the most suitable dictator.

As the Churchill hypothesis emphasizes, a regime does not have to be positively valued to be supported; it is enough to be viewed as the lesser evil. Similarly, the current Russian regime does not need the support of every Russian. "Divide and conquer" is a Machiavellian motto that gives any leader encouragement to exploit and even welcome multiple opponents. Comparing the extent of popular support for the current regime and alternatives (Figures 5.1, 5.3) shows that for most of the time the current regime has had a higher (or at least a less low) level of endorsement than alternative regimes. Even when this was not the case, the changing level was not sufficient to disrupt the current regime.

Whatever its level of popular support, the current regime has the added advantage of being organized in its own defense and able to use the administrative and other resources of the state to maintain its power. When the intensity of support for alternative regimes is taken into account, the strength of the status quo is enhanced, because the proportion of Russians strongly opposed to each alternative is greater than those in favor (see Figure 5.3). Thus, any attempt to mobilize support for a dictator or a return to Communist rule can be met by a countermobilization of those strongly opposed to a particular change in direction. Those participating in a countermobilization do not have to be positively in favor of the current regime: it is sufficient to regard it as a lesser evil.

While the alternatives to the current system are diverse, a factor analysis shows that support for four alternatives – suspension of parliament and elections, a tough dictatorship, military rule, and a return to a Communist regime – reflects a single underlying attitude. Hence, replies to these four related questions can be combined into a single additive scale of support for alternative regimes (see Appendix B for details).

For individuals, regime competition offers three alternatives. A person can reject all alternatives in favor of the status quo; this group offers the surest support for the status quo. At the other extreme, an individual can endorse a multiplicity of alternatives, thus implying that the current regime may be a greater evil. A third possibility is that only one alternative

Figure 5.5 *DISPERSION IN SUPPORT: ALTERNATIVE REGIMES*

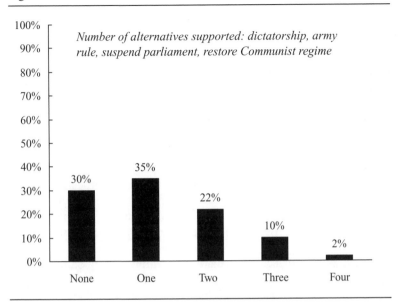

Number of alternatives supported: dictatorship, army rule, suspend parliament, restore Communist regime

Source: New Russia Barometer surveys.

is endorsed, thus raising the possibility that the current regime may be considered a second-best alternative.

Russians are widely dispersed in their views of alternative regimes (Figure 5.5). Over more than a decade, almost one-third reject all four alternatives; just over one-third endorse a single alternative; more than one-fifth endorse two alternatives; and one in eight endorse three or four alternative regimes. There is sufficient support for an average of at least one alternative to be endorsed. However, in every NRB survey, a majority of Russians withhold endorsement of a particular alternative.

Theories of why Russians differ

While differences in public opinion are recognized in the great majority of social science theories, there are big differences in the explanations offered for why people differ. Culture and socialization theories stress the influence of youthful learning on the adoption of political attitudes. By contrast, institutional theories stress the importance of the performance of government on attitudes, and political economy theories emphasize economic performance. A fourth set of theories, which can be tested only with surveys that extend over a decade or longer, stresses the importance of the passage of time.

Culture and socialization

*Hypothesis 1: Differences in regime support depend on what individuals learn from their roles in society.

The process of socialization begins as children learn values and norms about what is expected of them when they become adults. Within a society, individuals are socialized into different roles according to their gender, parental class, education, and other social differences. A society does not need to be totalitarian for nominally non-political forms of socialization to have political consequences, for example, being socialized into a minority racial or religious group, or having parents who get their offspring elite education. Insofar as each step in the process of youthful socialization influences subsequent life chances, an individual's adult roles will reflect youthful learning. Once political norms are internalized, whether in youth or early adulthood, they will tend to persist throughout a lifetime.

Political culture theories postulate that within a given society socialization promotes homogeneous core values; Russians have often emphasized distinctive cultural values, citing historical experiences or even a Russian "soul" (see, e.g., Berdyaev, 1947; cf. Duncan, 2000). However, a common history and common political institutions have not produced a consensus among Russians in support for the Russian Federation or for any one alternative. The preceding figures consistently show that Russians differ in their evaluation of regimes.

Socialization theories have been used to explain how an established regime maintains steady-state support as youthful socialization leads to the intergenerational transmission of support (cf. Easton and Dennis, 1969). However, the treble transformation of the Soviet Union introduced a fundamental discontinuity into the life of every Russian: adults are challenged to re-learn political attitudes and behavior, and new institutions become mechanisms of resocialization. When an election is held, people must deal with a ballot on which there are now many parties rather than just one. In order to function economically, everyone has had to learn enough about the market economy to live in an economy in which the state no longer guarantees an income for life. Resocialization can be influenced by prior socialization experiences: for example, those who enjoyed privileges in Communist times may be able to convert them into privileges in the new system. On the other hand, young people who had not entered school when the Soviet Union collapsed may take the current regime for granted and thus evaluate it differently from their elders.

Politics matters

* *Hypothesis 2: Differences in regime support depend on individual values and the performance of political institutions.*

By definition, regime change alters political institutions, and the repudiation of unpopular institutions that are a legacy from an unpopular predecessor regime can be popular. In evaluating the new regime, people can apply values that they had developed in Soviet times, especially values inconsistent with Communist ideology. There has also been the opportunity to learn and to express new values, as the Yeltsin administration ended many social controls introduced in the totalitarian period of the Soviet party-state.

Theories about the performance of institutions assume that individuals are always open to re-learning. Institutions described in the legal language of a constitution are expected to secure a predictable response from subjects, whether they confer opportunities or obligations. Many innovations of the new Russian Federation – for example, the privatization of major Soviet industries – required substantial re-learning by political elites as well as subjects. The massive transfer of institutional assets to private hands had consequences – including many that were not anticipated theoretically.

Political performance can change more readily than institutions, for every government has policies that can go wrong unexpectedly, thus damaging the reputation of the party in power and in a new regime potentially reducing support for institutions of government. Personalities at the top of government change, with implications for popular perception of government, for example, the succession of Vladimir Putin to the presidency in place of Boris Yeltsin. However, the evaluation of a given policy depends on individual values, and these vary: thus, Russians who favor democracy as an ideal are likely to evaluate "get tough" measures of the government differently from those who endorse a dictatorship. Presidential election results likewise show that Russians differ in how they evaluate leading political personalities.

Economics matters

* *Hypothesis 3: Differences in regime support depend on how individuals evaluate their household and national economic conditions.*

Socialization into the Soviet command economy stressed the material aspects of "building socialism"; inadvertently, it also made Russians materialistic, as the economy's deficiencies made many consumer goods scarce. The transformation to a market economy produced novel and hard evidence of the impact of political institutions on the national and the household economy.

Whereas major changes in political institutions may occur only once every decade or so, changes in the national economy can occur within a period of months, as can individual economic circumstances. Russia's transformation has produced extreme fluctuations in macroeconomic conditions and in the living standards of Russian households. Inflation moved into treble-digit numbers and then fell to double-digit and even single-digit numbers. The official gross domestic product contracted abnormally for half a dozen years and has since registered abnormal rates of annual growth.

Statements about the importance of economic conditions for politics raise the question: which economy? Is it the economy of the individual household or the national economy? Standard microeconomic theories of behavior assume that what counts is an individual's own economic circumstances as indicated by a measure of income. Transformation distributes costs and benefits differently between households. By contrast, macroeconomic theories emphasize collective concerns, such as inflation. Inflation is distinctive because enormous price increases tend to affect everyone in society similarly, whereas the benefits and costs of changes in the gross domestic product or unemployment affect people unequally (Rose, 1998). How the costs and benefits of economic transformation are evaluated can depend not only on household circumstances but also on whether individual values favor a market or a non-market economy.

Time matters

*Hypothesis 4: Differences in regime support depend on when individuals make evaluations and how long the new regime has been in place.

Insofar as political and economic performance influences regime support, fluctuations in these independent variables can cause regime support to fluctuate. The New Russia Barometer has been fielded at times when the regime's economic performance appeared good as well as at times when it appeared bad. Insofar as economic evaluations influence regime support, positive economic developments should boost support and negative developments depress it. Even though fluctuations in economic conditions may not follow a steady or predictable path, as long as the impact is consistent, the resulting change in regime support can be explained.

Big-bang events such as the ruble crash of 1998 have an immediate impact on what people make of the regime. Journalists tend to treat every day's headline as an event that wipes people's minds clear of all they had previously learned. However, such a theory of "instant resocialization" implies that there will be as many changes in popular attitudes each year as there are major events and that each headline event will have its effect washed away by the next event. If this were the case, the influence of events would be transitory rather than lasting.

Socialization emphasizes the importance of the sequence of events leading individuals to evaluate a particular event in the light of earlier experiences. If benefits of transformation come first, the lingering effects of these benefits will make subjects ready to bear subsequent costs. Insofar as political performance matters, dismantling the old regime's repressive institutions can quickly deliver the benefit of freedom and reduce dissatisfaction with subsequent evidence of shortcomings in its current performance. However, economic transformation delivers costs before benefits. According to the theory of populist myopia, this sequence immediately places support for the new regime in jeopardy (Stokes, 2001: 9ff.).

Cumulatively, the passage of time can create political inertia. At the start of a new regime, none of its subjects will have been socialized to support it and many will have accepted its predecessor. However, the longer it is in place, the more pressure it puts on adults to be resocialized, whether because of its positive achievements or on the pragmatic grounds that it is better to join than to fight the system. The longer a regime persists, the less alternative regimes will appear as likely to replace it. Insofar as this lowers popular expectations that regime change is possible, it will also lower support for alternative regimes and lead opponents of the regime to become resigned to accepting it.

Testing a lifetime of learning

The lifetime-learning model is open to multiple influences. It thus avoids the reductionist assumption that a single influence – whether the popularity of a president, household income, or an individual's education – is sufficient to explain why some people support the current regime and reject alternatives while others do the opposite. It also avoids false equality, assuming that each of the four above hypotheses are of equal importance. It can discriminate between influences that are more important, less important, and of no consequence. Insofar as Russians are crosspressured by different influences, such as an appreciation of freedom and the costs of transformation, the model can show the extent to which these influences reinforce or cancel each other out when individuals make judgments about a regime.

The next three chapters in turn test the extent to which socialization, politics, and economics influence how individual Russians evaluate their current regime and its alternatives. This is done by pooling the responses from New Russia Barometer surveys and weighting them equally, thus creating a mass data base with 26,000 respondents.[3] Since the NRB surveys include a multiplicity of indicators for each hypothesis, ordinary least squares (OLS) regression analysis is used to test the extent to which each indicator is important, net of all other influences.

More than fifty different political, social, and economic NRB indicators were initially tried out in preliminary analyses. Many things that are interesting in other contexts – for example, indications of how Russians have coped with the dislocations caused by economic transformation – were discarded because they had no influence on support for the current or alternative regimes. Because of their theoretical importance, a few indicators such as gender and church attendance have been retained in order to give evidence of their lack of influence. In order to focus attention on influences of substantive importance and to reduce both visual and statistical clutter, individual characteristics and attitudes that register little or no effect are excluded in subsequent stages of the analysis.[4]

In order to test whether and how time matters, different statistical procedures are required, because time is not an attribute that varies between individuals within a survey, but an aggregate characteristic common to all respondents within a single survey and differentiating them from respondents in other surveys. Introducing time along with individual-level data makes OLS procedures problematic, because, among other reasons, it biases aggregate-level standard errors, typically inflating estimates of their statistical significance.

In order to account for the influence of the passage of time, we turn to hierarchical level modeling (HLM), a set of statistical procedures that both corrects the standard errors associated with higher-level variables and permits tests of the interaction between higher-level time-related aggregate variables and individual-level variables (Steenbergen and Jones, 2002; Raudenbush and Bryk, 2002). HLM is often used to control for the effect of geographical context, for example, comparing respondents

---

[3] Thirteen Barometer surveys are pooled to test hypotheses about support for the current regime. NRB XII, undertaken as a post-Duma election survey in December 2003, is not included because it lacks a full set of independent variables. The first two NRB surveys are not included in the analysis of support for alternative regimes because the questions used to create the dependent variable were not asked then.

[4] We have run additional regression analyses to verify that discarded variables do not unexpectedly gain importance when additional variables are entered.

in different countries, but it can equally be used to "place" individual respondents at the particular month and year when they were interviewed in an NRB survey. By doing so, it avoids the OLS assumption that relationships between independent variables and regime support are constant across time. Hypothesis 4 postulates that time can have both direct and indirect influences on regime support. Hierarchical level modeling makes it possible to test the extent to which the passage of time cumulatively increases support for the current regime or decreases support for alternatives.[5] At the individual level, attitudes toward the old regime may have a different impact on support when memories of the old regime were fresh in 1992 than they do a decade later, while measures of current performance may increase in influence through time as individuals gain experience of the new regime.

The use of the lifetime-learning model as a theoretical framework for understanding why Russians differ in their support for alternative regimes makes it possible to relate complex statistics to everyday life. Chapter 6 looks at the extent to which age, education, gender, and other dimensions of social structure influence regime support. The following chapters examine the effects of political values and performance and then economic influences on regime support. Chapter 9 looks at the extent to which future expectations as well as current performance and the passage of time influence regime support. Since the lifetime-learning model is open rather than rigidly deterministic, the book ends by speculating about what could disrupt support for the regime.

---

[5] Because the NRB surveys were conducted at different times of year, time is measured in months in order to ensure that it is an equal-interval measure when calculating its effect.

6 Social structure and the evaluation of regimes

> It is not the consciousness of men that determines their being but, on the contrary, their social being that determines their consciousness.
>
> Karl Marx, *A Contribution to the Critique of Political Economy*

The unity of Russian society was a theme of both tsarist and Soviet writers, but every society is differentiated in many ways. Some differences have biological roots, such as gender and age; others reflect socioeconomic circumstances, such as income and education; and some are political, such as ethnic identity or pride in citizenship. The development of modern society increases differentiation within society, since the great bulk of the population no longer follows common rural pursuits, and modern communications make it easier for people to group themselves according to distinctive interests and tastes.

Socialization is a process in which individuals learn to fit into society in different ways, for example, as an unskilled worker or a highly educated professional. In this process, people develop distinctive interests and expectations about how the country ought to be governed. For adults continuing in a given role in society, whether as workers or members of an ethnic group, early socialization can reinforce initial evaluation. These interests and values can be invoked in the evaluation of the current and alternative regimes. Political sociology follows Marx in postulating that an individual's social being, that is, their position in the social structure, will influence their political consciousness.

Hypothesis 1: Regime support depends on what individuals learn from their roles in society.

Since society is structured in many ways, the critical question is: *which* social differences influence regime support? Marxist sociologists have argued that, when a regime reflects the interests of the capitalist class, support should not be given to it by those who are not capitalist. A multidimensional theory of political divisions propounded by S. M. Lipset and Stein Rokkan (1967) emphasizes cleavages along lines of religion, ethnic identification, and urban/rural residence too. Individuals who are members of churches, trade unions, farmers' organizations, business associations, and ethnic and cultural groups may be socialized to adopt values that affect support for alternative regimes. However, in the Communist party-state, it was not possible to develop organizations to promote these interests. All organizations, whatever the social characteristics of their members, were controlled by the party and propagated the party line.

Differences significant in one dimension of society, for example, tastes in sports or food, are unlikely to have a direct influence on regime support. Combining multiple distinctions to create ideal-type categories – for example, young, well-educated, secular urbanites and old, uneducated, rural churchgoers – reduces the size of each to a very small proportion of a national population. Simultaneously, it creates a majority in crosspressured categories, for example, uneducated urban residents or young rural residents, thus increasing the need for care in relating social differences to regime support.

The extent to which specified social differences actually influence Russians is an empirical question. The next section examines the relation between ethnicity, identity, class, education, place of residence, religion, and gender to support for the current and alternative regimes. Some but not all of these differences are associated with regime outlooks; however, the relationship is usually weak. In the second section, the influence of age on regime support is examined in terms of both an individual's position in the life cycle, and differences between generations socialized under Stalin and wartime and those during *perestroika*. Given a multiplicity of potential influences, including some that are interrelated, the concluding section tests which social differences are significant for regime outlooks net of the influence of all others. It also tests the extent to which the passage of time alters the influence of social structure on Russian regime support.

Social differences are inevitable; their influence is not

In established democracies, the regime leaves many areas of social life to individual choice and to the activities of civil society institutions independent of government. By contrast, the totalitarian aspiration of the Communist party-state sought to politicize every area of social life from the upbringing of children to painting. Transformation opened up the opportunity for many social differences to become politically salient. In theory, social differences could lead to 100 percent of older Russians opposing the current regime while 100 percent of younger Russians supported it.

However, political differences between social groups are almost invariably differences of degree: they may be statistically insignificant, trivial, or more or less substantial.

Ethnicity and identity

The Soviet regime was ambivalent about *ethnic* distinctions. On the one hand, Marxist ideology stressed that ethnic identification was unimportant compared to class differences. The Soviet regime offered careers open to many minority groups; for example, Stalin was a Georgian and Trotsky was of Jewish origin. Nonetheless, the Soviet Union institutionalized republics for historic nationalities such as Armenians and Ukrainians, and within the Russian Republic pseudo-autonomous jurisdictions were created with ethnic labels. Economic development also led many Russians to settle in non-Russian republics. A sophisticated study of interethnic relations conducted in the summer of 1991 found that Russians living outside the Russian Republic reported better interethnic relations than anxious elites had anticipated (VCIOM, 1997; Hosking, 2006).

Subjects of the Russian Federation today have reminders of their official nationality. In the Soviet era, nationality was inscribed in identity documents, and intermarriage between people with different official nationalities has created millions with ambiguous nationality status. The 2002 Russian census made a special effort to identify the ethnicity of subjects. However, since ethnicity is not biologically determined, there was substantial scope for individuals to choose how to respond. People could choose to reply with the nationality that was stamped in their Soviet identity card, even if its significance had lost meaning from one generation to another. Persons of mixed parentage could either state a hyphenated nationality or give a single choice. Those in a minority ethnic group could even state they were Russian in the belief this was "safest" to report on an official form. The 2002 Russian census recorded 79.8 percent of the population as Russian; 3.8 percent Tatar; 2.0 percent Ukrainian; 1.1 percent Bashkir; 1.1 percent Chuvash; and 1.0 percent gave no answer. Between 0.6 percent and 0.9 percent were recorded as Chechens, Armenians, Mordovians, Avars, or Belorussians. The remaining 7.9 percent were dispersed among 173 differently identified nationalities (Goskomstat, 2005).

When the New Russia Barometer asks people about their ethnic identity free of official associations, five-sixths say they are Russian, and the remainder are scattered among dozens of different non-Russian nationalities. Thus, even in a survey with 2,000 respondents, there are too few

Table 6.1 *Ethnicity, identity, and regime support*

Total (%)		Supports regime (%)	Rejects all alternatives (%)
	Ethnicity		
85	Russian	37	25
15	Non-Russian	34	25
	Pride in citizenship		
73	High	46	28
27	Low	41	28
	European identity		
40	Some	44	31
60	None	38	27

Source: New Russia Barometer surveys. For details of coding of indicators, see Appendix B.

people belonging to any one minority to be the basis for statistical generalization. Moreover, because of their geographical location, to study any minority ethnic group requires a specially drawn sample; for example, Brym (1994) sought to identify Jews by interviewing persons with German surnames. For this reason, a survey cannot simultaneously be a representative sample of a minority ethnic group and of the population as a whole, as the New Russia Barometer is.

The federation regime is much more closely identified with ethnic Russians than was the former Soviet Union, in which Russians were about two-thirds of the population. It does not make the nominally universalist claims of its Communist predecessor, nor does it claim the imperial inclusiveness of an expansive tsar. Both its presidents, Boris Yeltsin and Vladimir Putin, are ethnic Russians. Insofar as ethnicity is politically salient, ethnic Russians ought to be more inclined to support the new regime. However, the difference in support between Russians and non-Russians is only three percentage points (Table 6.1). And notwithstanding claims that Russian culture especially favors autocratic regimes, there is no difference between ethnic Russians and non-Russians in their readiness to endorse or reject alternative regimes. These findings justify the practice in this book of describing the population of the Russian Federation by their titular nationality, that is, as Russians.

Since citizenship in the Russian Federation is not based on nationality, the New Russia Barometer also asks if people are "proud of being a citizen of this country," a phrasing inviting everyone, regardless of their nationality, to indicate the psychological strength of their attachment to the community of the regime. Almost three-quarters express pride in the country. However, pride has little or no effect on regime support. There is no difference at all in the evaluation of alternative regimes between those who are proud of their country and those who are not, and the difference in current regime support is only five percentage points (Table 6.1).

There is a historic difference in identities between traditionalists who resist the importation of foreign ideas and those looking to Europe as a model (Neumann, 1996). Since the creation of the federation, the European Union has expanded to include eight former Communist bloc countries, and it now reaches the borders of Russia itself. However, the Russian Federation extends east from Eastern Europe; it covers eleven time zones and borders Iran, China, Japan, and Alaska.

For the great majority of Russians, Europe is remote: four-fifths know no foreign language; seven-eighths say they have no friends in the West, and for every Russian who has traveled in the West there are many who have never been outside the Commonwealth of Independent States (Rose and Munro, 2006). When the New Russia Barometer asks people to choose two identities from a list of six, only 4 percent say they think of themselves even secondarily as European. When asked a more directive question –whether they ever think of themselves as a European – an average of 16 percent say they often think of themselves as European, 24 percent sometimes do, 20 percent rarely do, and 40 percent never think of themselves as European.

Historically, European values have been used as a standard for criticizing "Asiatic" or "Byzantine" features of Russian regimes. Russians who sometimes or often see themselves as Europeans are six percentage points more in favor of the current regime. They are also four percentage points more likely to reject all alternative regimes.

Leading and lagging social positions

Theories of social structure emphasize the hierarchical nature of social differences: for any given dimension of social structure, some positions are superior to others (Geoffrey Evans, 1999). Class was a central ideological concept of Communism, but its application in Communist and post-Communist societies has been problematic. The Soviet Union rejected the occupationally based distinctions of class used in European societies. For example, it conferred high status on occupations such as coal mining, labor necessary to promote industrialization, and gave less prestige to service sector occupations such as accountancy. The transformation of the economy has forced a large proportion of the labor force to change their employer, their occupation, or both.

The ambiguity of the relationship between occupation and prestige is revealed in the way in which Russians have characterized businessmen. When the second New Russia Barometer asked how people who make a lot of money should be characterized, they were seen as using political connections by 84 percent; as taking advantage of other people, 71 percent; and as dishonest by 56 percent. On the other hand, businessmen were seen as intelligent by 65 percent; hard-working, 45 percent; and helping to make the economy grow, 33 percent.

Ambiguities in occupational stratification also exist in established market economies, leading to a subjective definition of social status derived from asking people to say where they place themselves on a social ladder. This allows people to register what is relevant in their own interactions with others. The New Russia Barometer measure of subjective social status asks people to place themselves on a social ladder in which the lowest rung is 1 and 7 is the top status. The use of numbers avoids giving politically charged or misleading verbal labels. Russians have no difficulty in recognizing differences in social status; only 1.5 percent are unable to locate themselves on the social status ladder. The median group of Russians does not choose the middle position on the status ladder; instead, they see themselves as below the middle, at the third rung of the ladder. Only 1 percent place themselves at the highest rung of the ladder, and 12 percent place themselves above the median point.

Whatever social status a Russian had prior to transformation – and more feel downwardly rather than upwardly mobile by comparison with Soviet times – a majority who now see their social status as above average give support to the current regime. Among those of below-average status, the level of support is seventeen percentage points lower (Table 6.2). Likewise, those above average in social status are more likely to reject alternative regimes.

An alternative measure of social position is education, for not only does it convey prestige but also more educated people tend to have better jobs, higher income, and more power in society. This was true in Soviet times, and it remains true today. Today, a majority of Russians have achieved either a vocational certificate as a skilled worker or an academic diploma entitling them to proceed to higher education. Among all adults, one-sixth have a university degree or its equivalent, while one-quarter have failed to obtain any qualification.

In times of transformation, people with more education should be better able to benefit from the opportunities it creates. Insofar as more-educated people are expected to be more in favor of democratic institutions, not only should they reject autocratic alternatives, but they may also be less in support of the current plebiscitarian autocracy. In fact, the

Table 6.2 *Social structure and regime support*

Total (%)		Supports regime (%)	Rejects all alternatives (%)
	Subjective status		
17	Above average	54	35
34	Average	48	33
49	Below average	37	25
	Education		
16	Higher	44	42
25	Technical	39	31
33	Secondary qualification	39	28
26	Low	33	17
	Urban/rural		
16	Million+ cities	38	34
34	Cities	40	31
27	Small towns	38	26
23	Rural	37	22
	Church attendance		
6	Monthly	40	24
17	Few times a year	34	23
29	Rarely	35	27
48	Never	36	25

Source: New Russia Barometer surveys.

most-educated group are eleven percentage points more inclined to support the current regime than are the least-educated Russians (Table 6.2). However, as hypothesized, the most-educated Russians are twenty-five percentage points more likely to reject autocratic alternatives than are the least-educated Russians.

A major goal of the Soviet regime was to abolish what Marx had denounced as "the idiocy of rural life." In pre-revolutionary Russia, the great majority of the population lived far from cities and basic public services such as schools and transport. The Soviet regime promoted urbanization as a necessary part of industrialization. Successive five-year plans developed major new industrial sites in remote regions safe from foreign invaders, and directed people to work there. By 1959 just over half the population was urban. By the time of the collapse of the Soviet Union, three-quarters was urbanized, with half living in cities of more than 100,000 people and one-sixth living in cities of more than 1 million.

It was state policy to turn peasants into the rural equivalent of a factory proletariat. Collective and state farms replaced the smallholdings of peasants, employing skilled labor, albeit on terms that encouraged shirking and production for private sale in the informal economy. Concurrently, the chronic food shortages of the command economy encouraged urban residents to grow food. By the end of the Soviet Union, a big majority of Russians growing food lived in cities rather than the countryside. Growing food was neither a hobby nor a source of income; people grew food in order to be sure that they got enough to eat (Rose and Tikhomirov, 1993).

While larger cities have offered greater opportunities to take advantage of transformation, the rural population has been insulated against insecurity insofar as its members are self-sufficient for food and basic necessities of life. Thus, there is no significant difference in support for the current regime among urban and rural residents. However, NRB surveys do show that people who live in bigger cities are more likely to reject all alternative regimes (Table 6.2). The rejection of autocratic alternatives is consistent with the traditional German dictum "Stadt macht frei" (a city gives a sense of freedom). The association between urban residence and resistance to alternative regimes is a force for maintaining a political equilibrium, since any attempt to change regimes would require political action in big cities.

In tsarist times, the Russian Orthodox Church was subservient to the tsar, who invoked divine authority for his despotic rule. The Soviet regime attacked religion: the Orthodox Church was rightly viewed as a bulwark of its predecessor, and its supernatural beliefs were in conflict with the materialism of Marxism-Leninism. Church institutions became subject to control by the Communist Party. Given traditional obeisance to civil authority, the Orthodox hierarchy accepted Communist *diktats* in order to survive under a totalitarian regime. In addition, the party waged an ideological war on religious beliefs, actively promoting atheism. While societies across Europe were concurrently experiencing secularization, governments did not promote this process with the intensity of the Soviet regime. In an attempt to mobilize support from Russians who remain committed to the Orthodox faith, President Putin has made well-publicized gestures in favor of religion.

When the New Russia Barometer asks people their religion, the population divides into three groups: about half say they are Orthodox; a quarter say they are atheist; and a fifth find it difficult to decide whether they have a religion. However, a nominal religious identification is not evidence of religious commitment, since many Russians who say they are Orthodox may do so to indicate that they belong to the country's majority ethnic group, just as many English people say they are Church of England.

Church attendance is a more meaningful measure of religious commitment. New Russia Barometer surveys find that almost half of adults never go to church, including many who are nominally Orthodox. The median person goes to a religious service no more than once a year; only 6 percent report going to church as often as once a month. There is a very small association between church attendance and support for the current regime and no statistically significant relationship between church attendance and support for alternative regimes (Table 6.2).

While gender is a biological fact, its political significance is socially constructed. In Soviet times, the regime's desire to industrialize mobilized a large proportion of women into the labor force, and women gained access to secondary and higher education. Factories in high-priority sectors of the economy provided many social services, including child care for working women, albeit such services were valued less by Russians than by Western advocates of the welfare state, because they were allocated according to the priorities of the economic plan rather than the needs of employees (Rose, 1996a). Abortion was commonly used for birth control; it was legalized by Lenin, then banned, and again made legal in 1955.

The Communist Party did not practice gender equality. Even after West European countries gave prominent political roles to women, the Central Committee of the CPSU did not. While women have begun to appear in public life in the Russian Federation, there is no positive policy to promote the role of women in politics. Another striking gender difference is that of health: today, as in Soviet times, the gap in life expectancy between Russian women and men is greater than in other modern societies (Boutenko and Razlogov, 1997: 9).

Individuals age and society rejuvenates

In a relatively stable society, the effects of age differences are likely to be limited because, however young or old people are, they are socialized as subjects of the same regime. Knowledge gained in childhood remains relevant for adult political participation. Life-cycle theories postulate stability arising by a different route. In youth a person may be optimistic about the possibilities of political change, while in middle age they accept the political status quo, and in old age they long nostalgically for a seemingly "golden" past or dismiss youthful beliefs as naive and misguided. As long as the proportion of young, middle-aged, and old in the population remains the same, the effects of people altering their views at different stages of the life cycle will cancel each other out.

In a society in transformation, adults find that political beliefs acquired in youth are no longer adequate to deal with the new regime. Russians depending on a state pension for their income cannot ignore the introduction of market prices. Those who remain committed to the Communist regime may refuse to support the new regime, but the fact of transformation makes reversion to the old regime difficult. Moreover, for younger people the past is outside their personal experience.

The passage of time causes the rejuvenation of society through the turnover of generations. Each year some youths become adults; concurrently their middle-aged relatives are coming to terms with what their life chances have allotted them; and some older adults are removed by death. Since New Russia Barometer surveys commenced in 1992, the extent of generational turnover is substantial. About one-quarter of the respondents interviewed in the first NRB survey are most likely now dead, and one-fifth interviewed in the fourteenth NRB survey were not yet adults when the first survey was conducted.

Regime support differs by age

The Soviet regime had the longest influence on the formation of political values and expectations of the oldest generation, including the assumption that regime was the only one that could or should govern them. By contrast, for younger Russians the old regime has little or no relevance to their own political socialization. Moreover, young people are in a better position to benefit from the effects of transformation, for they are more mobile and future-oriented than older people, whose working career was ended or ending when the Soviet Union collapsed. Insofar as social services have deteriorated since transformation, the dependence of older people on these services can encourage dissatisfaction with the new regime.

Insofar as age influences regime support, we would expect older people to be less likely to support the current regime and more likely to favor alternatives, and younger people to be more supportive of the new regime and less likely to endorse alternatives, with middle-aged people falling in between. New Russia Barometer evidence meets these expectations. When all NRB surveys are pooled, 32 percent of those over sixty endorse the current regime compared to 46 percent of Russian adults younger than thirty. Similarly, 37 percent of the youngest group of Russians reject all alternative regimes, while only 17 percent of the oldest group of Russians do so.

Generational theories attribute differences between age groups to historical differences early in life, for example, whether a person was socialized during war, peace, depression, or an era of affluence. Unlike life-cycle theories, generational theories postulate that individuals do not change their views as they grow older, but retain values formed in youth. Whereas there is regularity in the life cycle of individuals, there is no regularity in Russian history. Terror and war clearly define the oldest generation, and *perestroika* and what came after define the youngest. The New Russia Barometer database includes thousands of respondents born in very different generations. Russians born in 1931 or earlier were socialized politically during the Stalinist terror and the Second World War. At the other extreme, those born in 1976 or later became socialized during Mikhail Gorbachev's short tenure of office and only reached adulthood after the Soviet Union broke up. Since many changes in society occur gradually, for example, the relaxation of the party-state's efforts to mobilize its subjects, generational cohorts are here defined by decades, except for the oldest and youngest generations (Figure 6.1).

Between the generations born in the last years of the tsarist empire and in the last years of the Soviet Union. there are clear differences in support for the current regime (Figure 6.1A). In the post-*perestroika* generation, 57 percent support the new regime. Support then falls steadily with experience of the Soviet regime. Among those who remember Stalinism and the Second World War, only 29 percent support the current regime. The post-*perestroika* generation is also the most likely to reject alternative regimes: 42 percent do so. Here again, the oldest generation is the most likely to endorse at least one other regime: only 16 percent reject all alternatives.

Theories of generational change do not predict steady changes in the same direction from one generation to the next. However, this has occurred in Russia. The longer ago Russians were born, the less likely they are to support the new regime and the more likely to prefer an alternative regime. However, though differences between generations are sizeable, within each generation there is a division between those who do and those who do not support the current regime or its alternatives. For example, 43 percent of the youngest generation of Russians withhold support from the new regime and 29 percent of the oldest generation support it. Generational differences are thus a tendency rather than a categoric contrast.

Old Russians prepared to make new evaluations

Theories of generational determinism imply that the impact of early socialization tends to inoculate people against re-learning from subsequent events. Instead of changing evaluations in the light of experience, individuals will reinterpret new experiences in the light of the values and criteria reflecting the formative experience of their generation. If this is the case, then each generation's outlook would remain stable from one

Figure 6.1 *GENERATIONAL DIFFERENCES IN REGIME SUPPORT*

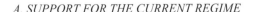

A. SUPPORT FOR THE CURRENT REGIME

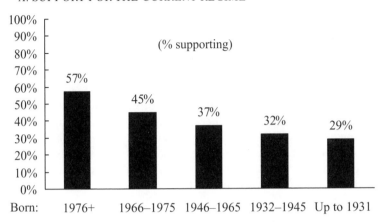

B. REJECTION OF ALTERNATIVE REGIMES

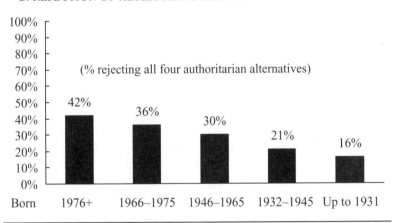

Source: New Russia Barometer surveys.

year or one decade to the next. However, the shocks of transformation have made every generation think afresh about politics and much else.

Regardless of early socialization, the regime support of each generation of Russians tends to go up and down from year to year. Within the youngest generation of Russians, support for the new regime has varied between 27 percent in 1996 and 75 percent in 2004. Similarly, among the oldest generation, support for the new regime has varied between 12 percent in 1992 and 57 percent in 2003. There have been equally big ups and downs in the rejection of alternative regimes. Whereas only 32 percent of the youngest generation of Russians rejected all four alternatives in 2001, 65 percent did so two years later. Among the oldest generation, 33 percent rejected all four alternatives in 2004 while only 11 percent did so in 2005 (Figure 6.2).

The ability of all generations to re-learn in the light of events is confirmed by all generations tending to go up and down together in their support for the current and alternative regimes (Figure 6.2). In the mid-1990s, the support of young, middle-aged, and older Russians went down. By the year 2000 all generations were becoming more positive about the new regime; then in 2005 the support of all generations again fell. A similar pattern occurs in support for alternative regimes. However, while generations tend to alter their views at the same time and in the same direction, their starting points remain different.

Combining the effects of social structure

The foregoing tables show some relation between some dimensions of social structure and regime support. However, simple correlations can be spurious, because they do not control for the relationship of social structure characteristics with each other: for example, the correlation between age and regime support may be due to age-related differences in education or the tendency of women to live longer than men. Ordinary least squares (OLS) regression is a standard procedure to test the extent to which each attribute of social structure influences regime outlooks net of the effect of other social structure attributes. Having identified the significant influence, we can then use hierarchical level modeling (HLM) to test to what extent the passage of time increases or decreases the influence of social structure on regime support.

Time changes the influence of social structure on current support

The evidence of the OLS analysis rejects the idea that a Russian's position in the social structure influences support for the current regime. When nine social structure indicators above are combined in a single equation, they can account for only 2.9 percent of the variation in regime support (Table 6.3). Since the pooled data includes 26,000 cases, it is relatively easy for indicators to achieve statistical significance. However, most potential influences fail to do so.

Relatively speaking, subjective social status and age have more influence on support for the current regime. The higher a person's self-assessed social status after transformation, the more positive their

Figure 6.2 *GENERATIONAL SUPPORT FLUCTUATES ANNUALLY*

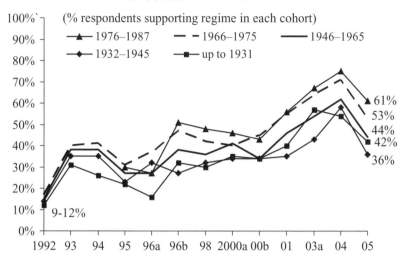

A. SUPPORT FOR THE CURRENT REGIME

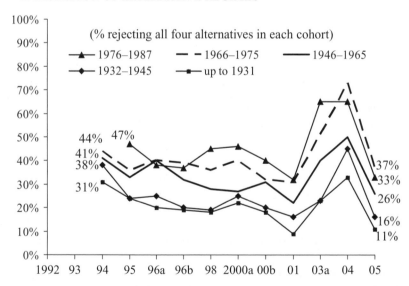

B. REJECTION OF ALTERNATIVE REGIMES

Source: New Russia Barometer surveys.

Table 6.3 *Social structure influences on current regime support*

	OLS			HLM[a]		
	b	se	BETA	b	se	P
Individual level						
Subjective status	4.6	.26	.11	4.3	.08	.000
Age	−.26	.02	−.09	−.29	.02	.000
European identity	2.4	.31	.05	2.8	.60	.001
Russian ethnicity	−3.8	.92	−.02			
Pride in citizenship	1.6	.61	—			
Education	.31	.23	—			
Town size	.33	.31	—			
Church attendance	.68	.41	—			
Female	−.63	.62	—			
Aggregate level						
Month				.21	.04	.000
Cross-level interactions						
Age × month				−.00	.00	.005
Identity × month				−.04	.01	.011
Variance explained:			$R^2 = 2.9\%$	*PSEUDO* $R^2 = 8.5\%$		

[a] Only significant variables included in HLM to preserve degrees of freedom.
−: Not significant at .001 level.

Source: New Russia Barometer surveys.

evaluation of the current regime net of all other influences. Conversely, the older a person is, the less likely he or she will be to give support to the current regime. The fact that education has no significant influence on support suggests that Russians learn more about their system of government from political realities than at school. Of the three measures of identity, identification with Europe and Russian ethnicity each achieve statistical significance; however, their degree of influence is small. Since support for the current regime varies much more among Russians than does pride in citizenship, it is not surprising that pride has no influence on regime support. Three additional indicators of an individual's role in the social structure – town size, church attendance, and gender – likewise fail to achieve any statistically significant influence on support for the new regime.

One explanation for the slight influence of social structure on support for the current regime is that an individual's social characteristics, such as gender and education, tend to be constant, whereas support for the regime fluctuates. The HLM analysis, which takes into account the passage of time, shows that influences on support for the current regime are not the same from one year to the next.[1] The month-by-month passage of time significantly increases support for the regime net of all other influences (Table 6.3). In addition, there is an interaction effect between age and the passage of time and between European identity and the passage of time. As time goes by, the gap between young and old in support for the current regime grows bigger. By combining the effects of time and of individual social characteristics, the hierarchical linear model can account for 8.5 percent of the combined variance, a substantial improvement compared to the effect of individual social structure characteristics.[2]

Steady influence of social structure on rejecting alternatives

Social structure contributes to resigned acceptance of the current regime, since it influences the rejection of alternatives. In the OLS analysis, social structure explains 8.9 percent of the variance in the evaluation of alternative regimes (Table 6.4).

Although education does not influence regime support, it has the most important effect on the rejection of alternative regimes: the more education a Russian has, the more he or she will not want a return to Communism, a dictatorship, getting rid of parliament and elections, or army rule.[3] Age is similarly important in the opposite direction: the older a Russian is, the more inclined he or she is to favor alternative regimes. While higher subjective social status also encourages the rejection of alternative regimes, its influence is substantially less than that of education.

The OLS analysis shows town size to have some influence too: even though Russians who live in larger cities are no more inclined to support the current regime, they are readier to reject alternative regimes. However, neither church attendance nor gender registers any statistically significant influence on the rejection of alternative regimes. Of the three

---

[1] The reduced maximum likelihood coefficients in HLM regressions can be interpreted roughly in the same manner as unstandardized b coefficients in OLS regressions, and hence are labeled "b" in the tables.

[2] Since the measures of variance accounted for in OLS and HLM analyses are not strictly comparable, a more exact measure of the effect of introducing the passage of time is to compare the variance accounted for by a hierarchical linear model that relies exclusively on significant individual characteristics (1.5 percent) and the variance accounted for when the passage of time is added at the second level (8.5 percent).

[3] For consistency in comparison with support for the current regime, the responses to questions about support for alternative regimes have been recoded to create a 201-point scale in which a positive answer reflects rejection of alternatives. For each alternative regime, strong rejection is scored as +100; somewhat negative, +50; no answer or don't know, 0; somewhat in favor of an alternative, −50; and strongly in favor, −100. An individual's readiness to reject alternative regimes is calculated by taking the mean of their responses to the four questions in Figure 5.5.

Table 6.4 *Social structure influences on rejecting alternative regimes*

	OLS			HLM[a]		
	b	se	BETA	b	se	P
Individual level						
Age	−.36	.01	−.15	−.37	.03	.000
Town size	3.2	.24	.08	3.7	.35	.000
Education	4.2	.17	.16	4.7	.32	.000
Subjective status	2.0	.20	.06	1.7	.38	.001
European identity	1.3	.24	.03	2.1	.33	.000
Russian ethnicity	.08	.71	—			
Pride in citizenship	1.2	.47	—			
Church attendance	.43	.31	—			
Female	.03	.48	—			
Aggregate level						
Month						
Cross-level interactions						
Age × month				−.002	.00	.009
Town size × month				.02	.01	.010
Variance explained:		$R^2 = 8.9\%$		$PSEUDO\ R^2 = 14.3\%$		

[a] Only significant variables included in HLM to preserve degrees of freedom.
−: Not significant at .001 level.

Source: New Russia Barometer surveys.

indicators of identity, ethnicity and pride in citizenship are completely without significance, and the influence of European identity is slight.

The passage of time has much less influence on the rejection of alternative regimes than on support for the current regime. Whereas the current regime gains support as it becomes more familiar and rooted in experience, the month-by-month passage of time does not change the extent to which alternative regimes are less or more attractive. Yet the two-level hierarchical level model accounts for 14.3 percent of the combined variance, because there is an interaction effect between time and two significant social structure influences.[4] The month-by-month passage of time increases the influence of age and of town size on evaluations of alternative regimes.

Social structure characteristics of individual Russians tend to be fixed: the shocks of transformation cannot alter a person's year of birth or gender, nor do they affect the education of the great majority of adults, who left school long ago. Relatively constant social characteristics tend to

---

[4] An HLM analysis using only individual-level variables accounts for 10.7 percent of the variance in the evaluation of alternative regimes.

encourage a degree of stability in the year-to-year evaluation of alternative regimes but are unable to prevent fluctuations up and down in support for the current regime.

Sociological theories are developed for many purposes besides explaining political attitudes. Hence, we should not be surprised that, whatever their significance in some domains of social life, gender, church attendance, and pride in citizenship show no significant influence on both support measures, and town size, Russian ethnicity, and education fail to register any significance for one measure of regime support. Age, subjective social status, and, to a minor extent, identification with Europe, are the only social characteristics significant for both dependent variables. Thus, an attempt to explain why Russians differ in their support for regimes solely in terms of social structure does little to advance understanding. As the next chapters will show, a Russian's place in the social structure has less influence on regime outlooks than the ways in which people respond to political and economic transformation.

7 The influence of political values and performance

> Many forms of government have been tried and will be tried in this world of sin and woe. No one pretends that democracy is perfect or all wise. Indeed, it has been said that democracy is the worst form of government, except all those other forms that have been tried from time to time.
>
> Winston Churchill, House of Commons, 1947

The structure of the regime that governs a country is determined by bargaining and competition between elites; it is not determined by the values of the general public. Survey studies of national political cultures may produce sophisticated analyses of how individuals acquire political values (Almond and Verba, 1963; Inglehart, 1997; Feldman, 2003). However, such studies are of little relevance to regime transformation, because individuals change slowly compared to the abruptness with which a regime can be transformed.

Logically, an individual cannot evaluate the performance of a regime without having criteria for making a judgment. Decisions about support for a regime depend not only on what a regime does but also on the values that individuals use to assess it. Even if a Marxist and a libertarian agreed in their description of the performance of the Soviet regime, their conflicting values would lead to opposite conclusions. Values define general principles applicable to performance in many contexts. They are thus more general than the views that public opinion polls collect about what people would like government to do about a current problem. Values are also more durable than attitudes toward candidates in a particular national election, for such attitudes become irrelevant when the next election offers fresh choices. Insofar as political values are sufficiently concrete to be applicable to the performance of an existing regime, they differ from abstract economic concepts of utility or welfare, which, as Ian Little (1963: 81–82) has commented, risk being "not about anything at all."

Regime support is the outcome of an interaction between individual values and the performance of the regime. Values about the ideal form of

124

rule, whether pure Communism or pure democracy, will lead to negative conclusions about regimes that embody all the imperfections of real political life. The Soviet regime recognized this, making a distinction between socialism as an ideal and "real existing socialism." The Churchill hypothesis likewise emphasizes a relative judgment: a regime does not have to conform to an ideal to be worthy of support. It simply needs to be better than any available alternative. A new regime can receive grudging acceptance as long as it is viewed as a lesser evil by comparison with what went before and other possibilities.

Because every subject holds a multiplicity of values, there are value conflicts between individuals but also within an individual. A Russian valuing both freedom and economic security was subject to conflicting pressures in the early years of the Russian regime, when it delivered both freedom and economic insecurity. Analysts who assumed that Russians would give priority to economic security predicted that this would led to the repudiation of the fledgling regime, while democrats regarded the introduction of competitive elections and freedom as giving it a firm basis of support.

Top-down and bottom-up evaluations of a regime's performance differ. Top-down evaluations such as a Freedom House or Transparency International score are holistic, producing a single numerical score for the regime in aggregate. Bottom-up surveys disaggregate public opinion into a number of categories, such as the percentage supporting the regime, the percentage negative, and those who are neutral. Even if a survey shows that a clear majority see the regime as free or honest, there will always be a minority that take the opposite view.

The performance of a regime is much more subject to fluctuation than are the political values of its subjects. The personalities and party in control of government can fluctuate from one election to the next. As Boris Yeltsin's erratic behavior demonstrated, within a president's term of office there are times when the president can claim credit for success and times when everything goes wrong. Events can unexpectedly detract from the performance of government, for example, a flood or a terrorist attack demonstrating a regime's inadequate capacity to cope with an emergency. However, some features of a regime tend to be institutionalized and resist change, for example, the Russian regime's reputation for corruption. Trust in political institutions may reflect judgments acquired through a lifetime of political learning or fluctuate with the performance of a regime.

Since support for the regime reflects the interaction between values and performance, individuals who hold fast to their values will alter their support when performance of the regime alters. Thus, a Russian who consistently values economic success above all else could withhold support from the regime when the economy was in turmoil in the 1990s and then enthusiastically support it during the economic boom that followed. Insofar as the performance of a regime is consistent, for example, in recognizing individual freedom, this can promote consistency in support.

The evaluation of political performance is a matching process. Thus:

Hypothesis 2: Regime support depends on individual values and the performance of political institutions past and present.

The next section focuses on the contrast between the democratic ideal that most Russians favor and the reality of their current regime. The second section shows how the legacy of the old regime affects Russian evaluations. Political performance in relation to the rule of law, political accountability and elections, and the personal appeal of Presidents Yeltsin and Putin is the topic of the third section. The conclusion draws together these diverse influences to show that politics has more influence than social structure on how Russians evaluate the current and alternative regimes – and how assessments have been influenced by the passage of time.

Democracy an ideal, not the Russian reality

The fall of the Berlin Wall was once hailed as "the end of history," making democracy the only ideal-type form of government (Fukuyama, 1992; Plattner, 1996). However, political ideals are stars to steer by rather than destinations that can be arrived at. As Robert Dahl (1989: 90; see also Dahl, 1971) emphasizes, "actually existing political systems, including democratic systems, do not measure up to their ideals." Soviet rulers accepted that their socialist regime was a stage on the road to the ever distant ideal of a Communist society (cf. Roberts, 2004). In a reciprocal manner, the theory that the Soviet Union was an exemplary totalitarian regime was challenged by critics who argued that the Stalinist system in actuality fell short of the totalitarian ideal-type.

Democracy today is a symbol; it is defined in hundreds of different ways by compounding different characteristics that may be incorporated in a particular definition. The greater the number of necessary attributes, the more likely a new regime is to fall short of being completely democratic. There is no agreement among scholars or politicians about the essential requisites of a democratic regime. Definitions often qualify the word by attaching adjectives, some positive, such as liberal democracy or social democracy, and some negative, such as references to a defective or pseudo-democracy. A catalogue of definitions has found more than 550 different adjectives to characterize "democracies." This is more than five times the number of regimes that today have any claim to be described as democratic (Collier and Levitsky, 1997).

What Russians mean by democracy

The Soviet system rejected the Western idea of democracy in favor of the doctrine of the dictatorship of the proletariat. The Communist Party claimed the right to dictate policies to transform society in the interest of the working class. The conviction that the party-state possessed the "correct" policies meant that the only choice at an election was to vote for the party or to invite suspicion as an enemy of the state. Since the creation of the Russian Federation, anti-Communists such as Aleksandr Solzhenitsyn have condemned the new regime as a "false democracy" conducting a "heartless experiment on unhappy Russia." Traditionalist church leaders have characterized the federation as a transitory stage in the move toward a regime governing in the Russian tradition of *sobornost*, which stresses collectivism and hostility to democratic pluralism (quotations in Sakwa, 2002: 474).

In a post-Communist society the meaning of democracy is problematic (cf. Brown, 2001a: 546ff.; Carnaghan, 2001; Gibson, 2001; Gibson and Duch, 1993). Yet it is also open to empirical enquiry. At the start of transformation, a twelve-nation survey of Central and Eastern Europe explored the meaning of the term through open-ended interviews and questions about the relationship to democracy of political liberties, multi-party elections, economic growth, and social equality. A factor analysis identified three important meanings in the minds of ordinary people: democracy was about respect for individual rights; representative political institutions; and promoting social and economic welfare (Simon, 1996; Rose, Mishler, and Haerpfer, 1998: 93ff.).

When NRB surveys have asked Russians what they think are the essential features of democracy, big majorities identify it with economic welfare as well as political rights and institutions (Table 7.1). Nearly everyone believes that equality of citizens before the law and economic prosperity are essential. There are differences in degree about whether guaranteeing a basic income, competitive elections, and freedom to criticize government or ignore it are essential or simply important. On average, only 3 percent dismiss any of these qualities as unimportant. The Russian view of democracy thus combines political and economic welfare values, themes endorsed by European social democrats but not by Anglo-American free-market democrats.

Table 7.1 *Russian views of essentials of democracy*

Q. The word democracy has many different meanings. How important do you think each of the following is in making a country's system of government democratic? Is it (a) essential, (b) important but not essential, (c) not very important, (d) unimportant?

	Essential (%)	Important (%)	Not very important (%)	Unim- portant (%)
Equality of all citizens before the law	91	6	1	1
Country is economically prosperous	88	9	2	1
Govt. guarantees all a basic income	79	15	4	2
Choice of candidates, parties at elections	60	25	11	5
Freedom to criticize government	54	27	14	5
Don't have to do what govt. says if you don't want to	50	30	12	7

Source: New Russia Barometer X (2001).

Is democracy desirable?

In post-transformation Russia, some politicians associate democracy with disorder, crime, or economic insecurity. Thus, the fact that Russians define democracy in terms familiar to Westerners is no guarantee that they regard it as desirable. Such doubts are also justified by a history of popular submission to and endorsement of undemocratic regimes (see Figure 5.3).

For a majority of Russians, democracy is a positive ideal (Figure 7.1). When asked to state a preference between a democratic regime or a dictatorship, more than two-thirds positively endorse democratic rule and less than one in ten endorses even a mild form of dictatorship. The median respondent gives democracy a rating of 8 on a 10-point scale. There is, however, a wide dispersion around the mean (standard deviation: 2.6). The endorsement of democracy as an ideal fluctuates little with the passage of time. Across seven NRB surveys asking the question, the mean has ranged between 6.6 and 7.6, and differences of opinion about the desirability of democracy have been consistent too.

Russians give less endorsement to the ideal of democracy than do citizens of the eight post-Communist countries that are now members of the European Union. In the 2004 New Europe Barometer survey, the mean response for democracy as an ideal was 8.1; the Russian mean of 6.6 was the lowest among all countries surveyed.

Figure 7.1 *DEMAND FOR AND SUPPLY OF DEMOCRACY IN RUSSIA*

Q. Here is a scale ranging from a low of 1 to a high of 10, where point 1
means complete dictatorship and 10 means complete democracy.
(a) Where would you personally like our country to be placed?
(b) Where would you place our country at the present time?

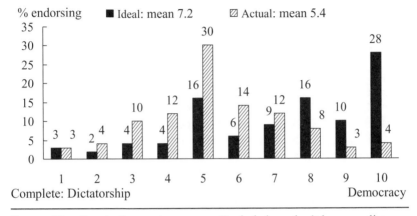

Source: New Russia Barometer surveys. Excluded are don't know replies,
averaging 6 percent for current and 5 percent for ideal democracy.

The qualified commitment of most Russians to the democratic ideal
is confirmed by replies to a question asking about the circumstances in
which democracy is preferable. In the 2005 NRB survey, only 25 percent
said democracy is always preferable to any other kind of government.
The largest group – 42 percent – said that under some circumstances an
authoritarian government could be better and 34 percent said it didn't
matter to them whether they had a democratic or an authoritarian regime.

Furthermore, Russians are in two minds about whether democracy is
suitable for their country. When the tenth New Russia Barometer asked
how suitable or unsuitable people thought democracy was to Russian
circumstances, the mean response on a 10-point scale, 5.4, was almost
exactly equidistant between the extremes of completely suitable or completely unsuitable. A total of 32 percent were inclined to see democracy
as unsuitable for Russia and 46 percent tended to see it as suitable, while
21 percent placed themselves at the psychological midpoint of the scale
or gave no answer.

For the median Russian, the actual character of the new regime is
ambiguous. When asked whether the regime was closer to the ideal of
democracy or of dictatorship, the median group places the regime at the

psychological midpoint between the two alternatives (Figure 7.1). Two-fifths regard the new regime as more democratic than dictatorial, and just under one-third see the new regime as some form of dictatorship. The tendency of Russians to view the new regime as somewhere between a democracy and a dictatorship has been very consistent: the mean has ranged between 5.3 and 5.7, and in each year the variations around the mean are substantial. The ambivalent popular judgment is consistent with describing the current regime as a plebiscitarian autocracy.

According to the "politics matters" hypothesis, Russians who want their country to be democratic ought to reject autocratic alternatives, and Russians who would like to see a dictatorship ought to endorse a change. Because many Russians do not see the regime as unambiguously democratic or a dictatorship, the implications for support are problematic. The hybrid character of the regime could make people who want democracy less likely to support it, or it could encourage them to ignore such ideals and evaluate the current regime by other criteria of political and economic performance.

The legacy of the past

A new regime is not created outside time: it is grounded in a particular place and launched with a legacy of institutions, personnel, and problems left behind by its predecessor. In short, inheritance comes before choice (cf. Rose and Davies, 1994). Whatever their aspirations for the future, governors cannot ignore the constraints of the past. In the words of Claus Offe (1996: 82):

Any regime change involves the forward-looking task of building a new political and economic order out of the ruins of the old. But it also involves the backward-looking task of removing those ruins, where they are not usable as construction materials of the new, but rather stand in the way of what is conceived as a smooth transition. The two tasks interact.

Subjects of a new regime likewise carry with them a legacy of experiences from the past, for a big majority have lived longer under the old regime than under the current regime.

Although the past is the starting point for a new regime, imposing "confining conditions," the fact of transformation creates the opportunity for what Kirchheimer (1965) describes as "revolutionary breakthroughs." The transformation of Russia in the early 1990s ruptured or loosened many bonds of the past. In such circumstances, the history that matters is not that found in old books. It is that which survives in the minds of ordinary Russians as an influence on regime support today.

A new regime can receive a "positive" or a "hard" legacy from its predecessor, depending on the extent to which the legacy has positive or negative consequences. When Norway became independent from Sweden in 1905, it positively benefited from the Swedish legacy of a modern bureaucratic state with representative political institutions. In Central and East European countries, post-Communist regimes have had a hard legacy: a bankrupt economy and an absence of the rule of law and civil society institutions. On the Churchill principle, leaders of a new regime could use this to promote "inverse legitimation," claiming that the new regime offered relief from an alien predecessor (Pridham, 2000: 49ff.).

The Russian Federation lacked a "usable pre-Communist past" that could be invoked by the leaders of new regimes in Central Europe (cf. Rose, Mishler, and Haerpfer, 1998: 63ff.; Linz and Stepan, 1996: 452). While Russian government has had many pasts, all represented a record of failure in the mind of the founder president, Boris Yeltsin. In the perceptive words of William Tompson (2004: 115): "Russia does not merely need a strong state; it needs a state different in kind to that which it inherited from the Soviet Union."

Positive evaluation of the past regime

When the New Russia Barometer asked people to place the pre-*perestroika* regime on the 10-point dictatorship/democracy scale, a big majority saw it as a dictatorship. The mean score was 3.5; 72 percent unambiguously characterized it as a dictatorship, and an additional 16 percent assigned it to the scale's psychological midpoint, 5. Only 12 percent described the Soviet regime as democratic. Moreover, 71 percent gave the past regime a lower rating on the democracy scale than the current regime, and an additional 10 percent gave the two the same rating.

Perceiving a regime as undemocratic need not make it unpopular, insofar as democracy is less important than economic security or the maintenance of order, conditions more evident before *perestroika* than afterwards. An undemocratic regime may be valued positively if it can claim credit for other valued goods, such as victory over Nazi Germany in the Second World War. Vladimir Putin implicitly endorsed this perspective when he declared in his April 2005 "state of the nation" address that the collapse of the Soviet Union was "the greatest geopolitical catastrophe of the twentieth century."

When asked to evaluate the pre-*perestroika* regime, a majority of Russians consistently give it a positive rating (Figure 7.2). In the first NRB survey in 1992, 51 percent were positive about the old regime; the proportion increased to 72 percent by 1998. Approval has remained on a high

Figure 7.2 *STEADY APPROVAL OF PAST REGIME*

Q. Here is a scale for ranking how our system of government works. The top, plus 100, is the best; the bottom, minus 100, the worst. Where on this scale would you put the political system we had before the start of perestroika?

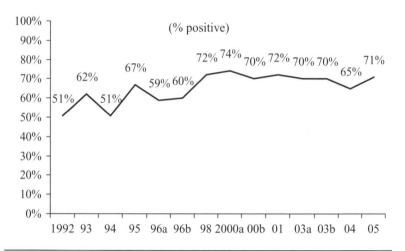

Source: New Russia Barometer surveys.

plateau since. Moreover, the percentage of Russians positive about the former Communist regime has always been greater than that endorsing the current regime. In 2005, 71 percent endorsed the old regime while 48 percent supported the current regime (see Figure 5.1).

The retrospective evaluation of the Soviet regime reflects a selective memory that ignores many of its problems during the pre-*perestroika* period. Archie Brown (1994: 125) has noted: "If the Brezhnev era (1964–1982) was both politically and socially the most stable of all periods of Soviet history, it was also the most cynical." Although the popular view of the old system is now positive, objective indicators show that it imposed enormous opportunity costs. For example, it was a source of poor health. The life expectancy of men increased everywhere in the OECD world, but it failed to do so in Russia. In 1965, male life expectancy in the Soviet Union was 63.8 years; it was exactly the same in 1985 (Boutenko and Razlogov, 1997: 9). For Russians who wanted to see the country progress – and Mikhail Gorbachev was in that category – the economic stagnation of the Brezhnev era was frustrating. When the sixth New Russia Barometer asked who was to blame for Russia's economic problems, more than half blamed the Communists for the problems arising from transformation.

Many Russians see positive features in the powers that be whatever the character of the regime. Across all NRB surveys, 24 percent positively evaluate both the old regime *and* the current regime, and in the 2004 NRB survey a plurality of 39 percent endorsed both. Since a substantial number of Russians compliantly endorse both regimes, those who are consistent reactionaries, favoring the past regime and rejecting the new, are substantial in number but not a majority. Over the period, they average 41 percent of NRB respondents. Only 13 percent are clearcut in supporting the new regime and rejecting the old.

Nostalgia about the Soviet regime encourages some Russians to support its restoration, but the two attitudes are distinct and to some extent have different determinants (Munro, 2006). Thus, the number of Russians who would like to see the return to the Communist system is only half the number of those who look back at it favorably. In 2005 the population divided into three substantial groups: those who neither approve of the Communist regime nor want it back (23 percent); those who approve of the old regime but would not want it restored (35 percent); and those who approve of the Communist regime and would like to see it restored (35 percent). Election results show that many who voice positive sentiments about the Communist system do not endorse it with their votes. In Duma elections, the Communist Party has always won less than a quarter of the vote, and in 2003 it took only 12.6 percent of the popular vote.

The past as a benchmark

Because Russians have experienced two different regimes, the past can be used as a benchmark for evaluating the new regime, and New Russia Barometer surveys ask for comparisons between past and current performance. Instead of asking whether people feel free in the abstract, Russians are asked whether they feel freer in the new regime than under the old in four different everyday activities: being free to say what you think, to join any organization you like, to choose in religious matters, and to decide whether or not to take an interest in politics (cf. Berlin, 1958; Rose, 1995b). Deciding for oneself whether to be interested in politics reflects the difference between a democratic regime in which taking an interest in politics is regarded as a civic virtue and a Communist regime in which feigning political interest was compulsory and a party card necessary to secure advancement and material goods.

An unintended legacy of the Soviet regime is that it makes an overwhelming majority of Russians feel freer in the new regime than in the old (Table 7.2). Over all NRB surveys, an average of 76 percent report feeling freer to decide about religious matters and to join any organization

Table 7.2 *Much greater sense of freedom from the state*

Q. Compared to our system of government before perestroika, would you say our current system is better, much the same, or worse than the old system in terms of whether:

	93	94	96a	96b	98	00a	00b	01	03a	04	05
						(%)					
Everybody has freedom of choice in religious matters											
Better	70	83	80	80	79	83	84	88	82	84	83
Much the same	29	15	17	16	16	14	14	11	16	14	14
Worse	1	2	3	4	5	2	2	1	2	2	2
Everybody has a right to say what they think											
Better	65	73	74	76	73	79	81	78	78	81	76
Much the same	27	18	21	20	21	15	13	16	18	16	19
Worse	8	8	6	4	6	5	6	6	4	3	5
One can join any organization one likes											
Better	63	77	82	79	75	77	76	81	81	83	78
Much the same	28	18	14	15	18	16	17	15	17	12	17
Worse	9	5	3	5	7	6	6	4	2	5	5
Everyone can decide individually whether or not to take an interest in politics											
Better	57	62	69	63	66	70	73	81	79	76	72
Much the same	39	33	27	32	27	23	23	16	18	20	21
Worse	4	5	4	4	7	6	4	3	3	3	7

Source: New Russia Barometer surveys.

of their choice, 75 percent feel freer to say what they think, and 70 percent say they feel freer to decide whether or not to take an interest in politics. In every NRB round, an absolute majority have expressed a greater sense of freedom on each of the four counts. Notwithstanding the well-publicized actions of the Putin administration resulting in jailing or exiling billionaire critics, this has not affected the sense of freedom of the great majority of Russians. Under President Yeltsin, an average of 42 percent said they felt freer than before on each indicator and, under President Putin, 57 percent feel freer on all counts. Among the limited minority of people who say that they do not feel freer than before, most say that things have remained the same rather than worsened.

Freedom from the state is a form of political disengagement. By contrast, exerting influence on the state is a form of engagement. When NRB surveys ask Russians to compare popular influence on the new regime with that in the pre-*perestroika* Soviet regime, 49 percent see it as much the same. Only 17 percent see the new regime as somewhat more open to influence by people like themselves, compared to 29 percent perceiving it as less open; the remainder are don't knows.

Nor is freedom from the state proof of good government, in the sense of bureaucrats treating everyone equally and fairly. When asked to compare fair treatment under the new regime with the Soviet regime, half think it is much the same, one-quarter regard the new regime as fairer than the Communist system, and one-quarter see it as less fair. When judged by absolute standards rather than comparatively, the performance of the Russian regime today falls far short of the ideal of equality before the law. In the fourteenth NRB survey, 83 percent said they did not think public officials treated people like themselves fairly and equally.

If the past influences regime support today, Russians who endorse the old regime should be more likely to approve alternative regimes and Russians who feel freer under the new regime should be readier to reject alternatives. The influence of the past on support for the current regime is problematic. As long as Boris Yeltsin was president, the new regime claimed to reject the Soviet system. However, President Putin has tried to associate the new regime with varied aspects of the Russian past, including the Soviet era.

Performance of a plebiscitarian regime

Because elections are held, Russia is no longer a despotism: it is a plebiscitarian regime. However, the performance of the new regime as regards the rule of law prevents it from being a democratic regime in which governors can be held accountable by the governed.

Rule of law

In a rule-of-law society, those who break the law are literally outlaws. However, in a society where laws are regularly ignored, then lawbreakers are behaving normally. In Soviet as in tsarist times, the chief lawbreakers were not anti-social criminals but government officials bending and breaking rules for political ends and private gain. This tradition has been maintained in the Russian Federation (cf. Sachs and Pistor, 1997).

There is a Russian ideal of a rule-of-law state (*pravovoye gosudarstvo*), just as there is an ideal of democracy. However, 71 percent of Russians do not think that the government lives up to this ideal. In addition, when the seventh NRB survey asked whether laws are often very hard on ordinary people, 61 percent agreed. This explains why 73 percent also endorse the epigram: "The harshness of Russian laws is softened by their non-enforcement." Confronted with public officials who break and bend rules, most Russians continue to use *blat* and other forms of "anti-modern" social capital to secure favors from public officials (Ledeneva, 1998; Rose, 2000b).

Whereas Transparency International uses a "top-down" methodology to assess the extent of corruption among political elites, the New Russia Barometer employs a bottom-up approach. It asks Russians what proportion of public officials they believe take bribes. The two main groups are those who believe almost all public officials are corrupt and those believing most officials are corrupt. The perception of corruption is higher in Russia than in the eight ex-Communist countries that are now new European Union member-states. While 89 percent of Russians consider most of their officials corrupt, in new EU member-states 69 percent do.

Participation with little accountability

In theory, elections allow everyone the opportunity to participate in politics and to hold the government accountable. However, the practice of a plebiscitary autocracy is to hold elections in which everyone can participate but the government is not accountable to its subjects.

A majority of Russians see elections with a choice of candidates and parties as an essential part of democracy (see Table 7.1). Popular commitment to elections was especially strong in 1996, when Boris Yeltsin was facing a Communist opponent whose victory would have created the prospect of a change in regime. While some Yeltsin advisors were promoting the idea of postponing the election on grounds of a national "emergency," an NRB survey in January 1996 found that 73 percent of Russians, including big majorities of both Yeltsin and Communist supporters, wanted the election held, while only 6 percent were against holding an election and 21 percent were don't knows. The first round of the presidential election was held in June, and Yeltsin won in the second-round ballot the following month.

Whatever Russians make of the conduct of elections, most do vote. Turnout in the federation's three presidential elections has averaged 67.5 percent, a figure higher than US presidential elections and much more honestly arrived at than in Soviet days.[1] In the four Duma elections since 1993, turnout has averaged 57.8 percent, similar to the turnout at the British general election of 2005. According to NRB surveys, most Russians who do not vote at a particular election do so for personal reasons such as ill health or inconvenience rather as a political protest. The Russian ballot allows electors to register an explicit protest by showing

[1] In *Virtual Politics*, Andrew Wilson (2005) draws on interviews with professional Russian campaigners specializing in dirty tricks and in organizing fraud in election administration to conclude that Russian elections depart from high standards of fairness. Yet the evidence cited above shows that elections also depart from the "too good to be true" results produced by the Soviet regime.

that they favor none of the candidates. In the first round of presidential elections, 2.3 percent on average have voted against all candidates, and in the Duma list ballots 3.7 percent on average have voted against all candidates.

At the start of the Russian Federation, a big majority of Russians rejected ideological labels such as Communism and capitalism (see Table 4.2). When NRB surveys have subsequently asked "Which broad political outlook are you most inclined to favor?," three-fifths choose an ideological symbol. A total of 22 percent endorse Communism and 9 percent social democracy; 19 percent are pro-market; 5 percent endorse the green movement, and the same percentage endorses great-power patriotism. The diversity of outlooks is consistent with competitive multiparty elections. The two-fifths who do not identify with any broad political outlook are roughly comparable to Americans who reject being labeled as liberal or conservative or who prefer being described as independent rather than as a Republican or a Democrat.

The introduction of competitive elections in Russia was a fundamental change from the Soviet era, for outcomes have shown that the Kremlin was not in control of the results. In the Duma elections of 1993, 1995, and 1999, no party won as much as one-quarter of the list vote. Moreover, the party that won the most votes was opposed to the Kremlin and the party favored by the Kremlin averaged only 16 percent of the list vote. In the 1996 Russian presidential election, Boris Yeltsin won only 35 percent of the vote on the first-round ballot, and his absolute majority in the second-round runoff was less than the share of the popular vote won by Lyndon Johnson in 1964 or by Ronald Reagan in 1984.

However, both electoral institutions and the practices of the political elite create major obstacles to Russian electors holding their governors accountable through conventional institutional channels such as political parties. President Yeltsin avoided establishing a party of his own and his presidential campaigns were run against the formerly dominant Communist Party. Likewise, in both the 2000 and 2004 elections, Putin ran as an independent rather than a party nominee. Insofar as Yeltsin and Putin have associated themselves with parties, they have preferred to be loosely linked to fuzzy focus groups which, like *borscht*, can have many different ingredients thrown in at the pleasure of the chef (see Rose, 2000a; Rose and Munro, 2003: chapter 11).

The electoral accountability of Duma members takes two very different forms. Half of Duma members have been elected by a proportional representation list system which requires candidates to stand as partisans. By contrast, half have been elected in single-member constituencies in which electors vote for an individual, and here a big majority of candidates have been independents. Since a candidate's position on the party list determines whether he or she gets a seat, list candidates are immediately accountable to party organizers. When independents arrive at the Duma, most join an existing party in order to gain advantages within the parliament, an opportunistic move inconsistent with their claim to be independents.

Political elites have frustrated accountability by generating dozens of list parties that appear on the ballot at a single election and then disappear. Some parties split the vote of a more popular party while others make the powers that be appear a lesser evil by comparison with extremist parties (cf. Lentini, 1995; Wilson, 2005: chapter 8). The turbulence in the supply of parties by elites has created a "floating system of parties," in which swings in votes between elections are principally caused by changes in the parties competing. Russian electors cannot hold accountable the party they voted for at the last election when it is no longer on the ballot at the next election (Rose and Munro, 2002: chapters 5–6; www.RussiaVotes.org). The only parties that have consistently fought and won seats at all Duma elections are the Communist Party and the Liberal Democratic Party of Vladimir Zhirinovsky, but their popular support is limited. In the Duma election of 2003, the two parties together won less than one-quarter of the list vote.

In a floating system of parties, electors cannot establish a long-term identification with a party. Surveys that seek to project the American concept of party identification onto Russian politics can lead to the creation of a party system that never appears on the ballot, because between the time of a survey in which people are asked to give a party identification and the time of an election the parties disappear (cf. Miller and Klobucar, 2000; Colton, 2004: 188ff.).

Under President Putin, elections have become less competitive, and this has further reduced accountability. During his first term of office, the Kremlin fostered the creation of a support party in the Duma, United Russia, consisting of earlier Putin backers and members of other parties who grabbed the opportunity to join what was clearly the party of power. In the 2003 Duma election, for the first time the government party won a plurality of list votes, 37.6 percent of the total. However, only 37 percent thought the Duma election was free and fair. By contrast, the 2004 New Europe Barometer found that in ex-Communist countries now in the European Union, an average of 78 percent see their parliamentary elections as conducted fairly. The reelection of President Putin in 2004 with a 57 percent lead over the runnerup was a result consistent with elections in post-Soviet regimes in Central Asia (cf. Tables 2.2, 3.1).

In established democracies, institutions of civil society provide another means of holding governors accountable. In the Soviet Union, membership in organizations that nominally appeared to be civil society institutions was compulsory. However, the organizations were in fact controlled by the Communist Party to advance the interests of the party-state. In consequence, institutions of civil society in the new regime are relatively weak and subject to pressure to give support to the Kremlin, or they run risks if they openly express criticism. Few Russians today want to belong to such organizations. In the fourteenth NRB survey, 95 percent reported not belonging to any type of voluntary community, charitable, sports, or other type of organization, and only 15 percent belonged to a trade union (cf. Howard, 2003; Table 7.1).

In theory, if there is trust in political institutions, individuals do not need organizations to represent their interests; in established democracies some assume that trust in political institutions is an important indicator of support for the current regime (Pharr and Putnam, 2000; Norris, 1999; but cf. Mishler and Rose, 2005). Consistently, New Russia Barometer surveys find low levels of trust in political institutions (Table 7.3). The two central institutions of representative democracy – the Duma and political parties – are the least trusted institutions: about one in ten Russians show any trust in either of them, while about three-quarters are actively distrustful and one in seven are skeptical about these institutions. The level of trust is less low in three authoritative institutions of the state: the army, the courts, and police. However, none can claim the trust of as many as half of Russians. Insofar as Russians differ in their attitude toward political institutions, it is in the degree of distrust.

Table 7.3 *Political institutions usually distrusted*

Q. To what extent do you trust each of the following institutions to look after your interests? Please indicate on a scale with 1 for no trust at all and 7 for great trust.

	Distrust (%)	Skeptical (%)	Trust (%)
Political parties	78	13	9
Parliament (Duma)	73	14	13
Police	68	15	17
Courts	59	18	23
Army	37	19	43

(Trust: Institution placed at points 5–7 on scale; skeptical: placed at midpoint, 4; distrust, points 1–3).

Source: New Russia Barometer surveys.

Presidential personality no substitute

Contemporary media, especially television, tend to personalize political coverage at elections, and even more in the years between elections when no other politician has the power of an incumbent president. While the personality of a president is relatively constant, his popularity fluctuates considerably. Shortly after the launch of the Russian Federation in March 1992, Boris Yeltsin's popularity was at its relative peak, a mean rating of 4.9 on a 10-point scale. However, he steadily lost popularity during his first term of office, dropping to a rating of 2.7. During his second term of office, Yeltsin became even more unpopular, having a mean rating as low as 1.8 in November 1998 (Rose and Munro, 2002: 85–86; Mishler and Willerton, 2003). The popularity of Vladimir Putin has been higher; his mean rating has ranged from 5.2 to 6.4. However, at any given moment Russians differ in their evaluation of the president. For example, in the fourteenth New Russia Barometer, the mean rating of President Putin was close to the midpoint of the scale, 5.8. Yet there were 27 percent who rated Putin at the top three points and 18 percent who rated him at the bottom three points.

It is a journalistic fallacy to confuse political regimes with political personalities, for example, speaking of Putin's Russia, Bush's America, or Blair's Britain. A regime is not a personal institution that expires with the passing of a leader. The Soviet Union demonstrated this: it persisted through six changes in leadership from Vladimir Lenin to Mikhail Gorbachev. While the 1993 Russian Constitution concentrates power in the presidency, it also includes a two-term limit on holding that office, which President Yeltsin respected.

Consistently, surveys show that Russians clearly distinguish between endorsing a president and the government: there is a big gap in the approval of the two (Figure 7.3). Since the beginning of Putin's first term of office, the Levada Center has asked separate questions about approval of the government of Russia and of Vladimir Putin as president. Over the years, Putin's approval has averaged 73 percent, while that of the government has averaged 37 percent.

Political performance matters

To hypothesize that regime support depends on political values and government performance is self-evidently reasonable, but it leaves open *which* particular values and attributes of performance matter most. It also leaves open whether influences on support for the current regime are equally important for rejection of alternative regimes and how these influences

Figure 7.3 *GAP IN APPROVAL OF PUTIN AND GOVERNMENT*

Q. Do you approve or disapprove of the performance of: (a) Vladimir Putin as president of Russia; (b) the government of Russia as a whole?

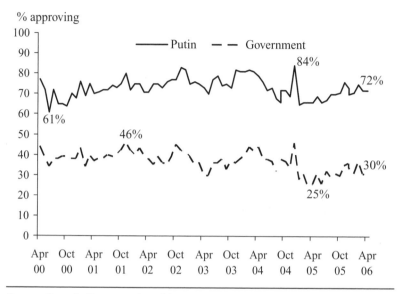

Source: Levada Center nationwide surveys, April 2000 to April 2006, as reported on www.RussiaVotes.org.

may be affected by the passage of time. To answer these questions, we turn again to OLS analysis to identify the most and least influential political as well as social structure influences, and to HLM analysis to take account of the passage of time as well. Statistical analysis confirms that politics matters, and it matters in different ways for current support and for alternative regimes.

Past and present politics matters for regime support

Whereas social structure could explain only 2.9 percent of the variance in current regime support, adding political evaluations increases the variance explained to 12.6 percent. Eight political measures achieve statistical significance compared to only four of the social structure influences; the influence of age, social status, and identities is secondary. Taking the passage of time as well as political variables into account[2] results in the

[2] The relatively small number of level-two observations, thirteen, restricts the degrees of freedom and limits the number of both first- and second-level variables that can be

Table 7.4 *Politics matters for current regime support*

	OLS			HLM[a]		
	b	se	BETA	b	se	P
Individual level						
Politics						
More freedom now	6.5	.38	.10	5.6	1.1	.000
Govt. fair, responsive	7.5	.38	.12	5.22	.99	.000
Pro old regime	−.10	.01	−.11	−.11	.02	.001
Approves president	2.8	.11	.16	4.98	.49	.000
Perception of corruption	−4.2	.55	−.04	−2.86	.55	.000
Democracy desired	1.2	.16	.04	1.33	.33	.002
Democracy achieved	.45	.20	—			
Trust political institutions	1.5	.18	.05			
Pro market ideology	9.7	1.8	.03			
Social structure						
Subjective status	3.1	.25	.07	3.41	.72	.000
Age	−.16	.02	−.05	−.16	.02	.000
Education	−.16	.22	—			
European identity	1.6	.30	.03			
Russian ethnicity	−3.8	.88	−.02			
Town size	.15	.23	—			
Aggregate level						
Month				.20	.02	.000
Cross-level interactions						
Corruption × month				−.08	.00	.000
Approves president × month				−.02	.01	.052
Variance explained:		$R^2 = 12.6\%$		$PSEUDO\ R^2 = 19.8\%$		

[a]Only significant variables included in HLM to preserve degrees of freedom.
−: Not significant at .001 level.

Source: New Russia Barometer surveys.

hierarchical linear model accounting for 19.8 percent of the reduction in variance compared to the 8.5 percent achieved by combining the passage of time solely with social structure influences (cf. Tables 7.4 and 6.4).

The legacy of the past has a significant influence on support for the current regime in three different ways. Not surprisingly, those who are more positive about the former Soviet regime are less likely to support the current regime. Equally important, the more people see the new regime as increasing their freedom by comparison with the Soviet regime – and

included in a hierarchical model. Because combining all of the political and social indicators previously employed would exceed this limit, the hierarchical linear models in Tables 7.4 and 7.5 exclude variables that were not significant in the preceding OLS analysis or otherwise appeared to be of minimal importance.

most Russians do – the more they endorse the new system. Because there is a strong statistical correlation between seeing the new regime as being fairer and more responsive than the old regime, the two measures are combined into a single composite indicator, and it too shows a significant influence on regime support.

When asked to evaluate the current performance of the regime, Russians tend to characterize it as corrupt, untrustworthy, and undemocratic. However, in the OLS analysis, these judgments have less influence on support than do evaluations based on a comparison of the current with the Soviet regime. This suggests that Russians have low but not uncritical expectations of government: if it performs badly, this will lower support for the current regime a little, but if its poor performance is viewed as less bad than that of the Soviet regime, this will actually increase support. For example, whether Russians perceive the current regime as democratic has no significant influence on support, while Russians who see the current regime as less unresponsive and less unfair than the old are more likely to support it.

The weak influence of distrust on regime support is consistent with other research showing that the political consequences of Russians' lack of trust are very limited (see Mishler and Rose, 2005). If trust were a major influence on regime support, as is hypothesized in theories of social capital (see Putnam, 2000), then, given the very low level of trust among Russians, support for the current regime should be a third or half as much as is the case today (cf. Table 7.3 and Figure 5.1). The multivariate analysis demonstrates that a lack of trust does not affect inclinations to support the regime nearly as much as comparisons of the current with the old regime.

The weak influence of democratic ideals indicates that a demand-side model of regime support is inappropriate for an autocratic regime in which political elites determine what subjects are asked to support. Since the great majority of Russians would like to have a democratic political system, demand-side models imply a strong negative relationship between endorsement of democracy as an ideal and support for the current regime. In fact, the opposite is the case: there is a weak but positive association between favoring democracy and favoring the current regime. In other words, the regime draws support almost equally from subjects who tend to favor democracy and those who favor dictatorship, an appropriate reflection of the hybrid nature of a plebiscitarian autocracy.

The effect of the month-by-month passage of time remains strong. Moreover, its influence on presidential approval and corruption leads to a more sophisticated understanding of how they affect regime support. In the OLS model, surveys from the Yeltsin and Putin years are pooled and approval of the president appears as a major influence on support (Beta: .16). However, the big difference in the approval ratings of the two presidents means that this association could be the spurious result of a differential influence of the two leaders. However, an HLM analysis controlling at the second level for whether the president was Yeltsin or Putin finds that this is not significant. The HLM analysis in Table 7.4 demonstrates two contrasting points. On the one hand, presidential approval does have a positive influence on support for the current regime. On the other hand, the passage of time reduces that influence from month to month. At the start of the Russian Federation, Russians could view Boris Yeltsin as a challenger to the Soviet regime. As the years rolled on, Russians gained experience of the new regime; this reduced the impact of presidential approval on regime support by more than one-third by the time Boris Yeltsin left office at the end of 1999. While Vladimir Putin has been a much more popular president to date, the increasing experience that people have of the new regime continues to reduce the relevance of presidential approval for regime support. By the time of the 2005 NRB survey, the passage of time had reduced the impact of presidential approval on regime support by three-fifths.

Seeing the regime as more corrupt is likely to reduce support, but in the OLS analysis the influence is limited (Beta: −.04). However, the HLM analysis shows that the passage of time makes corruption an increasingly strong influence on regime support. At the start of the new regime, it reduced support by relatively little, since Russians had no basis on which to evaluate its performance. By 2005, the well-publicized forms of corruption under the new regime (for example, involving the creation of ruble or dollar billionaires) increased fourfold the negative impact on regime support of the perception of corruption.

Ideals and legacy of past influence assessment of alternative regimes

The rejection of alternative regimes is influenced by politics as well as by social structure. Whereas the OLS analysis of the influence of social structure on alternative regimes accounted for 8.9 percent of the variance, adding political influences raises the amount to 21.1 percent, since seven political indicators are statistically significant too. The influences on rejection of alternative regimes are different from those affecting the current regime. They are also less affected by the passage of time. Thus, the variance accounted for by the hierarchical linear model is not much different from that of the ordinary least squares model (Table 7.5).

A political value – endorsement of democracy as an ideal – is the most important influence on the rejection of alternative regimes. The more

Table 7.5 *Politics matters for rejecting alternatives*

	OLS			HLM[a]		
	b	se	BETA	b	se	P
Individual level						
Politics						
Democracy desired	4.1	.12	.20	4.0	.14	.000
Pro old regime	−.15	.00	−.21	−.20	.02	.000
More freedom now	3.3	.29	.06	4.8	.59	.000
Approves president	.47	.08	.03	1.9	.37	.000
Perception of corruption	−1.1	.41	—	−1.4	.26	.000
Govt. fair, responsive	3.8	.29	.08			
Trust political institutions	.67	.13	.03			
Pro market ideology	12.8	1.3	.05			
Democracy achieved	−.42	.15	—			
Social structure						
Education	3.3	.16	.12	4.6	.30	.000
Age	−.23	.01	−.10	−.25	.02	.000
Town size	1.7	.17	.06			
Subjective status	1.2	.19	.04			
European identity	.81	.22	.02			
Russian ethnicity	.06	.66	—			
Aggregate level						
Month						
Cross-level interactions						
Approves president × month				−.02	.00	.001
Corruption × month				−.05	.00	.000
Variance explained:	$R^2 = 21.2\%$			$PSEUDO\ R^2 = 19.8\%$		

[a] Only significant variables included in HLM to preserve degrees of freedom.
−: Not significant at .001 level.

Source: New Russia Barometer surveys.

committed people are to democracy as an ideal, the more they are likely to reject dictatorship, army rule, a return to the Communist regime, or the suspension of parliament and the abolition of elections. Even though Russian democrats can be critical of the current regime, it is viewed as the lesser evil compared to other alternatives.

The legacy of the past is also important. The more people favor the former Soviet regime, the more inclined they are to endorse an alternative regime. Reciprocally, the more people see the new regime as freer, fairer, and more responsive to influence than the old regime, the readier they are to reject alternatives. However, current performance is of little importance. In the OLS model, neither corruption nor the extent to which the current regime is a dictatorship or a democracy has any significant influence on attitudes toward alternative regimes.

The additional variance explained by political ideals and the legacy of the past only marginally reduces the influence of social structure. After controlling for political indicators, in the OLS model five different social structure indicators appear statistically significant, albeit their influence ranges from the very limited to the substantial. Both of the two most important social structure measures – education and age – remain statistically and substantially significant influences on whether individuals endorse alternative regimes.

Political influences on the rejection of alternative regimes tend to be timeless. In the HLM analysis, the month-by-month passage of time has no significant influence. It does increase the influence of corruption: the longer the time since the founding of the new regime, the more support is given to alternative regimes by those who perceive corruption as a major feature of the new regime. The passage of time reverses the influence of presidential approval. Under President Yeltsin, there was a declining tendency for those who approved of the president to reject alternative regimes. However, for most of Vladimir Putin's time in office, those who approve of the president are more likely to endorse one or more alternative regimes.

Together, the analyses emphasize that political performance influences both regime support and the rejection of alternatives, but we cannot predict their level simply by looking at what the current regime does. The critical influence is how individuals evaluate the performance of the past as well as the current regime. While most Russians see great gains in freedom under the new regime, a majority also evaluate the old regime positively. When individuals are subject to such crosspressures, their overall judgment will reflect the relative weight given conflicting influences – and how these influences change with the passage of time.

While the foregoing analysis implies that an improvement in political performance could increase support, the history of Russian government emphasizes the obstacles to doing so. An alternative way of boosting support, which is consistent with Soviet thinking, would be to improve the performance of the Russian economy.

8   Finding the economic influences that matter

There is no such thing as a free lunch.

A maxim of economists

The creation of the Soviet economy was a political act that ruthlessly transformed a backward, agrarian economy into a large industrial economy. It was distinctive because decisions were not made by producers and consumers on the basis of market prices and calculations of risk and reward. Instead, prices and the allocation of resources were bureaucratically determined by five-year plans intended to maximize the resources of the state. Janos Kornai (1992) describes the system as a command economy because decisions were centralized in the higher echelons of the party-state rather than distributed throughout a market. The first seven chapters in Kornai's magisterial study of the command economy are about the organization of power.

The officially reported gross domestic product per capita of the Soviet command economy grew by 163 percent between 1950 and 1989. However, by comparison with the least-developed market economies of Europe, the achievement was unimpressive. In the same period, the Greek economy grew by more than 400 percent, the Portuguese economy by more than 350 percent, and the Spanish economy by more than 300 percent (Maddison, 1994: 22, 43). The inefficient allocation of resources to activities in which material costs outweighed benefits led to the gradual slowing down of Soviet economic growth and a widening gap in economic resources between the Soviet Union and its chief Cold War opponent, the United States. This was a major impetus behind Mikhail Gorbachev's attempt to reform the Soviet regime (cf. Winiecki, 1988; Brown, 1996). The disruption of the Soviet Union forced the transformation of the economy by destroying the power base of its commanders.

Institutions of a market economy have been introduced and reversed in a spasmodic trial-and-error process. At the start of 1992, the immediate challenge facing President Yeltsin's economic team was to fill an economic vacuum. There were shortages of goods and the value of money was uncertain. Enterprises replaced cash payments to suppliers and workers with barter or piled up debts that were eroded by inflation. Households relied on the food they could grow and paying little or nothing for housing and heating. After ministers decontrolled prices in order to end the shortage of goods, inflation went above 1,000 percent. President Yeltsin dismissed his pro-market advisors led by Yegor Gaidar and turned to experienced bureaucrats who had been important in the Soviet regime.

The Yeltsin administration gave political priority to reducing the power of the state by privatizing major state enterprises and valuable gas, oil, and mineral resources. However, the process of privatization differed from that in Britain and the United States, where property rights were clear and there was already a private sector to buy state-owned assets. In Russia, the Yeltsin administration pursued privatization without a private sector. The result was an economy in which the Kremlin dispensed favors to political supporters and get-rich-quick businessmen who repaid favors in kind. This climaxed in the "loans for shares" agreement that financed President Yeltsin's 1996 election campaign. After Yeltsin was reelected, businessmen received ownership of billions of dollars of natural resources at a fraction of their value. Favoritism and the lack of legal constraints on the disposal of state property created what has variously been labeled "crony capitalism" or a "kleptocracy," that is, rule by thieves (see e.g. Blasi, Kroumova, and Kruse, 1997; Freeland, 2000; Klebnikov, 2000; Reddaway and Glinski, 2001).

The weakening of the state's control of the economy under President Yeltsin has been replaced by the repatriation to the state of assets and power under President Putin. The horizontal pattern of the Yeltsin administration, in which Kremlin insiders exchanged favors with billionaire tycoons, has been replaced by a vertical system of controls in which tycoons are subordinate to the Kremlin and subject to having their property expropriated if they step out of line politically. The Putin strategy has been more consistent with Ivan the Terrible's expropriation of the boyars and the mercantilism of the French Sun King than with the doctrines of Adam Smith.

Since a national economy is a complex structure, the economic conditions that might influence the regime outlooks of Russians are multiple and, in an economy in transformation, they are much more uncertain than in an established economy (cf. Stokes, 2001: chapter 1). "Hard" numbers tend to go soft when inflation devalues wages or individuals are not paid at all. "Hard" measures of the gross domestic product are woefully incomplete when individuals rely on the unofficial barter economy, dollars, and household production without money to cope with the consequences of transformation.

The epigram made familiar by Bill Clinton's campaign staff – "It's the economy, stupid" – gains added salience when both the political regime and the economic system are in transformation. In its maximalist form, both neoclassical economists and Marxists can reduce all social behavior to determination by one or another form of economic influence. At a minimum, it can be hypothesized:

Hypothesis 3: Regime support depends on how individuals evaluate their household and national economic conditions.

The Clinton hypothesis is indiscriminate: it fails to identify which aspects of the economy are influential, rates of inflation and economic growth in the national economy, or the economic situation of an individual household that simultaneously faces job insecurity *and* new opportunities to make money.

The confusion created by transformation gives greater influence to how people perceive and evaluate economic conditions than to measures of material goods. Neoclassical economics postulates that individuals maximize their welfare, an assumption consistent with Russian distrust of collective institutions. From this perspective, regime outlooks ought to reflect individual and household standards of living. However, research in the United States pioneered by Kinder and Kiewiet (1981) offers a different theory. Individuals may accept responsibility for their own living standard, whether it is good or bad. However, the responsibility for preventing inflation and promoting economic growth is assigned to government. This implies that individuals who are satisfied with their household's living standard but dissatisfied with the state of the national economy will be less likely to support the regime, and those dissatisfied with their household situation but positive about the national economy will be more inclined to give support.

Given the problematic nature of economic influences, in this chapter the economy is viewed from both the top down and the bottom up. The first section outlines the performance of the national economy and how Russians have evaluated that performance. It also reports how Russians would like the economy to be organized. Since national conditions do not have the same effect on all individuals, the second section reports who benefits from and who pays the cost of transformation. There are substantial differences between the material impact that transformation has had and how these effects have been subjectively evaluated. While in a market economy changes are marginal and progressive, in an economy in transformation they are structural and erratic. The costs arising at the start of transformation are meant to be followed by benefits subsequently. The concluding section examines how Russian evaluations of their household and national economy have influenced regime support, and how this compares with the influence of politics with the passage of time.

Downs and ups of the national economy

The democratic assumption underlying many surveys of public opinion is that governors ought to supply what the people want, such as stable prices and economic growth. For this reason, politics can be described as a "happy" science, in which politicians promise popular benefits. However, economics is the dismal science, because its central maxim is that there are no benefits without costs. The absence of a free lunch was palpably evident during Russia's transformation.

Extent of creative destruction

Joseph Schumpeter's (1952) description of economic development as "creative destruction" is apt as a characterization of developments in Russia in the post-Communist era. The political power of the commanders of the command economy was destroyed. This was immediately followed by the creation of new enterprises, which have been challenged to survive or flourish by hook or by crook.

While institutional transformation is very visible, assessing the economic impact of transformation is very difficult, because the methods used to measure the market economy are fundamentally different from what Soviet ministries used to monitor targets in five-year plans. The planned economy paid more attention to inputs of physical resources, such as the weight of locomotives produced, than to valuing outputs in terms of their market price. The absence of markets in the Soviet system meant that the money values attributed to outputs tended to be arbitrary and higher than they would be in an open market. Because there were strong penalties for enterprises that failed to meet targets laid down in the plan, enterprise managers chronically overreported what was produced.

In the early years of economic transformation, it was far easier for official records to capture the contraction of the state-controlled sector than to estimate what was happening in the private sector, where much economic activity was off the books. Moreover, many enterprises operated a dual economy, returning losses to official agencies while profiting from cash-in-hand transactions or payments in foreign currencies that were not officially recorded. Inflation exacerbated problems, since all measures of economic trends require converting current money values into constant prices. However, in the early years of transformation, actual prices were anything but constant. While prices were continually rising, the rate of increase was erratic from month to month and quarter to quarter. As a consequence, aggregate official statistics for the Russian economy in transformation can give only an approximate estimate of economic change.

As a condition of giving billions of dollars of aid, organizations such as the International Monetary Fund and the World Bank required the Russian government to create statistical measures from the end of the command economy. This presupposed that Soviet-era statistics about net material product were comparable with the statistics used to produce standard national accounts and calculate the gross domestic product of a market economy. Even though this assumption was dubious, the demand from the international financial community led to the conversion of the accounts of the non-market economy into a notional measure of gross domestic product at the end of the Soviet era (Marer, et al., 1992; EBRD, 2005). Monitoring trends from 1992 onwards involved an additional assumption: that the inadequacies of official statistics at that time were also constant, an assumption that was undercut as a consequence of efforts to improve official statistics (cf. Rose, 2002).

By any measure, the output of the official economy contracted dramatically in the early years of transformation. In the first year of transformation, 1992, officially reported gross domestic product fell by 19 percent; in the following year the economy contracted by a further seven percentage points. By 1996, a presidential election year, the official economy was estimated to be only 60 percent of the size of the economy in the final year of the Soviet Union (Figure 8.1). Free-market economists argued that part of the contraction was a gain, not a loss, because the Soviet baseline included the production of goods that no one wanted to buy, and that evidence of factories laying off employees who added nothing to production was a sign of greater economic efficiency.

Since the shock fall in the value of the ruble in 1998, the official economy has consistently recorded growth. The effect of the crisis was positive: it cut imports and made it more profitable to export goods. In addition, the boom in world energy prices has especially benefited Russia because of the contribution of gas and oil exports to the value of its gross domestic product. When the Putin administration cut tax rates and took aggressive measures to collect taxes from enterprises, these actions encouraged firms to transfer activities from the unofficial economy or overseas bank accounts to the official Russian economy. The upshot has been that

Figure 8.1 *MACROECONOMIC TRENDS*

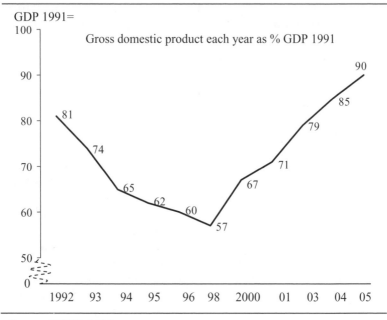

Source: EBRD, 2005.

between 1998 and 2005 the Russian economy has grown by almost half; annual rates of growth as high as 10 percent have been reported. The U-shaped path of the Russian economy illustrates both the costs and benefits of transformation – and how they have been distributed in the passage of time.

Because the command economy had used shortages, queuing, and bartering rather than prices to allocate goods and services, the introduction of market prices was a necessary step in establishing a market economy. However, government officials, including the Central Bank, were unaccustomed to managing a market economy. When prices began to rise, the Central Bank's instinct was to print money and give soft loans to enterprises in the belief that this would cushion the shock. But putting more money in the hands of consumers without increasing the supply of goods simply drove prices higher (see e.g. Aslund, 2002: 204ff.).

The more money the Central Bank issued, the more prices rose and the more the nominal value of the ruble dropped. In 1992, the first year of the Russian Federation, official statistics estimated inflation at more than 1500 percent. The following year the inflation rate was almost halved to 875 percent (EBRD, 2004: 40). However, because this increase was on top of that of the previous year, over a 24-month period prices rose by more than 2800 percent. The next year the annual rate of inflation again halved. This meant that in three years the price level had risen by more than 4000 percent. The career of the ruble since has shown a fall in the annual rate of inflation except for 1998, when inflation was 86 percent. A decade after the start of transformation, the annual Russian rate of inflation of 16 percent was within the range of a country such as Italy during most of its post-war history (EBRD, 2005).

The impact of quadruple-digit inflation has been great. As the value of the ruble fell, Russians in employment were running up the down escalator in pursuit of wage increases. Sooner or later enterprises offered increases in wages, government increased pensions, and new enterprises offered wages based on market values. However, increases in wages and pensions were not necessarily timed to match increases in prices.

Concern with inflation has remained strong among Russians. When the 2005 NRB survey asked whether rising prices or unemployment was the biggest threat to their family, 73 percent said that rising prices were a bigger threat than unemployment. The greater concern with inflation reflects the pervasive effects of price increases: in a market economy everyone needs money, whether employed, a pensioner, or a student. By contrast, unemployment does not immediately threaten almost half of the adult population who are retired or still studying (Rose, 1998).

While ordinary Russians could not follow the convoluted calculations of macroeconomic statistics, they had experienced how the national economy worked before and after transformation. When the New Russia Barometer asks people to evaluate the pre-*perestroika* economy, it is consistently viewed favorably; the only variation is in the size of the majority endorsing it (Figure 8.2). At the start of transformation, 62 percent of Russians viewed the old economy positively, 12 percent were neutral, and only 26 percent negative. After market mechanisms began to be established, attitudes toward the command economy became more positive. By the year 2000, a total of 83 percent endorsed the old economic system, and the proportion positive has remained high ever since.

When asked in a follow-up question to evaluate the current economic system, a neutral term that avoids ideologically charged references to the market, a very different picture emerges (Figure 8.2). At the start of transformation, 82 percent of Russians were negative about the new economy and only 10 percent positive. Throughout the 1990s, less than one-third expressed positive evaluation of the national economy. It was not until 2003 that as many as half of Russians had a positive view of the current economic system, rising to 61 percent in 2004. However, the proportion favorable fell to 47 percent in 2005.

Figure 8.2 *EVALUATION OF ECONOMIC SYSTEMS*

Q. *Here is a scale evaluating how well an economy works. The top, plus 100, is the best and the bottom, minus 100, is the worst. Where on this scale would you put:*
   (a) The economic system before the start of perestroika?
   (b) Our current economic system?

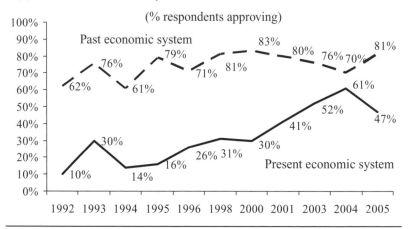

Source: New Russia Barometer surveys.

No agreement about how the economy ought to be run

Because many Russians have no opinion about philosophical debates concerning capitalism and socialism (see Table 4.2), asking people to choose between economic systems in the abstract risks collecting unreliable data. However, people cannot opt out of the realities of the market place. Kornai's (1992: 228ff.) description of a socialist economy as one in which consumers experienced chronic shortages and queuing translates economic abstractions into terms readily recognizable to Russians. Russians are also familiar with a market economy in which there are lots of goods in shops but the prices are high by comparison with the past.

Given people's experience of being consumers in two very different economic systems, the New Russia Barometer asks whether they prefer an economy with shortages and queuing or a window-shopping economy in which there are lots of goods for sale at prices that are often too high for many people to afford. Only 1 percent of Russians have no opinion about which system they prefer, but there is no agreement about which system is better (Figure 8.3). An average of 49 percent have endorsed a market economy and 51 percent a command economy, and this division is

Figure 8.3 *DISAGREEMENT ABOUT IDEAL ECONOMIC SYSTEM*

Q. Which of the following statements would you agree with? It is better when there are plenty of goods in the shops even if they are expensive, OR it is better when prices are kept low by the state even if there are few goods in the shops.

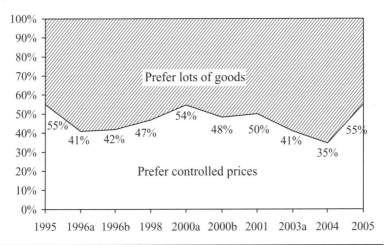

Source: New Russia Barometer surveys.

consistent over time. In Russia, there remains a categoric difference between those who believe the economy ought to be in the hands of bureaucrats allocating goods and services or in the hands of private entrepreneurs who profit by producing goods that people want to buy.

Downs and ups of the household economy

National economic statistics give an aggregate picture: they do not deal with the circumstances of individuals and households. By definition, statistics about the conditions of the average Russian say nothing about the distribution of costs and benefits between Russians. When the national economy grows or contracts by five percentage points, this does not mean that every Russian's income has risen or fallen by the same amount. Some people will see their income rise or fall more than the average while others will see it change less. Even when national statistics are about conditions concerning everyone, such as inflation, the effects are not identical: inflation tends to hurt people on fixed incomes most, while benefiting those who can push up their earnings when prices rise. A major advantage of NRB surveys is that the data can be used to identify those Russians who have materially benefited or see themselves as benefiting from transformation and those who feel its costs.

Stresses of transformation

In Soviet times, the whole of the labor force was employed by state-owned institutions and assured a job for life. Typically, enterprises had a surplus of labor; the difficulties of recruiting new staff and the absence of any hard budget constraints were incentives to hoard labor. A high priority for liberals within the Yeltsin government was to reduce the economic power of government departments where the old economic commanders were still in place and to create a new class of private owners to run the economy. Initially, it sought to do this by a program of voucher privatization, in which every Russian household was given vouchers with which they could buy a small number of shares in large enterprises. Effectively, this favored existing enterprise management at the local level and former Communist Party apparatchiks with inside knowledge. The process was caricatured as *nomenklatura* privatization.

Working in private enterprise has offered a greater risk of unemployment and the prospect of higher wages. When the 1995 New Russia Barometer asked about a preferred choice of employer, there were massive differences between age groups: 69 percent of older Russians said they would prefer a job in the state sector, while among young Russians 69 percent preferred a job in a new private company, a joint venture combining foreign and Russian capital, or self-employment. At that time, more than half of Russians were employed in the public sector, while 31 percent were employed in privatized enterprises and 12 percent in firms newly created since 1991. By 2005, the NRB found that the proportion working in new private enterprises had trebled to 36 percent and those in privatized enterprises were 26 percent, while state employees had fallen to 38 percent. The loss of social services provided to employees of an enterprise had less of an impact than expected, because many workers did not work for enterprises that provided such benefits. Benefits were first of all allocated according to the priority that the state's planners gave to an industry rather than according to individual need (Rose, 1996a).

In a market economy, unemployment can deprive people of wages, while in an economy in transformation there is also the risk of not being paid wages by an employer. In 1995, when the New Russia Barometer first starting collecting data about the non-payment of wages, 52 percent in work sometimes went without pay. By the time of the presidential election in mid-1996, 78 percent of Russians were making forced loans to their employers by receiving wages late or not being paid at all. An indicator of the pathologies of public finance is that late payment of wages was more likely among state employers than in the new private sector, where workers would quit their job rather than work without pay. It was not until 2000 that half the labor force was paid on time throughout the year. A sign of the institutionalization of the market by 2005 is that 71 percent of those in work were paid on time. However, the majority suffering from some degree of interrupted income remain people in employment rather than the unemployed.

Coping thanks to a multiplicity of economies

When the economy was transformed by top-down decisions taken in Moscow, this led to warnings that the new regime would be repudiated if it could not maintain the living standards and the social safety net offered by the Soviet regime. However, such forecasts overlooked the strategies that Russians had devised to cope with the shortcomings of the command economy.

Russians have long relied on a portfolio of economic activities to cope with uncertainties (Rose, 1993). The introduction of the market legalized working for cash in hand in the unofficial shadow economy, but not many people could pay cash. Households relied more on "social" economies in which no money changed hands. Families grew some of their own food, made repairs and improvements to their houses, and turned to friends and relatives for help. Thus, when non-payment of wages was at its height in 1996, only 15 percent were relying solely on what they were meant to be paid from the official economy. A majority, 55 percent, relied on a defensive portfolio of economies that included growing food and exchanges with others without money as well as on a nominally paid job or pension; 19 percent were enterprising, being paid cash in hand in an unofficial economy as well as having an official income; and 11 percent were marginal, depending solely on others to help them survive without a regular official income.

The combination of inflation and reliance on multiple economies makes money wages a misleading indicator of household living standards. The New Russia Barometer has developed two complementary measures of economic welfare and illfare. Instead of a poverty index calculated in unstable rubles of uncertain value, a destitution index measures the frequency with which Russians go without critical necessities – food, clothing, and electricity and heat. In a time of transformation, many people may sometimes go without meat for their Sunday dinner, patch their clothes, or be without electricity for a few hours. Destitution arises only when people frequently go without necessities.

Widespread destitution has not resulted from the dislocations of transformation. It was a challenge that Russians could meet by falling back
on household production or help from friends. Buying new clothes is the
biggest financial problem of Russian households. Consistently, a majority
of Russians say that they sometimes or often are unable to buy clothes
that they really need. Until 2001, the median Russian sometimes had
to go without food; by 2005 almost half said they never went without
food during the course of a year, and an additional fifth rarely went without food. In the Russian climate, heating is a critical necessity (see Hill
and Gaddy, 2003). Because the country has great energy resources, the
state can subsidize the cost of heating. Thus, an average of three-fifths of
Russians have never had to go without heating during the year, and an
additional one in seven has rarely gone without heating.

While no one wants to do without new clothes, ample food, and heating, the dislocations of transformation force people to do without. The
critical point is the frequency with which people do without necessities.
The more infrequently this happens, the easier it is to make temporary
adjustments, for example, having a dinner consisting only of potatoes,
or buying secondhand rather than new clothes (see Rose, 1995a). The
NRB evidence shows that doing without has been an occasional or rare
event rather than a continuing problem. On average, 25 percent said
they never lacked any necessities during a year, 36 percent rarely did so,
and 30 percent sometimes went without necessities. The group that often
went without necessities is the smallest, 9 percent of Russians. Moreover,
the longer the time period used for assessing deprivation, the smaller the
size of the group that has often gone without necessities.

Affluence is the opposite of destitution, and transformation has offered
opportunities for individuals to become more prosperous. In a market
economy, having durable household goods is an indicator of prosperity
and decades of shortages have made Russians avid consumers. From
an economic standpoint, the fact that a car, a color television set, or a
video cassette recorder (VCR) is *not* a necessity makes ownership a sign
that a household has discretionary income sufficient to buy what most
people think of as "good" goods. While food can be grown at a *dacha*,
major consumer goods are factory-made and can be acquired only by
paying anything from a month's to more than a year's income (Rose
and Krassilnikova, 1996). Since goods such as VCRs or Internet access
became available only after the market was introduced, they are especially
clearcut indicators of post-transformation prosperity.

Today, the great majority of Russians have a color television set produced in a market economy (Figure 8.4). Almost half of households have
an additional home entertainment system, such as a cassette or digital
video recorder. Car ownership remains limited to a quarter of households

Figure 8.4 *CONSUMER GOODS SHOW DISCRETIONARY INCOME*

Q. Does your household have any of the following...?

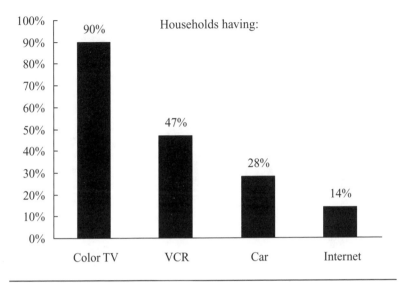

Source: New Russia Barometer surveys. Internet users include 9 percent connecting outside the home.

while Internet use is rising, whether at home, a friend's house, school, work, or an Internet cafe (Rose, 2006b). A sign of growing affluence is that 20 percent of Russian households have access to at least three of these consumer goods, more than twice the proportion, 8 percent, who lack all of them.

The assessment that Russians make of their household's economic circumstances cannot be automatically inferred from official economic statistics or from the material circumstances of individual households. Individual views about economic satisfaction are subjective judgments. At the start of transformation when economic difficulties were great, 26 percent nonetheless rated their household's economic conditions as satisfactory, while 74 percent said it was unfavourable. Since then, the shortages of the non-market economy have disappeared and a majority of homes have enjoyed enough discretionary income to buy new consumer goods. However, the proportion of people reporting themselves satisfied with their household's economic situation has remained low: an average of 23 percent say they are satisfied economically compared to 77 percent reporting they are dissatisfied with their household's economic condition (Figure 8.5).

Figure 8.5 *STEADY DISSATISFACTION WITH HOUSEHOLD ECONOMY*

Q. All in all, how do you rate the economic situation of your household today?

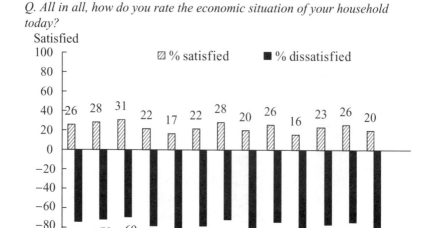

Source: New Russia Barometer surveys.

When Russians are asked to compare their household's economic situation at present with what it was before *perestroika*, in every NRB survey the largest group feel that their living standards have fallen. In January 1992, when comparison was between the legacy of Gorbachev and that of Brezhnev, 56 percent said their household's economic situation was worse at the end of the Soviet Union than before reforms began. Notwithstanding the spread of household consumer durables since 1991, in 2005 a total of 58 percent felt their living standards had fallen. Over the period as a whole, 51 percent have reported their living standards falling, 18 percent say that they have remained much the same, while 31 percent feel that their living standards are rising. Thus, even if Russians are living better today than twenty years ago, many nonetheless feel worse off.

Politics pervasive; economic influences contingent

The time frame in which economic evaluations are made is important. The costs of transformation are front-end loaded, whereas the benefits require the passage of time to unfold. Because an economy is constantly in flux, whether perceptions of economic conditions increase *or* decrease support for the regime can depend on when a survey is done. Since transformation began, every Russian has witnessed the national economy contracting greatly and then growing rapidly. To divide Russians into "winners" and "losers" from economic transformation is a gross oversimplification. In the course of a decade and a half, many households have experienced both pains *and* gains.

The New Russia Barometer questionnaire has been explicitly designed to collect data about how people evaluate the national economy as well as their household's living standard. It has included subjective and material indicators of current economic conditions and comparisons with the past. Thus, it can test theories about alternative types of economic influences – and whether or not their influence remains constant with the passage of time. Adding economic indicators to the regression analyses in previous chapters provides an empirical test of under what circumstances and to what extent economic influences may be important for regime support. The evidence shows that the influence of economic conditions is contingent.

Subjective evaluations of the national economy affect regime support

When economic influences are included in regression equations about support, this more than doubles the total amount of variance explained. Whereas an OLS analysis with political performance and social structure accounts for 12.6 percent of variation in regime support, the addition of economic influences increases the variance explained to 38.2 percent (Table 8.1). Likewise, when economic influences are added to the multilevel model, the variance accounted for increases to 38.9 percent. This occurs even though the majority of economic indicators fail to register any statistical significance.

Russians do not evaluate their economic system on the basis of official statistics produced by Goskomstat or by intergovernmental agencies in Washington. Whereas official data about the gross domestic product in a given year produces a single aggregate number, individuals evaluations are variable. For example, in 2005 when the national economy was booming, less than half of Russians gave the economy a positive rating. How Russians subjectively evaluate the national economic system is the critical influence on regime support, after controlling for all other social, economic, and political conditions. In the OLS analysis, the standardized Beta coefficient of the current economy (.52) is far greater than for any of the fifteen other potential influences in the regression. In addition, Russians who subjectively approve of the old command economy are, net of all other influences, less likely to endorse the current regime.

The HLM analysis includes the cumulative rate of growth in the gross domestic product as an additional influence. Just as regime support

Table 8.1 *Economic influence on current regime support*

	OLS			HLM[a]		
	b	se	BETA	b	se	P
Individual level						
Economy						
Pro current economic system	.52	.00	.52	.52	.01	.000
Pro lots of goods in market	1.51	.29	.03	1.30	.40	.007
Pro old economic system	−.05	.01	−.05			
Destitution	−.07	.14	—			
Number of consumer goods	1.84	.94	—			
Satisfied household economy	.73	.25	—			
Change household economy	−.14	.18	—			
Politics						
Approves president	1.72	.08	.11	2.55	.33	.000
More freedom now	4.59	.34	.07	4.48	.66	.000
Democracy desired	.74	.13	.03	.88	.15	.000
Pro old regime	−.09	.01	−.09	−.07	.02	.004
Perception of corruption	−.11	.46	—	−1.46	.19	.000
Govt. fair, responsive	1.73	.26	.03			
Trust political institutions	.33	.10	—			
Social structure						
Subjective status	.83	.21	.02			
Age	−.05	.02	—			
Aggregate level						
Month				.22	.02	.000
Cumulative economic growth				.51	.11	.001
Cross-level interactions						
Corruption × month				−.05	.00	.000
Variance explained:		$R^2 = 38.2\%$			$PSEUDO\ R^2 = 38.9.\%$	

[a] Only significant variables included in HLM to preserve degrees of freedom.
−: Not significant at .001 level.

Source: New Russia Barometer surveys.

fluctuates, so a distinctive feature of the GDP measure is that the economy has reversed direction (cf. Figures 8.1, 8.2). But aggregate changes in the national economy, while statistically significant, are much less important than differences between individuals in their subjective evaluation of the current economic system. The latter variable remains just as important as in the OLS analysis. Moreover, changes in aggregate GDP are much less important than most political influences.

Neoclassical theories of economics are bottom-up theories, emphasizing the importance of individuals maximizing their utility. This implies that subjective evaluations and material indicators of a family's economic condition ought to be even more important than evaluations of the national economy. Thus, when the transformed economy started to deliver what are regarded as "good" goods in market economies, such as color television sets or cars, this should have boosted regime support among households that benefit. However, Kinder and Kiewiet's (1981) theory of sociotropic voting postulates that these egocentric concerns are secondary in importance to the state of the national economy.

Contrary to neoclassical economic theories about the maximization of private benefits, all four household economic indicators fail to achieve statistical significance in the OLS analysis. Whether an individual is destitute or has lots of consumer goods makes no difference for his or her support for the current regime (Table 8.1). Likewise, whether a person is satisfied or dissatisfied with their household's current economic condition or by comparison with the past also makes no difference to their evaluation of the current regime. The failure of individual economic conditions to influence regime support reinforces the finding that education and social status, which tend to correlate with individual economic conditions, do not influence support.

The evaluation of the current economy is most important for regime support, but it is not all-important. After controlling for the influence of economic evaluations, in the OLS analysis five measures of political performance and values remain significant (cf. Tables 8.1 and 7.4). While the influence of these political factors is lessened, they remain significant, unlike the indicators of household economic conditions.

The HLM analysis again confirms the importance of the passage of time. The month-by-month passage of time again shows a substantial influence on support for the current regime, and it is much greater than the secondary influence of the change in gross domestic product. As shown before, not only does an individual's perception of the corruption of the regime reduce support, but also the downward pressure intensifies substantially with the passage of time. Thus, the increased benefit that the new regime has gained from the improved popular evaluation of the national economy in recent years has been offset by the intensification of the negative influence of corruption.

Politics not economics drives rejection of alternative regimes

Adding economic measures to the analysis of alternative regimes shows how contingent is the influence of the economy. The addition of eight economic indicators to the OLS analysis does little to account for the rejection of alternatives; the variance explained is increased by only 3.3 percentage points (Table 8.2 and 7.5). Likewise, adding economic

Table 8.2 *Economy adds little to rejecting alternatives*

	OLS			HLM[a]		
	b	se	BETA	b	se	P
Individual level						
Economy						
Pro lots of goods in market	5.0	.25	.12	6.06	.71	.000
Pro current economic system	.07	.00	.09	.08	.01	.000
Pro old economic system	−.05	.01	−.06			
Destitution	−.74	.12	−.03			
Number of consumer goods	2.0	.74	—			
Satisfied household economy	.46	.22	—			
Change household economy	−.31	.16	—			
Politics						
Democracy desired	3.8	.12	.18	3.89	.12	.000
Pro old regime	−.11	.01	−.15	−.18	.01	.000
More freedom now	2.4	.30	.05	4.03	.49	.000
Approves president	.07	.07	—	1.08	.30	.004
Trust political institution	.30	.08	.02			
Pro market ideology	12.3	.75	.09			
Govt. fair, responsive	1.8	.23	.04			
Perception of corruption	−.69	.40	—			
Social structure						
Education	2.8	.19	.10	4.15	.02	.000
Age	−.15	.01	−.06	−.17	.02	.000
Town size	1.5	.22	.04			
Subjective status	.53	.19	—			
European identity	.27	.22	—			
Russian ethnicity	.60	.64	—			
Aggregate level						
Month						
Cumulative economic growth				.53	.09	.000
Cross-level interactions						
(none significant)						
Variance explained:		$R^2 = 24.5\%$		$PSEUDO\ R^2 = 24.4\%$		

[a] Only significant variables included in HLM to preserve degrees of freedom.
−: Not significant at .001 level.

Source: New Russia Barometer surveys.

influences to the HLM analysis adds 4.6 percent to the variance accounted for.[1] Whereas evaluations of the current national economy had an exceptionally strong influence on support for the current regime, its influence on the rejection of alternative regimes is of secondary importance. The

[1] Since five economic influences registered a slight influence or failed to achieve statistical significance in the OLS analysis, they have been omitted from the HLM analysis.

same is true of a preference for a market economy offering goods in abundance.

Political performance and values remain most important for the rejection of alternative regimes. Net of all economic influences, the extent to which a Russian is committed to the democratic ideal is again most influential. The legacy of the past remains important too: approval of the Communist regime increases endorsement of alternatives more than any economic influence. The influence of social structure remains strong. A Russian's education has more effect on rejecting alternative regimes than does his or her assessment of the current or former economic system or preference for a market or a command economy. Age remains important too.

The Soviet regime socialized Russians to think of the national economy as a political economy, for the system made it very evident that political power rather than market forces controlled the allocation of material resources. Since official data about the national economy were Potemkin statistics, Russians learned to ignore statistics that are the primary focus of attention of international policymakers. Instead, they have relied on their own subjective judgments to evaluate the country's economy and the political regime which is held responsible for it.

9 The impact of the passage of time

Politics is the strong and slow boring of hard boards.

Max Weber

When the facts change, I change my mind. What do you do?

John Maynard Keynes

Support for a regime is never static, as is implied by theories of democratic consolidation. A steady-state equilibrium is momentarily at rest thanks to the tension created by multiple influences, some favoring support for the current regime while others push in the opposite direction. Therefore, a change in any one influence will affect the overall equilibrium – and this is especially true if all other conditions remain constant. If multiple influences cancel out by changing in opposite directions, then aggregate regime support will appear steady, but underneath the surface there are pressures that could challenge it. When major influences change substantially and do not cancel each other out, this will create a dynamic challenge. Since society is constantly in flux, the longer the passage of time, the less realistic it is to expect the influences contributing to regime support to remain unchanged or to neutralize each other.

The direction in which influences change will always receive attention. Anything increasing support for the current regime will be welcomed. Likewise, anything decreasing support will sound political alarm bells. The scale of change is equally relevant, for, even if a change is statistically significant, its impact may not be large enough to be politically significant: for example, a 3 percent compared to a 30 percent movement in the evaluation of the current economic system.

The tempo of change and the length of time it is sustained also influence the dynamics. A quick change in regime support can capture political attention because of its unexpectedness but, if its cause quickly disappears, then it will be only an ephemeral event. A monthly opinion poll secures a headline if one month's result is different from that of the previous month but, as Weber emphasizes, politics is often slow-moving and boring. In what historians call the *longue durée*, the cumulative effect of seemingly small changes can have a big impact on regime support. However, from the perspective of impatient dissidents, the current regime's resistance to change can appear like granite.

In a lengthy time perspective, there are fluctuations in regime support. As long as changes are small in scale and there are incremental adjustments in countervailing directions, there is a steady-state equilibrium, for changes are limited; the net effect is that support cycles around a stable mean. However, if influences on support are large, fast-paced, and sustained, this creates a dynamic challenge for the regime's leaders to adapt their behavior. As an economic advisor to many British governments, Keynes was an advocate of quickly adapting the economy in response to evidence of change in order to maintain an economic equilibrium. If a challenge is due to passing events, adaptation can produce a return to the previous status quo. However, if the challenge is major, a dynamic cycle will end only if reforms are introduced that modify the regime in order to maintain support.

The lifetime-learning model recognizes many opportunities to alter political evaluations with the passage of time. Resocialization starts when, for example, the regime's political performance, national economic conditions, or an individual's own position in society stimulate a change in attitudes. A change in underlying causal influences will lead to a change in an individual's support for the current or alternative regimes. However, some underlying conditions do not vary much with the passage of time: for example, support for democracy as an ideal appears to have been little altered by transformation and its aftermath.

Even if the total population of a country remains constant, there is a slow but steady turnover of generations. The economy tends to be continuously in flux, and economic cycles occur when economic conditions reverse. Some aspects of political performance may be persisting, but others, such as the popularity of the president, are inherently unstable. As previous chapters have documented, the passage of time can also increase or decrease the intensity with which influences such as corruption have an impact on regime support.

Hypothesis 4a: Regime support changes with alterations in the variables that significantly influence support.

In the unprecedented circumstances of transformation, hopes and fears for the future are subjective and malleable. Political elites, whether democrats or Leninists, can assert that today's costs will be rewarded by a better tomorrow. Expectations are equally important for the rejection of alternative regimes. If people favoring an alternative regime do not expect it to come about, they are more likely to give resigned acceptance to the status quo. Insofar as future expectations differ from current and past judgments (cf. Munro, 2006), they may exert an independent influence on regime support. With the passage of time, what was once the future becomes the all-too-real present, the present becomes the past, and the future can be imagined afresh in the light of previous experience.

Hypothesis 4b: Regime support changes when future expectations alter.

Political inertia – that is, the tendency of a regime in place to remain in place from one year to the next and from one presidential term to the next – can encourage the gradual accretion of support for the regime and the erosion of support for alternative regimes. As a result, people may support the regime simply out of habit. Resigned acceptance of the powers that be avoids the frustration of preferring an unattainable alternative.

Hypothesis 4c: Regime support increases the longer a regime is in place.

The great majority of surveys of public opinion in new regimes are undertaken soon after their launch, when interest is highest and there has not been enough time to arrive at an equilibrium of support. Such data cannot be used to understand the process by which regime support settles down with the passage of time. Because the New Russia Barometer has been surveying public opinion since the start of the Russian Federation, it is extraordinarily suited to test under what circumstances and to what extent the passage of time influences support for the current and alternative regimes. The next section reviews patterns of stability and change in the chief conditions affecting regime support. The second section tests the extent to which expectations of the future feed back as influences on support for the current and alternative regimes. The concluding section uses HLM analysis to test the extent to which political inertia has influenced regime support.

Stable and variable influences

The passage of time is a necessary but not a sufficient condition for political re-learning. If national conditions remain stable and an individual's position in the social structure is stable too, then there is no stimulus to alter attitudes to the regime. If changes occur in conditions that have no significant influence, for example, the Russian regime is perceived as more democratic or more dictatorial, this will not be sufficient to change regime support. To have any impact, changes must occur in the limited number of variables that have previously been identified as significant (cf. Tables 8.1, 8.2). Such changes can take the form of a steady trend in one direction or fluctuations that intermittently vary in opposite directions. Meteoric events can also create an unexpected challenge to rethink regime support.

Since the past is past, the Soviet regime cannot change but people can alter their evaluation of it, for example, as a consequence of disappointment with the current regime or as more information about the *gulag* enters the public domain. On the other hand, the intensity of political socialization in the Soviet era could create barriers against learning to think afresh about the old regime. In fact, Russian attitudes toward the political past tend to be stable. For more than a decade of New Russia Barometer surveys, the overall pattern of replies to questions about the pre-*perestroika* Soviet regime have tended to be much the same: a majority have consistently tended to give a favorable assessment of the old regime. While there have been fluctuations in attitudes, they are less than half the fluctuation that has occurred in the evaluation of the current regime (cf. Figures 5.1, 7.2).

When Russians are asked to compare their freedom today with freedom under the old regime, the pattern of replies shows an even higher degree of stability. The freedom of action gained in the new regime has not been taken for granted. In 1995 an average of 76 percent said they felt freer on four different indicators of freedom; in 2005, the proportion was virtually identical: 77 percent felt freer (Table 7.2).

Russians see corruption as a fact of life persisting from tsarist and Soviet times to the present. Therefore, views about corruption tend to be stable too. The chief fluctuation is not between those who see the government as honest or as corrupt but in the proportion seeing all or simply most officials as corrupt. For example, in the 2005 New Russia Barometer, 43 percent said they thought almost all officials were corrupt and 46 percent thought most officials corrupt. Only 8 percent believed that corruption is rare – and this small minority change little through the years.

Democratic ideals express "timeless" values, and those most committed to these ideals will hold to them whatever the performance of government or the state of the economy, or their own personal circumstances. While individual Russians differ in whether a democracy or a dictatorship is their ideal, the majority of Russians endorse democracy as an ideal, and they do so consistently.

Approval of a president relates both to personal qualities and political performance. Given the radical difference in the personalities of Presidents Boris Yeltsin and Vladimir Putin, it is not surprising that approval ratings of the president have not been stable since the first NRB survey. Even though personality remains relatively constant, monthly opinion polls show that evaluations have fluctuated during Vladimir Putin's term of office as well as that of Boris Yeltsin. In turn, these fluctuations reflect intermittent changes in political and economic performance. When the economy is perceived as booming and regime support rises, approval of the president also rises – and the opposite can also occur (White, Rose, and McAllister, 1997: 167ff.; Mishler and Willerton, 2003; Rose, Munro, and Mishler, 2004: 208ff.).

In a market economy, small, short-term fluctuations in economic conditions gradually form a business cycle, in which there is a spurt in growth and inflation, followed by a slowing down of growth and more stable prices. Theories of political economy likewise emphasize short-term fluctuations, as governments tend to overspend in pursuit of popularity before a general election and compensate by imposing cuts once election victory is achieved. In an economy in transformation, the amplitude and direction of change are likely to be erratic before a pattern becomes evident.

Evaluations of the current economic system have intermittently moved up and down. Amidst the uncertainties of economic transformation in 1992, only 9 percent were positive about the current economy; the proportion has since risen as high as 60 percent positive. However, in some years endorsement has fallen rather than risen, for example, between 2004 and 2005 (Figure 8.2). While the regression equations provide evidence of a predictable effect of economic evaluations on support for the current regime, the direction and size of that effect in a given year depend on the percentage of Russians who feel positive or negative about the economic system.

Economic theories such as capitalism and socialism or Communism are expressions of values as well as stylized models of how an economy is meant to operate and, to a greater or lesser extent, how it actually operates. Hence, asking Russians whether they prefer an economy with lots of goods to buy at high prices or one with shortages and low prices is a question of values as well as economic performance. This interpretation is substantiated by the fact that, while Russians have become more familiar with a market economy with the passage of time, this has not produced a trend in favor of or against it. When first asked their preference for a market or a command economy in 1992, 45 percent endorsed the market economy. In eight subsequent surveys, there have been intermittent movements up and down. In the 2005 NRB survey, the proportion of Russians approving the market was again 45 percent (see Figure 8.3).

Demographic changes are a textbook example of a slow but steady trend, as older members of society die off and youths become young adults. Russia today is distinctive because this process is producing a contraction of the country's population due to a combination of low birth and high death rates. Demographic change has gradually altered the political socialization experiences of the youngest and the oldest generations in the population. However, the year-to-year turnover of generations is slight. Annually, between 1.5 and 2 percent of the adult population is removed by death and a lesser but similar number added by the maturing of youths. Although the direction and extent of demographic trends are clear, the political effects are weak. Regression analyses find that age has no significant effect on support for the current regime and only a secondary influence on support for alternative regimes (cf. Tables 8.1, 8.2).

Events as short-term challenges

Major political events can be like meteors, unexpectedly attracting attention by flashing a very public challenge to the regime's leaders – and then disappearing almost as rapidly as they emerged. Whereas events in an established democratic regime only affect election prospects, in a system in transformation, events can influence support for competing regimes. Because their occurrence is abrupt and their impact, if any, immediate, events can easily override any influence arising from the annual turnover of generations. However, because events tend to be brief in duration, the influence of an event is likely to have a short half-life and fail to persist with the passage of time.

Compared to the irreversible shock of transformation, the major events of a political year are much more frequent but much less intense. To meet the incessant demands for headlines, the media will manufacture events to fill the available space. In the course of a year, morning and evening news bulletins require 730 "events," new or recycled, to lead their bulletins. The very immediacy of events calls into question the durability of their influence. Since each night's headline event is soon superseded by another event, the impact of one can quickly subside as another captures the media's attention. Furthermore, events of interest to politicians within the ring roads of Moscow may be ignored by ordinary people. For example, a change in prime ministers is unlikely to stimulate much of a popular response, since about half of Russians do not know the name of the country's prime minister.

Some major political events can be staged by the regime's leaders: for example, Vladimir Putin has shown a readiness to make public appearances and proclamations to exploit Russian holidays from different eras and with contradictory political implications, such as Orthodox religious holidays and holidays from the Stalin era. Political events can also be unexpected and often bad news, such as hostage-taking by Chechen guerrillas. However, a crisis is, by definition, a short-term event, and it is likely to have a long-term influence only if its consequences ramify and endure.

Events are not interpreted in a political vacuum: Russians can respond to events according to their prior political predispositions. Since these predispositions have been developed over a long period of time, a single event may simply reinforce rather than override what has gone before. For example, the collapse of the ruble in August 1998 was undoubtedly a major economic event. However, it did not make people shift their opinion from positive to negative, for a substantial majority were already negative about the regime.

Expectations encourage resigned acceptance

A political equilibrium is expectation-based: it requires that subjects expect it to remain the only game in town in the future. However, in a regime in transformation, expectations cannot be as certain as in a long-established regime. Expectations can influence current behavior through a feedback process (see Easton, 1965). If an event is considered unlikely to occur, this will encourage its dismissal as "not practical politics," whereas if it is considered likely support for alternatives may increase. However, what happens if expectations are not met? Gurr's (1970) demand-side theory predicts that, if expectations are not met – that is, if there is a gap between what people would like to happen and political outcomes – this will lead to frustration and aggressive behavior disrupting the political equilibrium. By contrast, a supply-side approach predicts that, if subjects find their expectations are not met, then they will avoid frustration and disruptive behavior by lowering their expectations to match the performance of the regime.

Economic expectations: optimistic, pessimistic, and patient

Because the future has not yet arrived, expectations cannot be classified as true or false; they are subjective assessments of what is likely to happen. Immediately after asking people to evaluate the current economic system, the New Russia Barometer asks people to evaluate the economic system as they expect it to be in five years. Consistent with transformation, Russians view the economic past, present, and future differently. The median Russian is very positive about the old Soviet economy; close to neutral in evaluating the current system; and optimistic about the national economic system in the future.

Insofar as future expectations affect current support, optimism may offset negative judgments about the current performance of the economic

Figure 9.1 *ECONOMIC EXPECTATIONS*

Q. Here is a scale for ranking how the economic system works: the top, plus 100, is the best; the bottom, minus 100, the worst. Where would you put our economic system in five years?
Q. What do you think the economic situation of your household will be in five years? Much better; A little better; About the same; A little worse; Much worse.

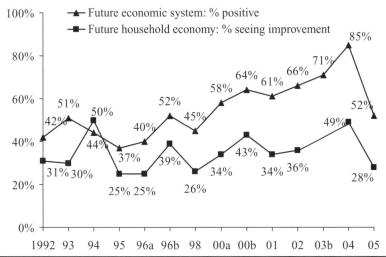

Source: New Russia Barometer surveys.

system. Over a decade and a half, the percentage of Russians optimistic about the economic future has always been greater than those positive about the current economic regime (cf. Figures 9.1 and 8.2). Since the year 2000, a majority of Russians have consistently been optimistic about the future state of the economy; this indicator rose to 85 percent in 2004, before falling sharply the following year (Figure 9.1).

The expectation that Russians have about their future household economic situation, however, tends to be negative. Even though official statistics about the national economy have been positive for half a dozen years, the subjective evaluation of the household economy has fluctuated around predominantly unfavorable expectations. On average, only 34 percent have expected their household's economic situation to be better in five years, and in 2005 the proportion of optimists was below average (Figure 9.1). Over the years, the largest bloc, 43 percent, see their situation remaining much the same. Since households tend to be dissatisfied with their current economic situation, expectations of no change are simply a lesser evil compared to a worsening in family fortunes, the expectation on average of 23 percent of Russians.

The evidence about economic expectations is ambivalent. Russians tend to be optimistic about the future of the national economic system but pessimistic about the future economic situation of their own household. Since it is national rather than household economic conditions that influence support for the current regime, the conflicting pressures between the two sets of expectations should be resolved by a boost to regime support from positive expectations about the future of the national economy – and to be further reinforced if these expectations are realized. Moreover, patience remains a continuing bulwark against frustration. In 2005 as in 1993, the largest group of Russians did not know whether they would ever be satisfied with their economic circumstances.

Expectations of regime change

In addition to asking about wanting parliament and parties closed down, the New Russia Barometer asks whether people expect this to happen. The question has historical justification, since President Yeltsin did close down parliament in September 1993, and the current constitution gives the president the legal power to dissolve the Duma and force a new election. While so dramatic a political event is rare, it has a particular resonance in Russian history.

Even though there is a high level of distrust of the Duma, this does not lead people to expect its disappearance. In the March 1994 NRB survey, 38 percent thought suspension might happen again and the same proportion was uncertain. By the second term of the Yeltsin presidency, the median Russian viewed the suspension of parliament as not very likely, and this has tended to remain the case since. By 2005 three-quarters of Russians thought the suspension of the Duma was not very likely or not at all likely. While Russians have always disagreed in their expectations, the overall mean has moved toward the expectation that the Duma and political parties, whatever their faults, will remain active (Figure 9.2).

Consistently, there is a substantial gap between what people would like to happen to the regime and what they expect to happen. Russians divide into four categories. The largest group are confident that the current regime will remain in place and would not like to see the Duma suspended. Their number is augmented by anxious supporters, who would not like to see parliament suspended but think it could happen. Anxious supporters are likely to be alert to threats to regime change. While a substantial minority of Russians endorse the principle of getting rid of parliament and parties, most who do so are pessimistic about this actually happening (cf. Figures 5.4, 9.2).

Figure 9.2 *EXPECTATION OF SUSPENSION OF PARLIAMENT*

Q. Some people think this country would be better governed if parliament were closed down and all parties were abolished. How likely do you think this is to happen in the next few years?

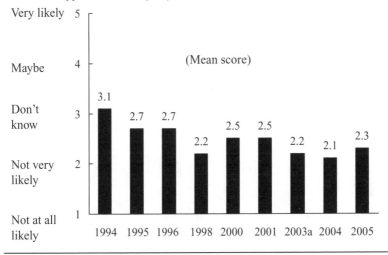

Source: New Russia Barometer surveys.

Expectations influence support for the current regime

Political and economic expectations influence both current regime support and preferences for alternative regimes, but they do not do so equally. In the OLS analysis, economic expectations do have some influence on regime support: people who are more optimistic about the economic future are more likely to support the regime (Table 9.1). However, the evaluation of the economic system today has a much stronger influence on support than do future expectations. Consistent with earlier findings, expectations of the national economy are much more influential than hopes about one's household situation. Political expectations and patience are statistically insignificant and the other influences are scarcely altered (cf. Tables 9.1 and 8.1). The addition of four indicators of future expectations to the OLS model of support for the current regime increases the proportion of variance accounted for in the OLS model by only 0.8 percent.

Political expectations do have a major influence on whether Russians support alternative regimes; adding expectations to the OLS model boosts the total variance accounted for to 27.7 percent (cf. Tables 9.1 and 8.2). A person with a low expectation of getting rid of parliament is substantially less likely to support autocratic alternatives, while those

Table 9.1 *Influence of expectations: OLS model*

	Regime support			Rejection of alternatives		
	b	se	BETA	b	se	BETA
Expectations						
Expect suspension parliament	−.25	−.24	—	−6.7	.21	−.17
Economic system in five years	.09	.01	.09	.03	.00	.04
Future household economy	1.45	.29	.03	.59	.25	—
Time before household content	−.34	.22	—	−.45	.19	—
Economy						
Pro current economic system	.47	.01	.47	.04	.00	.05
Pro old economic system	.04	.01	.04	−.05	.01	−.06
Pro lots of goods in market	1.38	.29	.02	4.86	.25	.11
Destitution	−.03	.05	—	−.64	.12	−.03
Politics						
Democracy desired	.58	.13	.02	3.6	.11	.17
Pro old regime	−.08	.01	−.09	−.11	.00	−.15
More freedom now	4.30	.34	.06	2.20	.29	.04
Pro market ideology	1.52	.86	—	11.43	.74	.08
Govt. fair, responsive	1.13	.26	.02	1.67	.23	.04
Trust political institutions	2.05	.23	.04	1.40	.20	.04
Approves president	1.51	.08	.09	.06	.07	—
Perception of corruption	−.78	.46	—	−.18	.39	—
Social structure						
Education	−.28	.18	—	2.77	.16	.10
Age	−.03	.02	—	−.15	.01	−.06
Town size	−.45	.25	—	1.74	.21	.04
Subjective status	.83	.21	.02	.52	.18	—
Variance explained:	$R^2 = 39.0\%$			$R^2 = 27.7\%$		

−: Not significant at .001 level.

Source: New Russia Barometer surveys.

who think suspension of parliament could happen are more likely to support such a measure. The influence of political expectations is as strong as commitment to democracy as an ideal (Beta: .17). Expectations of regime change are also a stronger influence on current regime support than evaluations of the national economy.

Expectations are particularly important in an autocratic regime. Instead of trying to win the normative commitment of subjects, as would be the case in consolidating support for a democratic regime, autocratic leaders need only make subjects believe that there is no alternative to the current regime. When subjects see little or no chance of changing regimes, then they can avoid frustration by giving resigned acceptance to the powers that be.

The cumulative impact of inertia

Because the turbulence of transformation cannot persist for decades, the cumulatively increasing force of political inertia can encourage people to become resigned to it or even give positive endorsement. In the *longue durée*, the passage of time itself becomes an influence. Moreover, the impact of time can be substantial because it is cumulative – the pages of the calendar are always turned in the same direction. As Aristotle noted, it is a sophist fallacy to assume that, because each month has only a little impact, the total is little. The more months that pass, the greater the cumulative impact.

The years between the first New Russia Barometer survey in 1992 and the most recent in 2005 provide substantial time for political inertia to take effect. However, most studies of public opinion cannot show the cumulative effect of inertia because they are based on a single survey that is a snapshot at a single point in time or a pair of surveys before and after an event such as an election. Conclusions from such surveys may be projected forward, but subject to the qualification that "all other conditions remain equal." However, this is very unlikely in the aftermath of transformation. As previous chapters have shown, the impact of political inertia operates both directly and indirectly. Directly, the steady month-by-month passage of time can increase regime support; indirectly, political inertia can strengthen or weaken the impact that other variables have on support for the current or alternative regimes.

Passage of time increases support for current regime

When the effects of the passage of time are added to an hierarchical linear model that includes major influences identified in preceding analyses, the results are significant. The pseudo-R^2 accounts for 42.7 percent of the variance in support for the current regime, substantially more than is accounted for in preceding chapters (cf. Tables 9.2 and 8.1).

Political inertia has an impact on support for the current regime both directly and indirectly. The scale of the impact can most clearly be understood by using HLM statistics to calculate the cumulative impact of monthly changes from 1992 to 2005. The reduced maximum likelihood (RML) coefficient shows the extent of change in regime support in a single month. The impact refers to the extent of change in the 201-point scale of support for the current regime resulting from the passage of one

Table 9.2 *Comprehensive multilevel model*

	Regime support			Rejection of alternatives		
	b	se	P	b	se	P
Individual level						
Expectations						
Expect suspension parliament				−7.4	.56	.000
Economic system in five years	.10	.02	.000			
Economy						
Pro current economic system	.47	.02	.000	.10	.01	.000
Pro lots of goods in market				8.2	.81	.000
Politics						
Democracy desired	1.2	.15	.000	4.2	.14	.000
More freedom now	4.1	.57	.000			
Approves president	2.6	.32	.000	1.7	.34	.000
Perception of corruption	−1.6	.12	.000			
Pro old regime	−.07	.02	.005			
Social structure						
Education				5.3	.33	.000
Aggregate level						
Passage of months	.25	.02	.000	.05	.02	.046
Cross-level interactions						
Corruption × month	−.04	.00	.000			
Democracy desired × month	−.01	.00	.001			
Approves president × month				−.01	.00	.000
Approves current economy × month				.001	.00	.000
Variance explained:	*PSEUDO R^2 = 42.7%*			*PSEUDO R^2 = 22.6%*		

Source: New Russia Barometer surveys. Only significant variables included in HLM to preserve degrees of freedom.

month's time. The RML coefficient for the direct impact of the passage of months appears small, one-quarter of a point. But adding up 160 months of seemingly little change cumulatively has a big impact (Figure 9.3).

In the course of twelve months, political inertia creates a three-point increase in support and, as the years pass, the impact becomes increasingly large. By the beginning of 2005, it adds forty points to mean support for the current regime. Russians who were initially positive become more so, those neutral become positive, and the intensity of those negative toward the regime is reduced. Because the positive effect of the passage of time is independent of other influences, it is a countervailing force when economic or political influences tend to depress regime support.

Figure 9.3 *CHANGING IMPACT OF DETERMINANTS OF SUPPORT*

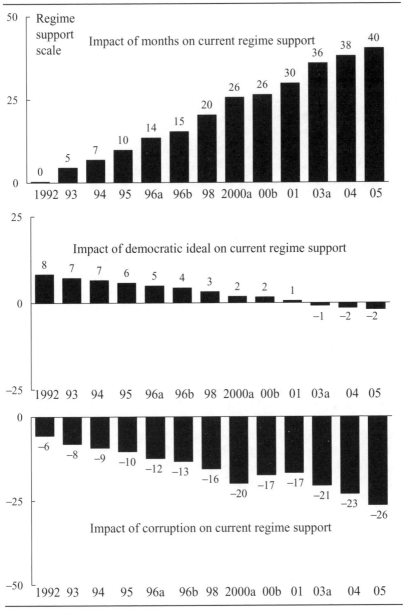

Source: New Russia Barometer surveys. Calculated from Table 9.2.

Indirectly, the passage of time substantially reduces regime support by interacting with other influences that affect individual evaluations.[1] Corruption provides a striking example of the importance of the interaction effect. While a big majority of Russians consistently see the regime as corrupt, the passage of time substantially increases the negative impact of corruption on support (Table 9.2). Whereas corruption reduced support for the current regime by only six points in 1992, by 2005 it reduced regime support by twenty-six points. As Russians have become more accustomed to their new regime, they have also become less tolerant of its corruption.[2]

The influence of the desirability of democracy and the passage of time interact in opposite directions. Over the period as a whole, Russians who view democracy as desirable have tended to be positive about the new regime. However, the passage of time has reduced its effect to the point that it has become negative. Initially, commitment to the ideal of democracy boosted support for the current regime by eight points. However, the longer Russians have observed the performance of the current regime, the less inclined those who value democracy as an ideal are inclined to support the current regime. The trend that started under President Yeltsin has continued under President Putin. By 2003, the passage of time resulted in those committed to democratic ideals being slightly less likely to support the current regime (Figure 9.3).

The dynamic character of most variables in the HLM analysis is different, because they fluctuate with the passage of time rather than steadily changing in the same direction. The impact of time is registered when the mean level of an independent variable alters from one year to the next. The impact of the current national economic system is thus doubly important, for not only is its impact on support for the current regime big (b coefficient: .47), but also it reverses. When the new economic system was seen at its worst in 1992, this depressed regime support by twenty-two points net of all other influences. However, when economic evaluations improved the following year, the negative impact was cut in half. The

---

[1] To calculate the overall impact of a variable with a significant interaction effect with the passage of time, the monthly interaction coefficient must be multiplied by the number of months since the start of the Russian Federation and the product added to the product of the coefficient for the independent variable and its mean value.

[2] In Table 9.2, the b coefficient for corruption (–1.6) measures its impact at the start of the time series. In month one, when the mean level of perceived corruption was estimated at 3.50 on a 4-point scale, the effect of corruption on support was –1.64 × 3.5 = –5.7. In each subsequent month, the interaction term, –.04, is then added. Thus, the impact of corruption on support in the first month is –1.64 (that is, –1.6 + –.04); in month two, –1.68 (that is, –1.6 + (2 × –.04)) and so forth. By month 161, the impact of corruption on support is 8.04.

up-and-down pattern has continued, peaking in its positive effect in 2004 only to reverse the following year.

The HLM analysis confirms that the influence of presidential approval on regime support reflects how popular the president is at a given point in time rather than who is president, since it has gone up and down within Vladimir Putin's period in office as well as during that of Boris Yeltsin. During Yeltsin's period in office, presidential approval boosted support for the regime between eight and eleven points. During Putin's time in office to date, his popularity in a given year has boosted regime support by eight to sixteen points on the 201-point scale of regime support.

In theory, the impact of freedom on support for the current regime could fall with the passage of time, as an appreciation of gains since the Soviet era could fade, and the apparent influence of the security services within the Putin administration could make ordinary Russians feel less secure. In practice, this has not happened. The appreciation of gains in freedom has been consistently high for more than a decade; its impact on support for the current regime has remained constant too. Whatever the state of the economy or the performance of the Kremlin, the perceived gains in personal freedom have boosted support for the current regime by fourteen to seventeen points. Endorsement of the Communist regime has not been reduced by the passage of time either, but the HLM analysis shows that its impact on support for the current regime has been small (Table 9.2).

Since regime support is the result of a multiplicity of pressures, the combined effect of steady and time-dependent influences is more important than that of a single influence. At the launch of the Russian Federation in 1992, support for the fledgling regime was extremely low, and influences favoring the regime, such as an appreciation of freedom, tended to be canceled out by those that were negative, such as the evaluation of the national economy. In the next few years, the chief variable influence on support was the evaluation of the national economy.

The development of a steady-state equilibrium of support has been primarily due to the passage of time turning a new regime into a familiar fact of life. Without the positive effect of political inertia, support for the current regime in 2005 would have been much the same as it was in the early 1990s. Between 1992 and 2005, the cumulative impact of political inertia increased support for the regime by forty points (Figure 9.4). Concurrently, other significant influences have been pushing in different directions. The passage of time has increased the depressing impact of corruption and made endorsement of the democratic ideal a negative influence too. However, the impact of the evaluation of the national economic system has become much less negative and at times positive.

Figure 9.4 *TIME IMPORTANT FOR CURRENT REGIME SUPPORT*

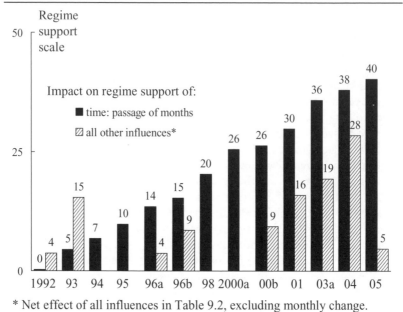

* Net effect of all influences in Table 9.2, excluding monthly change.

Source: New Russia Barometer surveys.

Furthermore, presidential approval and, even more, the appreciation of freedom have been consistently positive influences. Whatever its political and economic performance, the longer the current regime has been in place, the more Russians appear resigned to accept the regime that elites supply.

Constant influences on rejection of alternative regimes

Whereas political inertia is a primary influence on support of the current regime, the chief influences on the rejection of alternative regimes are timeless. The level of democratic idealism, education, and expectations of the suspension of parliament tend to be stable; there is no interaction effect with the month-by-month passage of time, which has little cumulative impact on the rejection of alternative regimes (Table 9.2; Figure 9.5). Altogether, in the HLM analysis, relatively stable influences account for most of the variance of rejecting alternative regimes.

Since NRB surveys ask Russians to evaluate a range of undemocratic alternatives, it is logical to expect that those more committed to democracy as an ideal will also be more likely to reject alternative autocracies, and this is the case. The combination of little variation in commitment

Figure 9.5 *STEADY INFLUENCES ON REJECTING ALTERNATIVES*

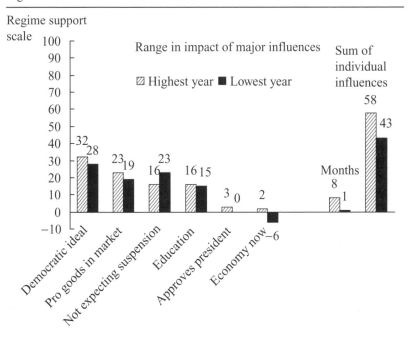

Regime support scale

Source: New Russia Barometer surveys. Presidential approval and economy here include an interaction term for months. Calculated from Table 9.2.

to democratic ideals and a large coefficient unaffected by the passage of time results in democratic idealism increasing the tendency to reject alternative regimes by twenty-eight to thirty-two points over a decade.

Consistent with liberal theories linking economic and political choice, the second biggest impact is the endorsement of a market compared to a shortage economy. Preferences for the market economy consistently add nineteen to twenty-three points to the 201-point scale for the rejection of alternative regimes. The passage of time does not alter the influence of market values, thus indicating that the commitment is normative rather than based on the cumulative experience of the actual operation of a corrupt Russian market subject to significant political controls.

Expectations of the suspension of parliament and elections are important too. The less likely Russians think suspension of parliament is, the more likely they are to reject alternative regimes. There is no interaction between this judgment and the passage of time, but there are fluctuations in expectations of parliament remaining in place. Thus, its effect on the evaluation of alternative regimes fluctuates between sixteen and twenty-three points.

Because education is acquired early in life, there is very little likelihood of individuals being resocialized by getting more education after they reach their mid-twenties. Since it is an especially stable independent variable, the substantial influence of education on the evaluation of alternative regimes is also unaffected by the passage of time. In each NRB survey, education increases the readiness of Russians to reject alternative regimes by fifteen or sixteen points.

The HLM analysis shows that the month-by-month passage of time does little to increase the rejection of alternative regimes. From 1992 to 2005, it has increased the readiness of individuals to reject alternative regimes by only seven points. This is much less than the effect of political inertia on support for the current regime, and it is also much less than the impact of expectations of regime change on support for alternative regimes (cf. Figures 9.3, 9.5).

Indirectly, the passage of time exerts a little influence on attitudes toward alternative regimes through the interaction of time with approval of the president and with the evaluation of the national economy. At the start of the Russian Federation, the more Russians approved President Yeltsin, the more likely they were to reject alternative regimes. However, the monthly passage of time has reduced the impact of approval of the president. Thus, Putin's higher approval ratings have not made Russians more likely to reject alternative regimes. By Vladimir Putin's second term of office, approval of the president neither increased nor decreased an individual's readiness to endorse alternative regimes (Figure 9.5). The interaction of the passage of time and the current national economic system increases the effect of the economy on the rejection of alternative regimes a little, but the effect is much less than that of the fluctuations in the level of endorsement of the economic system.

The very limited influence of the passage of time, combined with stability in the mean level of major influences, results in little change from one year to the next in the readiness of Russians to reject alternative regimes. The mean level of rejection was +44 in 1995 and +53 in 2005.

The steady rejection of alternative regimes is important in maintaining an equilibrium of support for the current regime. The rejection of alternative regimes makes the current regime the "only game in town." However, projecting this conclusion into the future depends on all other conditions remaining equal or their combined impact canceling out. This is a reminder that the political equilibrium of today could be disrupted in the future if all other conditions do not remain equal.

10   What could challenge the new equilibrium?

> You can't step into the same river twice.
>
> Heraclitus

> If things are going to stay the same, there will have to be some changes made.
>
> Giuseppe Lampedusa, *The Leopard*

A primary object of the winners of the initial battles of transformation is to achieve an equilibrium of popular support for the new regime through a combination of political performance, economic measures, and the passage of time. In Central and Eastern Europe, there has been dynamic progress from the confusion of the first elections in 1990 to securing popular acceptance and locking the new regimes into the European Union.

Once a steady-state equilibrium is achieved, the next concern of leaders is to maintain support. Fluctuations in the major influences on popular support are facts of political life. The more evenly balanced forces are, the greater the risk that a small change in the impact of one influence will have big consequences for the regime. Whether an equilibrium is democratic or autocratic, political leaders must remain watchful of challenges to the institutions that empower them. Vigilance is not only the price of liberty; it is also the price that autocrats must pay to maintain a repressive regime. The more that political elites ignore changes in the sources of their support, the greater the risk that such pressures will create a major challenge.

In the medium term, the question is not whether a challenge to a regime will arise but when and how it will occur. For example, in the Soviet Union, the death of a CPSU general secretary from time to time forced the Communist elite to determine the new head of the regime. For more than half a century the elite succeeded in changing party secretaries while the regime remained intact. The countdown to the end of Boris Yeltsin's second term as president created a challenge of leadership succession for which there were no precedents and few rules. In a plebiscitarian autocracy, which offers some opportunities for the expression of popular opinion, challenges to the regime can come from the bottom up as well as from the top down, or from a collision between different sets of pressures.

This chapter's title emphasizes uncertainty, by asking what *could* challenge the equilibrium of support a decade and a half after the launch of the Russian Federation. The next section considers the likelihood of change in the trajectories of significant influences on regime support. Since the future is never certain, the second section considers risks that could challenge the regime if they came to pass, such as the outbreak of another ethnic conflict like Chechnya or another nuclear accident like Chernobyl. The concluding section examines the consequences of the constitutional rule limiting the president to two successive terms of office. The rule creates uncertainties not only about the succession to Putin, but also about whether or not the rule will be enforced, repealed, or bent.

Likelihoods and uncertainties

Any list of potential political challenges is speculative; since 1989 forecasts of the doom of post-Communist regimes have been as much in error as were earlier forecasts of Soviet stability. However, it is an exaggeration to assert that everything in politics is uncertain: some political challenges are more speculative than others. Focusing on the likelihood of the persistence of major influences on regime support can put bounds on speculation.

A number of significant political, economic, and social influences on support for the current and alternative regimes were identified as significant in chapters 6, 7, and 8; chapter 9 showed the extent to which their influence has or has not changed since the first New Russia Barometer survey was conducted in 1992. Here, we consider how these influences *might* change in the future in ways that could strengthen or challenge a steady-state equilibrium.

Trajectories of significant influences

The logical complement of the passage of time increasing support for the new regime is that it would reduce the impact of the old regime. Approval of the Communist regime would cease to depress support for the current regime and, if Russians increasingly take freedom for granted, the contrast with an unfree past would no longer boost support for the new regime. However, resocialization has not yet resulted in Russians unlearning lessons from the past. The HLM regression analysis finds no evidence of a reduction in the impact of either influence on regime support with the passage of time (Table 9.2). Both remain consistently albeit unequally significant – and push in opposite directions.

There can be no certainty that the impact of political inertia will remain the same in the future as in the past. As of 2005, political inertia was annually adding three points to the level of support for the current regime. If there were a gradual reduction in this impact, the force of political inertia could still add ten points or more to support before leveling off completely, with political support at a higher plateau.

Concurrently, the passage of time could further reduce the expectation of a change in regimes. The 1991 coup and the 1993 shootout at the White House were reasons to think that a change could happen at any time. However, since then, four Duma elections and three presidential elections have given Russians ample opportunity to learn about the new regime. Even though the Duma and parties are much distrusted, they are also increasingly familiar. Insofar as familiarity lowers the expectation of an end to an elected Duma, this will increase Russian rejection of alternative regimes, thereby strengthening resigned acceptance of the current regime (cf. Table 9.2).

A striking feature of the HLM analysis is that the passage of time has been steadily increasing the negative impact of corruption on support for the current regime. The longer the new regime has been in place, the more it has encouraged Russians to reject the current regime. By 2005, for every three points that political inertia added to regime support, corruption subtracted two points (Figure 9.3). President Putin's repeated statements of the need to "do something" about corruption shows his awareness of the problem. However, the repetition of this exhortation indicates that the obstacles to reducing corruption remain formidable. Therefore, it would be unrealistic to assume that corruption will fall in the foreseeable future. Corruption thus has the potential to create increasing tension in the equilibrium of support, as its strong negative impact pushes against the positive impact of other influences. However, it is uncertain whether this negative pressure will increase or level off in the future.

When the new regime was launched, Russians committed to democratic ideals were significantly more likely to support the regime that had replaced the Soviet party-state. While support for democratic ideals has remained substantial, the passage of time has steadily reduced its impact, as democratic idealists became disillusioned with the "real existing democracy" of the Yeltsin administration and with the "sovereign democracy" that President Putin has introduced, confirming the popular assessment that the current regime is halfway between a democracy and a dictatorship. In consequence, the HLM analysis calculates that Russians more in favor of democracy as an ideal are less likely to support the current regime. However, if this trend continues in the future it does not mean that idealistic democrats will start demanding a change of regimes, for idealists are also much more likely to reject the alternative regimes on offer (cf. Figure 9.3, Table 9.2).

Of all the influences on support for the current regime, popular approval of the current economic system has the strongest impact. The coefficient used to calculate its impact is not altered by the passage of time; the HLM analysis indicates that each one-point change in Russians' evaluation of the current economic system adds or subtracts just under half a point on the scale measuring support for the current regime. Economic evaluations have a fluctuating impact on support, going up or down each year in accordance with swings in subjective assessments. By contrast, a preference for a market economy with lots of goods and high prices rather than a shortage economy has a steady impact on the rejection of alternative regimes, and the proportion of Russians holding this view has remained relatively steady for more than a decade.

As the preceding analysis has emphasized, the evaluation of the economic system cannot be inferred from macroeconomic statistics about the country's gross domestic product. Since every NRB survey shows that Russians differ in their subjective economic evaluations, this adds to uncertainties about the future direction of economic evaluations. For example, if many Russians perceive increased national wealth as due to the exploitation of natural resources and political corruption, this could even reduce support for the current regime.

Expectations of the economy in the future are much more malleable than expectations of institutional survival. The proportion of Russians with positive expectations of the future economy has ranged from 37 percent in 1995 to 85 percent in 2004. Future economic expectations have consistently been more positive than evaluations of the current economy. However, since the impact of future economic expectations is less than one-quarter of that of endorsement of the current economy, it would take a big change in economic expectations to have much impact (see Table 9.2).

Much social change of little political relevance

While the turnover of generations is steady, its political effects are easily exaggerated. While the age cohort least inclined to support the new Russian regime can be expected to die by 2020, the cohort that replaces it will consist of Russians who are almost as unsupportive of the current regime. It will not be until after 2020 that a majority of Russian adults will belong to post-Soviet generations, and only after 2050 will almost all the country's population belong to post-Soviet generations.

The demographic inevitability of the turnover of generations makes it tempting to extrapolate intergenerational differences in regime support into the future. However, any extrapolation is subject to the necessary qualification: all other conditions remaining equal. The longer the span of time – and generational changes take decades to register substantial effects – the more realistic it is to assume that the political and economic performance of the regime will *not* remain constant. In turn, this produces adult resocialization that leads to changes in regime support among all generations (Figure 6.2). Moreover, regression analysis finds that, after taking into account all other influences, age has no significant effect on regime support and a limited effect on the endorsement of alternative regimes (Table 9.1).

Risks

The future is full of risks, unwelcome events that may *or* may not happen, such as a submarine disaster or an explosion in a shopping center. At any given moment, the probability of a risk being realized is low. Since Russia's governors have lots to worry about here and now, they can, like their Western counterparts, ignore risks on the grounds that a disaster is unlikely to happen while they are in power. In areas of Russian life where the government has a direct responsibility, for example, nuclear safety, ignoring risks increases the possibility that something could go badly wrong. Moreover, the motto "Never say never in politics" is a reminder that the passage of time can increase the possibility that something unwanted will happen.

Even if a risk is not realized, the fact that something could go wrong – for example, another nuclear accident on the scale of Chernobyl – can generate popular anxiety. The 2005 New Russia Barometer asked about the likelihood of events that would be disasters if they came to pass. For three of the four events – being unable to heat their house, another Chechnya, or an HIV-AIDS epidemic – the median Russian thought this might happen or was even very likely. Such disasters are viewed as more likely to happen than is the suspension of parliament (cf. Table 10.1, Figure 9.2). Only a very small percentage thought there was no risk of such events.

In Russia, adequate heat through the long and cold winter is essential. In Soviet times a majority of Russian households received heat from a communal source without paying a significant charge, and energy was consumed very inefficiently. The federation regime has continued this practice, using its political power over energy tycoons to make them

Table 10.1 *Likelihood of future disasters*

Q. *Now let's consider some things that might happen in this country in the next few years. How likely do you think the following would be:*

	Very likely (%)	Maybe (%)	Not very likely (%)	Not at all (%)
Cost of energy would stop us heating our house	25	46	23	5
Another ethnic conflict like Chechnya	16	54	27	3
Big HIV-AIDS epidemic	15	42	36	7
Another Chernobyl	7	36	44	12

Source: New Russia Barometer XIV (2005).

provide domestic gas and oil at costs far below world market prices. As a consequence, Russians are much less likely to do without heat than without food or clothing, according to NRB destitution surveys. Months before the NRB survey, President Putin had spoken of gradually raising the price Russians paid for energy to world market levels. Thus, notwithstanding Russia's rich endowment of energy resources, there is a widely perceived risk of heating becoming so expensive that homes would be cold in winter: 71 percent saw this as very likely or possibly happening in the next few years.

The Chechen war has challenged the territorial integrity of the Russian Federation, but its political impact has been blunted by a resigned consensus. Levada Center surveys have consistently found that Russians approve the war against Chechens but expect that fighting will end in a stalemate; few Russians expect peace and order to result (www.RussiaVotes.org/slide473.htm). While Chechens constitute less than 1 percent of the population of the Russian Federation, there are upwards of 28 million non-Russians living in the federation, including approximately 10 million with a Muslim heritage. When the NRB asked about the risk of another ethnic conflict like Chechnya breaking out within Russia's borders, 70 percent thought it might happen or was very likely.

The spread of HIV-AIDS is a worldwide problem, and international public health specialists have tracked its diffusion in the Russian Federation. Official figures estimate that 330,000 people are infected by HIV-AIDS; unofficial estimates are at least three times higher. While the government has not denied that there could be an HIV-AIDS problem, Russian health services are not well organized to deal with the threat nor is it a high priority. An NRB question about the risk of an HIV-AIDS epidemic showed widespread popular awareness of the problem; less than 1 percent had no opinion about the issue. The median Russian thinks an epidemic might happen and almost one in six thinks it very likely.

The potential disaster that causes least concern among Russians is one for which there is a precedent: a nuclear power station accident like that in 1986 at Chernobyl in Ukraine. It caused the premature death of tens of thousands of former Soviet citizens living in the adjacent area. Four in seven see a nuclear accident as not very or not at all likely, compared to three in seven seeing it as possible or likely. Concern with this risk has dropped twelve percentage points by comparison with responses in the 2001 NRB survey.

Unexpected disasters threaten regimes everywhere, and concerns spotlighted by the New Russia Barometer – very high fuel prices, ethnic violence, HIV-AIDS, and nuclear safety – are voiced in established democracies too. The ubiquity of risks is a reminder that living in a modern society does not remove all risks, and the vulnerability of a new regime is greater than that of an established regime.

Whether a disaster challenges support depends upon how the mass of the population apportions blame in the light of the government's response. For example, the spread of HIV-AIDS can be blamed on stigmatized minority groups in the population, such as homosexuals, prostitutes, and drug-takers. If another nuclear accident occurred in a neighboring CIS state, even if the fallout affected people in Russia, the blame could be projected onto another government. Bombs or insurrection by an ethnic minority could be blamed on the ethnic minority. However, while Chechen guerrillas receive much blame for the inability of Moscow to control that territory, the Russian government has been blamed for its failure to free Russians taken hostage by Chechens in a Moscow theater and in a Beslan school.

The one measure for which the regime could not easily escape blame would be raising energy prices to world market levels, since this would be seen as determined by government rather than by impersonal market forces. The Kremlin has demonstrated its readiness to use energy pricing for foreign policy goals. It has put political pressure on Ukraine, Moldova, and Georgia by increasing the cost of buying Russian energy and incidentally raising questions about the security of its energy supplies to EU member countries. The potential for a move to the market challenging the political equilibrium was shown in January 2005, when the government proposed replacing subsidies of local services providing benefits in kind to the many with cash benefits targeted at needy individuals. This led to demonstrations that were not large by the standards of the United States or Europe but that were unprecedented in Russia. In response, the government deployed a mixture of concessions, coercive measures, and partial implementation of this unpopular reform.

2008: changing leaders or changing regimes?

A rule-of-thumb test of a new regime reaching a steady-state equilibrium is that control of government twice changes hands without disruption (Huntington 1991: 266ff.). The first turnover provides a public demonstration that the regime is different from the person or group that initially created it. A second succession reinforces this point, and creates the expectation among elites that subsequent successions will occur within the rules of the regime, whether the rule is that the choice of government should be decided by a free election or by non-accountable elites. Control of government did not change hands between parties until twenty years after the founding of the Federal Republic of Germany and twenty-three years after the founding of the Fifth Republic in France. The second turnover in Soviet leadership did not occur until thirty-six years after the Russian Revolution. The passage of time before two turnovers in leadership gives scope for political inertia to encourage resigned acceptance, if not positive support.

Political succession is a much more difficult problem in autocracies than in democracies. In a democratic regime, rulers are chosen by free elections conducted according to the rule of law. However, in an autocracy, the death or deposition of a dictator creates the opportunity for a lawless and violent power struggle among elites. In a plebiscitarian autocracy, the outcome is less certain (see Schedler, 2006). The only example of succession in the Russian Federation to date – Vladimir Putin becoming acting president due to the resignation of Boris Yeltsin and then using the advantages of incumbency to win popular election – demonstrates the scope for the unexpected to happen.

The 1993 Constitution of the Russian Federation includes a term-limits clause. Article 81, paragraph 3, states: "No one person shall hold the office of President of the Russian Federation for more than two terms in succession." Vladimir Putin's second term of office is due to expire after the presidential election scheduled for March 9, 2008. If these rules are followed, there will be a second turnover of leaders without a change of regime. If the rules are not followed, this will create a significant challenge to the regime.

Events around the 2008 election will show the extent to which the current equilibrium is proof against challenge or even disruption. Logically, the challenge of succession could be resolved by a competitive election to choose a new president or by a plebiscitarian election in which Putin's endorsement of a hand-picked successor made the outcome a foregone conclusion. Alternatively, the constitution could be amended to allow Putin to stand again, or existing rules could be broken or bent to keep power in Putin's hands by means not authorized by the constitution.

What Putin has said and done

Prior to his presidential election victory in 2004, Vladimir Putin declared that he would leave office at the end of his second term. Since winning reelection, he has reaffirmed this view with statements such as: "I will not amend the basic law and it is impossible under the constitution to be elected three consecutive times" (Buckley, 2005). However, this has not stopped speculation inside the ring roads of Moscow and elsewhere about what the president will actually do as the end of his second term approaches. The speculation is fueled by those close to Putin, who have a personal interest in his retention of power, and their own retention of influence on that power, since their influence will decline sharply whenever Putin leaves the Kremlin.

Tens of millions are formally eligible to stand for the presidency, being Russian citizens aged thirty-five or older and having resided in the country for the ten years preceding the election. However, in order to be elected president, an ambitious politician must first get his or her name on the ballot. The case for limiting the number of candidates and parties through restrictive election laws is familiar in the literature of two-party Anglo-American politics, and similar arguments have been made by President Putin.

Presidential nomination procedures concentrate the power to place names on the ballot in a very limited number of hands. To nominate a candidate, a party must first be officially registered under the supervision of the Ministry of Justice. If it wins seats in the Duma, it is assured the right to nominate a presidential candidate. At the 2003 Duma election, only four parties won enough votes to secure list seats: the pro-Putin United Russia Party, the Communist Party, the Liberal Democratic Party of Vladimir Zhirinovsky, and the nationalist Motherland Party (Rodina). A law adopted in 2005 abolished single-member Duma districts and raised the threshold for winning proportional representation seats in the Duma to 7 percent of the popular vote, a significantly higher standard than the previous threshold of 5 percent.

The deadline for parties nominating their candidate for the March 2008 presidential election is six weeks after the Duma election. The nomination procedure requires each party to hold a conference to adopt its nominee. President Putin has said that he will recommend a successor to be endorsed by United Russia, the party that he favors. Given the patronage powers of the Kremlin, Putin's choice should be United Russia's choice. If popular votes for list parties are the same in 2007 as before, the Communist Party, the Liberal Democratic Party, and Motherland will also have the right to nominate presidential candidates. If pro-market parties that contested the 2003 Duma election under different labels could agree a merger and maintain their share of the 2003 popular vote, 7.6 percent, they could also qualify to nominate a presidential candidate.

The Central Election Commission, which administers electoral laws, has fifteen members, all of whom must be lawyers. Five members are appointed by the president, five by parties in the Duma, and five by the Federation Council in consultation with regional legislators and governors. The commission verifies whether nomination papers meet the complex rules to qualify for a place on the presidential ballot; it has the power to disallow candidates and parties whose papers are ruled out of order. In 2004, eleven candidates put their names forward for the presidential ballot and four had their nominations disallowed.

Because of the term-limits law, jockeying for President Putin's endorsement has already begun. Since United Russia can nominate only one candidate, Putin's endorsement will inevitably create bruised egos and frustration among those passed over. However, in 2008 it will not be easy for disaffected politicians to get on the presidential ballot – and the longer Putin delays identifying his successor, the greater will be the difficulties in organizing a competing candidacy. For example, it can take a year to create a new party according to stringent legal requirements and have the new party's registration accepted by federal authorities. Even then, there is no guarantee that a new party will win enough votes to qualify for seats in the Duma and the right to nominate a presidential candidate.

The law allows presidential candidates independent of parties to be nominated if they can collect at least 2,000,000 valid signatures. Recognizing the probability that election officials will rule out many signatures, up to 300,000 additional signatures can be filed to replace disallowed names. No more than 50,000 signatures may come from any one of the country's eighty-eight regions. Soliciting 2,000,000 signatures nationwide requires funds that can be obtained only from very rich backers. Following the exile or jailing of billionaire tycoons who have shown political opposition to President Putin, any rich person who backed an electoral challenge to Putin's nominee would risk losing their wealth or their liberty, or being forced into exile. Strict rules about campaign finance may also be invoked against an independent candidate.

Since a successful plebiscite requires the appearance of opposition candidates, the Kremlin takes a special interest in who comes forward for a place on the ballot. In the cynical words of a leading Russian political technologist, "If the Kremlin decides it needs an opposition, then it will create one" (Wilson, 2005: 272). There is precedent for the boast, since one of the four Duma parties with a right to nominate a presidential candidate, the Liberal Democratic Party of Vladimir Zhirinovsky, was apparently created with the assistance of the security services in the closing years of the Soviet Union (Umland, 2005).

The Kremlin is also prepared to promote the disruption of opposition parties that appear to be gaining "too much" support. Before the 2003 Duma election, it encouraged the formation of the left-nationalist party Motherland to draw votes from the Communist Party. In the Moscow mayoral race in December 2005, the biggest rival to United Russia, Motherland, was ruled off the ballot by the High Court on the grounds that its campaign appeals were racist. When the newly formed Democratic Party of former prime minister Mikhail Kasyanov called a party congress to elect him as its leader in December 2005, the congress had to be canceled when "unidentified persons" took over the central Moscow building where it was due to meet and held a conference for a party using the same name.

Amending or bending the constitution

If the two-term limit were removed from the constitution, President Putin could be a candidate and win reelection. In justification of doing so, he could cite the practice of many established democracies that do not have any term limits. For example, Margaret Thatcher led her party to three successive British election victories; Tony Blair did the same for his. Amending the constitution is one way in which a regime can adapt to dynamic challenges while maintaining continuity overall. Bending or stretching the rules is another method that can give powerholders what they want without a formal break in the institutions of the regime. For example, Boris Yeltsin's naming of Vladimir Putin as acting president did not violate the constitution, but it was hardly anticipated within the letter of that law. President Putin has demonstrated skill in taking administrative actions and enacting new laws that enhance his power; these have cumulatively strengthened the autocratic element of the regime. Changes in election laws have been to the advantage of the Kremlin too.

Three steps would be required to repeal the term-limits clause of the Russian Constitution: the change must be endorsed by two-thirds of the members of the Duma; three-quarters of the members of the upper chamber of the Russian parliament, the Federation Council, must approve the change; and two-thirds of the subjects (that is, territorial regions) of the federation must also endorse it. These requirements were designed to create a barrier to rapid or self-serving constitutional amendments. However, following the 2004 presidential election, Kremlin initiatives have given President Putin substantial influence over the Duma, the Federation Council, and the regions (Remington, 2005). Hence, Putin would expect prompt endorsement of a constitutional amendment to repeal term limits – if he decided to propose such a change.

Stretching or bending the constitution involves actions that do not explicitly violate its rules – if only because they are so novel and ingenious that they have not been anticipated and forbidden. One example that has been canvassed is that the president's term could be extended to seven years on the grounds that a lengthier time period ensures more continuity and order in government. If such a law stipulated that a seven-year presidency was a different office from a four-year presidency, then the Kremlin might claim that Putin was eligible to serve up to twenty-two years in office, that is, two four-year terms and then two seven-year terms.

Since the constitutional prohibition on a third term explicitly refers to the Russian Federation, Putin could remain in the Kremlin if the federation were to be superseded by another state. Moscow political gossips raise the possibility of a revamped union between the Russian Federation and Belarus, in which power in the union would rest with the president of the union, a new office that Putin would be eligible to fill. However, such a maneuver would have implications for Russia's national interest going far beyond Putin's career. If Putin wanted to concentrate on international politics, he might create a new office as head of the Commonwealth of Independent States, to which national security and foreign policy powers would be transferred, and nominate a politically weak successor to carry out reduced duties of the presidency, or even abolish that office and transfer domestic responsibilities (and difficulties) to the prime minister.

The eruption of events threatening the security of Russia – for example, a series of major terrorist attacks in Moscow and other Russian cities attributed by the Kremlin to Chechens or another Islamic group – might lead the president to declare an emergency that would suspend elections and other constitutional provisions. A federal law of 2001 gives the president emergency powers for thirty days, with the approval of the Federation Council.

An election or a plebiscite?

Both elections and plebiscites involve a popular vote, but the connotations of the two terms are very different. The language of elections is conventionally associated with free and democratic choice. By contrast, the connotation of a plebiscite is negative, "an unfair, unfree and uncompetitive vote of confidence for a leader and regime" (Uleri, 2000: 199). By contrast with a free election, a plebiscite is a vote that those in power are certain to win by whatever means necessary. Even if there are multiple candidates on the ballot, an election is a plebiscite if it is seen as a vote to confirm the position of those in power.

By comparison with totalitarian elections of the Soviet Union, many ballots in its successor states have been "semi-free" elections. This type of election gives opposition parties a place on the ballot and a chance to seek popular support, albeit often on unfair terms. While the intention of governors is to make an election a plebiscite, the consequences can be different from what is predicted. Even if the opposition has no chance of winning the official count, popular demonstrations can force an incumbent to make concessions or, in the case of Kyrgyzstan, lead to the president handing over power to a successor. In Ukraine, a combination of popular protests, judicial decisions, and the refusal of the security services to crack down on the opposition voided the election of the official presidential candidate and produced a free election. However, in Belarus in March 2005, Aleksandr Lukashenka campaigned with a heavy hand, intimidating and suppressing the opposition; the official report of the election gave the president 82.6 percent of the vote (see Table 2.2).

The Russian presidential election of 2004 was a placid plebiscite. There was never any doubt that Vladimir Putin would be reelected on the first-round ballot. This was the position not only of the Kremlin and of external observers but also of candidates nominally described as competing with the president. Opposition parties showed their rejection of what they saw as an abuse of administrative resources by refusing to nominate their strongest candidate. The chief justification for alternative candidates appeared to be that they fulfilled the plebiscite's need for opposition without placing the outcome in doubt. Media coverage gave Putin a very disproportionate amount of attention and marginalized his opponents.

For a presidential election in the Russian Federation to be valid, a turnout of at least 50 percent of the registered electorate is required. Although the outcome was never in doubt in 2004, turnout was 64.3 percent. Of those who voted, 3.4 percent cast a vote "against all," an option offered on the Russian ballot. An NRB post-election survey found that half or more who reported that they did not vote were not principled abstainers but did not participate because of apathy, absent-mindedness, the weather, or personal circumstances.

The 2004 presidential election has been described by Timothy Colton (2005: 114) as "the attenuation" of electoral competition; no one could imagine any of the opponents of the Kremlin's candidate "was up to the task of filling the president's shoes." The thoroughly documented report on the election by the Organization for Security and Co-operation in Europe (OSCE, 2004: 1) concluded that the electoral process overall "did not adequately reflect principles necessary for a healthy democratic election." Nonetheless, the international team conceded that a majority of Russian voters endorsed Vladimir Putin as president.

Learning to want what you get

In a democratic regime, governors are supposed to supply what citizens want. Consistently, New Russia Barometer surveys show that people would like a government that lives up to democratic ideals, respects the freedom of individuals, and is not corrupt. The current regime shows more respect for freedom than its predecessor, but it is corrupt and does not respect democratic ideals. On left-versus-right issues, a substantial proportion of Russians endorse a welfare-state approach consistent with European social democratic parties, and while some prefer to take more individual responsibility for their wellbeing, as Anglo-American free market parties recommend. However, this is not the choice that voters are offered at the ballot box.

In an autocratic regime, subjects are expected to want what is supplied by governors and, in both the literal and practical senses, the choice before Russian voters at the next presidential election will be what elites supply. In turn, elite choice is restricted by election laws that the Putin administration has promoted. The laws make it difficult for parties to be formed, to win a place on the ballot, to gain Duma seats, and to nominate a presidential candidate. Together, the laws place major obstacles in the path of any counterelite that would like to challenge whatever actions President Putin takes in anticipation of the 2008 election.

When the 2005 NRB survey asked Russians what President Putin should do at the end of his second term, respondents divided (Figure 10.1). A plurality, 42 percent, wanted the president to leave voters free to choose his successor. The median group, more than a third of the total, were don't knows. Almost a quarter of Russians either wanted Putin to change the law and stand again or appoint his successor. Together, those without an opinion or letting Putin decide what happens constitute a majority; this indicates that, whatever choice President Putin makes, he will have a substantial amount of passive or active acceptance.

Given a plebiscitarian system, many Russians have become resigned to elections having little relevance. In 1996, there was widespread media discussion about the possibility of President Yeltsin suspending the

Figure 10.1 *HOW SHOULD THE NEXT PRESIDENT BE CHOSEN?*

Q. At present, the constitution says that Vladimir Putin is ineligible to be a candidate for a third term as president in 2008. What should he do in this situation?

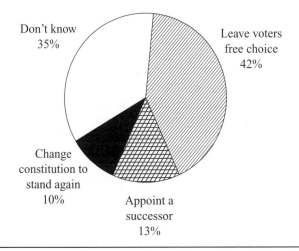

Don't know
35%

Leave voters
free choice
42%

Change
constitution to
stand again
10%

Appoint a
successor
13%

Source: New Russia Barometer XIV (2005).

presidential election rather than risk electoral defeat in what appeared to be a close contest with a Communist opponent. At that time, 74 percent of NRB respondents thought it right to hold elections compared to 26 percent having doubts. However, now a majority indicate doubts about the value of holding an election. Following the 2004 presidential election, 58 percent of NRB respondents said it would have been better to save money and not hold a presidential ballot.

Whenever the next Russian election is called, the first decision facing subjects is whether or not to vote. In Soviet times, Russians summed up their resigned acceptance to the command economy with the saying, "They pretend to pay us and we pretend to work." Today, Russians might characterize their resigned acceptance to what the ballot offers by saying, "They pretend to represent us and we pretend they do so." The 2005 NRB survey found that only 9 percent think that most elected politicians care what people like themselves think and only 10 percent trust political parties. Indifference to elections and alternative candidates can encourage abstention.

Whereas the Soviet regime mobilized Russians to vote, the new regime has been inclined to demobilize subjects. The resigned acceptance of subjects is accepted on the principle that those who are not against us are with us. If there was a prospect of turnout falling below the legally required minimum of 50 percent, administrative resources could be utilized to raise turnout by removing the names of non-voters from the electoral register before the election campaign began. In addition, the number of votes counted on election night could be greater than the number of people who turned out to vote (cf. OSCE, 2004).

The tightening of procedures for the nomination of presidential candidates is a barrier to protest candidates appearing on the ballot. However, the ballot does offer voters the opportunity to vote "against all." Paradoxically, to vote against all the candidates on the ballot is a sign of civic engagement. It not only requires a person to have standards by which existing candidates are judged wanting, but also to believe that it is worthwhile to express an opinion. The maximum use of this option was in the second round of the 1996 presidential election contest, when 4.8 percent were recorded as voting against all. In the 2004 presidential election, 3.4 percent of votes were reported as against all.

Figure 10.2 *RUSSIANS ADAPTING TO TRANSFORMATION*

Q. Have you and your family already adapted to the changes that have happened in the country during the past ten years?

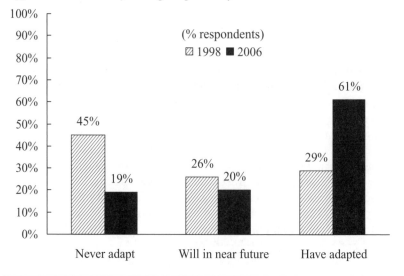

Source: Levada Center nationwide surveys, October 1998; June 2006.

An autocratic regime wants its subjects to adapt to what rulers supply – and this has gradually been happening. In 1998, when Russians were first asked if they had adapted to the upheavals of the past decade, only 29 percent said that they had done so and one-quarter hoped to do so in the near future. The largest bloc of Russians said that they would never adapt (Figure 10.2). These replies showed that Russians underestimated their capacity for re-learning. By June 2006, an absolute majority, 61 percent, reported that they had adapted to transformation; another fifth expected to do so in the near future. The proportion saying that they would never adapt is now down to one in five, and they are disproportionately old.

Today, four-fifths of Russians have accepted life as it is in the new Russian regime. Adaptation does not mean that Russians are satisfied with the political performance of the new regime. In a 2006 Levada Center survey, 49 percent said they were dissatisfied with the direction in which the country was going. Adaptation is a process of learning to cope with the difficulties of everyday life rather than being overcome by them. Before a majority had adapted, in 1998 as many as 51 percent of Levada Center respondents said they found their current situation "unbearable." By May 2006, the position had reversed: only 20 percent said they found their current situation unbearable, while 51 percent reported it difficult but bearable and 22 percent described it as not so bad (www.RussiaVotes.org/).

Whoever is Russia's leader in 2009 will benefit from the political equilibrium that has been developed through the passage of time. This will be the case whether there is a new president in the Kremlin or Vladimir Putin is able to retain his current power. How the situation is to be evaluated is both a normative and empirical question. In established democracies and in Central and East European regimes that have become members of the European Union, popular preferences and political institutions tend to be congruent. In Russia the situation is different. While Russians would prefer to live in a democratic regime, they appear resigned to accepting the real existing system of plebiscitarian autocracy supplied by the country's political elites.

Appendix A: New Russia Barometer samples

Every NRB survey bar one has been conducted by the same organization, initially known as VCIOM, the Russian Center for Public Opinion Research, and then as the Levada Center, the most senior and established not-for-profit survey research institution in Russia. Its leading personnel are social scientists well versed in both the theory and the practice of survey research (see www.levada.ru for details). Continuity in organization and personnel is especially beneficial for the long-term trend analysis reported in this book.

All New Russia Barometer surveys are conducted with multistage stratified samples. The starting point is the division of the population geographically, in order to cover the whole of the Russian Federation except for war zones and difficult-to-reach extremities, areas with a small percentage of the national population. The data used for stratifying the population come from the censuses and official statistics collected by Goskomstat (www.gks.ru). Initially, the country is stratified into seven to ten large economic and geographical regions, and each is assigned a number of interviews proportionate to its share of the national population. All cities with a population of more than 1 million people are selected, and within each region regional centers, towns, and villages are selected with a probability proportionate to their population. Then, cities are stratified by ward and rural areas by villages in order to select Primary Sampling Units; an average of ten interviews is conducted in a sampling unit, thus ensuring a wide dispersion of interviews within big cities such as Moscow.

Within each Primary Sampling Unit, an interviewer is assigned a random address for interviewing, and households are approached on a random route basis. Within each selected house, the interviewer normally interviews the person whose birthday comes next, which may be supplemented by an age-by-sex-by-education grid. Face-to-face contact in the home is especially important in Russia, since a substantial fraction of the population did not have a home telephone when NRB surveys started, and mobile phones create further difficulties for sampling and interviewing. In common with West European countries and the United States, the rate of response has declined substantially: it was 82.7 percent of the effective universe in the 1992 NRB survey and 64.3 percent in the 2005 survey.

Levada Center field supervisors verify up to one-fifth of the interviews by return visits to households, post, or telephone. Quality checks of the questionnaire are undertaken in the Center's office. The profile of respondents according to age, education, and gender is compared with census estimates for the population and, as appropriate, weights are calculated to match the census figures.

Fuller details of each sample can be found at www.abdn.ac.uk/cspp/NRBsamples.shtml, and questions and answers to all questions are contained in the Studies in Public Policy (SPP) series of the Centre for the Study of Public Policy at the University of Aberdeen. The relevant SPP number is given along with distinctive details of each sample below.

New Russia Barometer I: January 26–February 25, 1992 (SPP 205)

The survey was conducted by VCIOM in consultation with Dr. Irina Boeva and Dr. Viacheslav Shironin, economists in the former USSR Academy of Sciences, and supported by a grant from the Centre for Research into Communist Economies, London. The universe consisted of Russians in the urban population, 73.3 percent of the total population of Russia in the 1987 census. The effective sample consisted of 2,547 persons; a total of 2,106 interviews were completed. The survey was confined to urban areas because of difficulties at that time in carrying out fieldwork in rural areas. Subsequent comparison with urban and rural respondents in NRB II showed that in the great majority of political questions there was no significant difference between urban and rural respondents, and the impact on economic behavior and attitudes was predictable and, with a few obvious exceptions, such as growing food, marginal. (For full details, see Boeva and Shironin, 1992: 40–43.)

New Russia Barometer II: June 26–July 22, 1993 (SPP 216)

The survey was financed by a grant from the British Foreign Office Know How Fund to study popular response to privatization. The universe of the sample was the population of the whole of the Russian Federation aged sixteen and above, rural as well as urban. Respondents under the age of eighteen were excluded from the analysis. There were a total of 1,975 interviews, and a response rate of 83 percent. VCIOM used a multiple regression analysis to derive appropriate weights for gender, age, education, and town size.

New Russia Barometer III: March 15–April 9, 1994 (SPP 228)

This survey was a collaboration between the CSPP and the Paul Lazarsfeld Society, Vienna. Fieldwork was undertaken by MNENIE Opinion Service, Moscow, under the direction of Dr. Grigory A. Pashkov. Financial support came from a group of Austrian banks and a grant to the CSPP from the British Know How Fund. The questionnaire was piloted with 100 interviews in Rostov on Don and Petrozavodsk, February 26–28, 1994. The universe for the sample was the population of the Russian Federation aged eighteen and above. The target number of responses was 3,500; in the event, 3,535 interviews were completed.

New Russia Barometer IV: March 31–April 19, 1995 (SPP 250)

This survey was financed by a grant from the British Foreign Office Know How Fund and, like all subsequent surveys, was conducted by VCIOM and its successor, the Levada Center. A total of 2,770 contacts were made, and 1,998 were interviewed face to face, a response rate of 72.1 percent.

New Russia Barometer V: January 12–31, 1996 (SPP 260)

This post-Duma election survey, organized by VCIOM, was financed by the CSPP. A total of 4,508 contacts were made and 2,426 persons were interviewed, a response rate of 53.8 percent. The data were weighted to match the regional census population in gender, age, education, town size, and, because of proximity to the general election, party preference. VCIOM collected data on the voting preference of its interviewers; they were widely dispersed across the political spectrum. Yabloko was the only party favored by more than a tenth of interviewers; the Communist Party was second and Our Home Is Russia third in interviewer preferences.

New Russia Barometer VI: July 25–August 2, 1996 (SPP 272)

This post-presidential election survey was organized by VCIOM and again financed by the CSPP. The timing of the presidential election shortly before the start of the summer holidays posed a dilemma. To maximize the number of people at home when an interviewer called would have meant postponing fieldwork until September. But given the uncertainties of President Yeltsin's health and the political situation in Chechnya, as well as completely unforeseeable events, delay would have risked spoiling the study by introducing post-election events into an election survey, as well as decreasing the accuracy of reported voting. That risk was minimized by starting interviewing in late July, even though this invited a lower response rate during the holiday season. Therefore, all interviews were concluded before the presidential inauguration made very visible the state of the president's health and before quarrels about Chechnya had become another running story. In all, 3,379 households were contacted with someone at home; in 965 cases no one at that point met the requirements of the interviewer's age-by-sex-by-education sampling grid. Of the 2,414 households where an interview was sought, there were 1,599 completed responses, 66.2 percent of the total. VCIOM weighted the data to match the regional census population in terms of gender, age, education, town size, and, because of the election, voting.

New Russia Barometer VII: March 6–April 13, 1998 (SPP 303)

In addition to standard NRB trend questions, the seventh NRB survey included a lengthy special-purpose section of questions about social capital. It was financed by a grant from the Social Capital Initiative of the World Bank, funded by the Development Fund of the Government of Denmark. Altogether, 5,903 contacts were made with households, 1,868 did not have a respondent matching grid requirements, and in 1,035 no one answered. In 3,000 households there was a respondent meeting the sampling specifications, and 2,002 interviews were satisfactorily completed, a response rate of 66.7 percent.

New Russia Barometer VIII: January 13–29, 2000 (SPP 328)

This survey took place just after the 1999 Duma election and Christmas holidays. It was funded by the British Economic and Social Research Council, and fieldwork was conducted by VCIOM. Fieldwork occurred just after the Duma election and the seasonal holidays. Altogether, 4,326 addresses were visited; there were 1,940 completed interviews with adults aged eighteen or above, 65.6 percent of the effective sample.

New Russia Barometer IX: April 14–18, 2000 (SPP 330)

The ninth New Russia Barometer survey was funded by the British Economic and Social Research Council, and ECOHOST (European Centre on Health of Societies in Transition) of the London School of Hygiene and Tropical Medicine for health questions. VCIOM undertook field-work promptly after the presidential election, while events were fresh in the minds of Russians and post-election events could not yet influence attitudes. In 2,019 households, there was a person meeting the specifications of the sample grid, and 1,600 interviews were completed, 79.2 percent of the total households.

New Russia Barometer X: June 17–July 3, 2001 (SPP 350)

The tenth NRB survey was funded by the British Economic and Social Research Council with fieldwork by VCIOM. In 3,254 households a resident met sample specifications, and 2,000 interviews were completed, 61.5 percent of effective contacts.

New Russia Barometer XI: June 12–26, 2003 (SPP 378)

The eleventh NRB survey was funded by the CSPP with fieldwork by VCIOM. The data collected provided public opinion near the end of President Putin's first term of office. In 2,095 households, a resident met the sample specifications, and there were 1,601 valid respondents, 76.4 percent of effective contacts.

New Russia Barometer XII: December 12–22, 2003 (SPP 384)

The twelfth NRB survey was conducted as part of the VCIOM–Analytica survey immediately after the Duma election. It was funded by the British Economic and Social Research Council. There were 2,022 contacts within the sampling frame and 1,601 interviews, a response rate of 79.2 percent.

New Russia Barometer XIII: March 18–23, 2004 (SPP 388)

This survey started a week after the reelection of President Vladimir Putin. It was conducted by the Levada Center, Moscow, staffed by former members of VCIOM, and funded by a grant from the British Economic and Social Research Council. Contacts were made with 2,130 individuals with characteristics fitting the sample design; there were 1,602 completed interviews, 75.2 of the effective contacts.

New Russia Barometer XIV: January 3–23, 2005 (SPP 402)

The final NRB survey reported in this book was timed to occur after the aura of President Putin's election victory had evaporated. It was funded by grants from the British Economic and Social Research Council and the Epidemiology Department of University College London Medical School. Of the 3,278 persons eligible for interviewing, there were 2,107 respondents, 64.3 percent of the total contacted.

Appendix B: coding of variables

	Range of codes	Mean	Standard deviation
Dependent variables			
Supports current regime	+100 best to −100 worst	−12.20	48.93
Rejects alternative regimes Mean: Communism, army rule, dictatorship, abolish parliament	+100 strongly rejects; 50 somewhat rejects; 0 no opinion; −50 somewhat favors; −100 strongly favors	30.39	41.30
Political values & performance			
Pro old regime	+100 best to −100 worst	23.77	54.21
Democracy desired	10 strongly favors democracy to 1 strongly favors dictatorship	7.23	2.57
Democracy in Russia today	10 complete democracy to 1 complete dictatorship	5.43	2.02
Freedom now and then Mean: speech, joining organizations, religion, political participation	5 much better now; 4 somewhat better now; 3 much the same; 2 somewhat worse now; 1 much worse now	3.74	.79
Govt. fair, responsive Mean: people can influence government, government fair	5 much better now; 4 somewhat better now; 3 much the same; 2 somewhat worse now; 1 much worse now	2.44	1.07
Trust in political institutions mean for trust in: army, Duma, police, parties, courts,	7 trust to 1 distrust	3.17	2.72
Presidential approval	10 total approval to 1 total disapproval	4.68	3.29
Corruption in government	4 almost all corrupt; 3 most corrupt; 2 less than half corrupt; 1almost no corruption	3.23	.86
Pro market ideology	1 pro market; 0 other ideologies, no ideology	.24	.43

(cont.)

Economy			
Pro old economic system	100 best to −100 worst	35.77	47.85
Pro current economic system	100 best to −100 worst	−24.19	49.86
Gross domestic product	Cumulative growth 1991 = 100	73.77	9.77
Household situation:			
Current	5 very good; 4 fairly good 3 neutral; 2 fairly unsatisfactory; 1 very unsatisfactory	2.27	1.06
Compared to five years ago	5 much better today; 4 somewhat better today; 3 much the same; 2 somewhat worse today; 1 much worse	2.67	1.38
Destitution	4 often; 3 sometimes 2 rarely; 1 never	2.34	1.82
Mean doing without: food, clothing, electricity			
Consumer goods: phone, car, color TV, VCR	100 has all goods to 0 has none.	47.68	31.59
Prefer lots of goods, high prices to controlled prices, shortages	4 strongly for lots of goods; 3 somewhat for goods; 2 somewhat prefers controls; 1 strongly prefers controls	2.53	.96
Expectations			
Expect parliament suspended	5 very likely; 4 maybe 3 don't know; 2 not very likely; 1 not at all likely	2.51	1.13
Regime in five years	100 best to −100 worst	13.89	47.02
Economic system in five years	100 best to −100 worst	7.40	50.01
Household economy in five years	5 much better; 4 somewhat better; 3 much the same; 2 somewhat worse; 1 much worse in five years	3.08	1.02
Social structure			
Age	Age in years	44.11	16.65
Gender	1 woman; 0 man	.55	.50
Subjective social status	5 highest to 1 lowest	2.00	1.43
Church attendance	4 weekly or monthly; 3 a few times a year; 2 once or twice a year; 1 never	1.81	.93
Education	6 degree; 5 some university; 4 technical college; 3 academic secondary; 2 vocational; 1 less	2.91	1.44

(cont.)

(*cont.*)

	Range of codes	Mean	Standard deviation
Town size	4 million plus; 3 100,000–999,999; 2 town; 1 village	2.42	1.01
Russian ethnicity	1 self-declared Russian; 0 other ethnic group	.85	.36
Pride in citizenship	3 definitely; 2 somewhat; 1 little or none	2.09	.80
European identity	4 often; 3 sometimes; 2 rarely; 1 never	2.16	1.12

Note: For most variables in the analysis, missing data are a very low percentage of replies. Respondents with missing data on support for the current regime are deleted from the analysis. Questions about rejection of alternative regimes were first included in NRB III; hence, the analysis of this variable excludes the first two NRB surveys. Where a reply is missing for an independent variable, the mean for all answers in that year is substituted. In the few cases in which a question was not included in an NRB round, a mean for the year was calculated by interpolating between the yearly means for the variable in the two adjacent surveys and substituted. Sensitivity tests indicate that alternative methods of handling missing data, including multiple imputation procedures, have no appreciable effects on either the relative sizes or statistical significance of estimates.

References

Alexander, Gerard, 2002. *The Sources of Democratic Consolidation*. Ithaca: Cornell University Press.

Almond, Gabriel A. and Verba, Sidney, 1963. *The Civic Culture*. Princeton: Princeton University Press.

Aron, Leon, 2000. *Boris Yeltsin: A Revolutionary Life*. New York: HarperCollins.

Aslund, Anders, 2002. *Building Capitalism: The Transformation of the Soviet Bloc*. Cambridge: Cambridge University Press.

Bacon, Edwin, 2004. "Russia's Law on Political Parties: Democracy by Decree?" In Cameron Ross, ed., *Russian Politics Under Putin*. Manchester: Manchester University Press, 39–52.

Bahry, Donna, 1987. "Politics, Generations and Change in the USSR." In Millar, 1987, 66–99.

Bartolini, Stefano, 2000. "Franchise Expansion." In Richard Rose, ed., *The International Encyclopedia of Elections*. Washington, DC: CQ Press, 117–130.

Baumgartner, Frank R. and Jones, Bryan D., 1993. *Agendas and Instability in American Politics*. Chicago: University of Chicago Press.

Berdyaev, Nikolai, 1947. *The Russian Idea*. New York: Macmillan.

Berlin, Isaiah, 1958. *Two Concepts of Liberty: An Inaugural Lecture*. Oxford: Clarendon Press.

Blasi, Joseph R., Kroumova, Maya and Kruse, Douglas, 1997. *Kremlin Capitalism: Privatizing the Russian Economy*. Ithaca: Cornell University Press.

Boda, Michael D., ed., 2005. "The 'Free' and 'Fair' Elections Issue," *Representation*, 41, 3, 155–227.

Boeva, I. and Shironin, V., 1992. *Russians Between State and Market: The Generations Compared*. Glasgow: CSPP Studies in Public Policy No. 205.

Boutenko, Irene A. and Razlogov, Kirill E., 1997. *Recent Social Trends in Russia 1960–1995*. Montreal: McGill-Queen's University Press.

Brady, Henry E. and Collier, David, eds., 2004. *Rethinking Social Inquiry: Diverse Tools, Shared Standards*. Lanham, MD: Rowman & Littlefield.

Breslauer, George W., 1978. "On the Adaptability of Soviet Welfare-State Authoritarianism." In Karl W. Ryavec, ed., *Soviet Society and the Communist Party*. Amherst: University of Massachusetts Press, 3–25.

2002. *Gorbachev and Yeltsin as Leaders*. New York: Cambridge University Press.

Brooker, Paul, 2000. *Non-Democratic Regimes: Theory, Government and Politics*. Basingstoke: Macmillan.

Brown, Archie, 1994. "The Brezhnev Era, 1964–1982." In Brown, Michael Kaser and Gerald S. Smith, eds., *The Cambridge Encyclopedia of Russia and the Former Soviet Union.* Cambridge: Cambridge University Press, 122–125.

    1996. *The Gorbachev Factor.* Oxford: Oxford University Press.

    2001a. "Evaluating Russia's Democratization." In Brown, ed., *Contemporary Russian Politics: A Reader.* Oxford: Oxford University Press, 546–568.

    2001b. "Vladimir Putin and the Reaffirmation of Central State Power," *Post-Soviet Affairs,* 17, 1, 45–55.

    2004. "Vladimir Putin's Leadership in Comparative Perspective." In Cameron Ross, ed., *Russian Politics Under Putin.* Manchester: Manchester University Press, 3–16.

Brunner, Georg, 1990. "Elections in the Soviet Union." In Furtak, 1990, 20–52.

Brym, Robert J., 1994. *The Jews of Moscow, Kiev and Minsk: Identity, Antisemitism, Emigration.* Basingstoke: Macmillan.

Buckley, Neil, 2005. "Putin Rules Out Third Term as President," *Financial Times,* 13 April.

Bunce, Valerie, 1995. "Should Transitologists Be Grounded?," *Slavic Review,* 54, 1, 111–127.

    2003. "Rethinking Recent Democratization: Lessons from the Postcommunist Experience," *World Politics,* 55, 2, 167–192.

Campbell, Angus, Converse, P. E., Miller, W. E. and Stokes, D. E., 1960. *The American Voter.* New York: John Wiley.

Canache, Damarys, Mondak, Jeffery J. and Seligson, Mitchell A., 2001. "Meaning and Measurement in Cross-National Research on Satisfaction with Democracy," *Public Opinion Quarterly,* 65, 506–528.

Carnaghan, Ellen, 2001. "Thinking About Democracy: Interviews with Russian Citizens," *Slavic Review,* 60, 2, 336–366.

Carothers, Thomas, 1999. *Aiding Democracy Abroad.* Washington, DC: Carnegie Endowment for International Peace.

Central Election Commission, 2004. *Vybory Prezidenta Rossiiskoi Federatsii.* pr2004.cikrf.ru, April 2.

Churchill, Winston, 1947. Speech to House of Commons, *Parliamentary Debates,* London: HMSO, November 11, col. 206.

Clark, John and Wildavsky, Aaron, 1990. *The Moral Collapse of Communism: Poland as a Cautionary Tale.* San Francisco: ICS Press.

Cohen, Ira J., 1985. "The Underemphasis on Democracy in Marx and Weber." In R. J. Antonio and R. M. Glassman, eds., *A Weber–Marx Dialogue.* Manhattanville: Kansas State University Press, 274–295.

Collier, David and Levitsky, Steven, 1997. "Democracy with Adjectives: Conceptual Innovation in Comparative Research," *World Politics,* 49, 3, 430–451.

Colton, Timothy J., 2000. *Transitional Citizens: Voters and What Influences Them in the New Russia.* Cambridge, MA: Harvard University Press.

    2004. "Parties, Citizens and the Prospects for Democratic Consolidation in Russia." In Michael McFaul and Kathryn Stoner-Weiss, eds., *After the Collapse of Communism.* Cambridge: Cambridge University Press, 173–206.

    2005. "Putin and the Attenuation of Russian Democracy." In Alex Pravda, ed., *Leading Russia: Putin in Perspective.* Oxford: Oxford University Press, 103–118.

Conquest, Robert, 1990. *The Great Terror: A Re-assessment.* London: Pimlico.

Converse, Philip E., 1964. "The Nature of Belief Systems in Mass Publics." In David Apter, ed., *Ideology and Discontent.* New York: Free Press.

Cook, Linda J., 1993. *The Soviet Social Contract and Why It Failed.* Cambridge, MA: Harvard University Press.

Daalder, Hans, 1995. "Paths Toward State Formation in Europe." In H. E. Chehabi and Alfred Stepan, eds., *Politics, Society and Democracy: Comparative Studies in Honor of Juan J. Linz.* Boulder, CO: Westview Press, 113–130.

Dahl, Robert A., 1971. *Polyarchy: Participation and Opposition.* New Haven: Yale University Press.

1989. *Democracy and Its Critics.* New Haven: Yale University Press.

Dalton, Russell, 2004. *Democratic Challenges, Democratic Choices: The Erosion of Political Support in Advanced Industrial Democracies.* Oxford: Oxford University Press.

Davies, Sarah, 1997. *Public Opinion in Stalin's Russia: Terror, Propaganda and Dissent, 1934–1941.* Cambridge: Cambridge University Press.

Diamond, Larry, 1999. *Developing Democracy: Toward Consolidation.* Baltimore: Johns Hopkins University Press.

2002. "Thinking About Hybrid Regimes," *Journal of Democracy,* 13, 3, 21–35.

Duncan, Peter J. S., 2000. *Russian Messianism: Third Rome, Holy Revolution, Communism and After.* London: Routledge.

Durkheim, Emile, 1952. *Suicide: A Study in Sociology.* London: Routledge.

Dyson, Kenneth H. F., 1980. *The State Tradition in Western Europe.* Oxford: Martin Robertson.

Easton, David, 1965. *A Systems Analysis of Political Life.* New York: John Wiley.

1975. "A Re-Assessment of the Concept of Political Support," *British Journal of Political Science,* 5, 435–457.

Easton, David and Dennis, Jack, 1969. *Children in the Political System: Origins of Political Legitimacy.* New York: McGraw-Hill.

EBRD (European Bank for Reconstruction and Development), 2004. *Transition Report 2004: Infrastructure.* London: EBRD.

2005. *Transition Report 2005: Business in Transition.* London: EBRD.

Eckstein, Harry, 1988. "A Culturalist Theory of Political Change," *American Political Science Review,* 82, 3, 789–804.

Elster, Jon, Offe, Claus and Preuss, Ulrich K., 1998. *Institutional Design in Post-Communist Societies.* Cambridge: Cambridge University Press.

Emmons, Terence, 1983. *The Formation of Political Parties and the First National Elections in Russia.* Cambridge, MA: Harvard University Press.

Evans, Alfred B. Jr., Henry, L. A. and Sundstrom, L. M., eds., 2006. *Russian Civil Society: A Critical Assessment.* Armonk, NY: M. E. Sharpe.

Evans, Geoffrey, ed., 1999. *The End of Class Politics?* Oxford: Oxford University Press.

Feldman, Stanley, 2003. "Values, Ideology and the Structure of Political Attitudes." In D. O. Sears, Leonie Huddy and Robert Jervis, eds., *The Oxford Handbook of Political Psychology.* Oxford: Oxford University Press, 477–598.

Finer, S. E., 1997. *The History of Government.* Oxford: Oxford University Press, 3 vols.

Fish, M. Steven, 1995. *Democracy from Scratch: Opposition and Regime in the New Russian Revolution*. Princeton: Princeton University Press.

2005. *Democracy Derailed in Russia: The Failure of Open Politics*. New York: Cambridge University Press.

Fitzpatrick, Sheila, 1999. *Everyday Stalinism. Ordinary Life in Extraordinary Times: Soviet Russia in the 1930s*. New York: Oxford University Press.

Franchetti, Mark, 2004. "Don't Vote for Me, I'm Only Throwing the Poll for Putin," *Sunday Times* (London), 10 January.

Freeland, Chrystia, 2000. *Sale of the Century: The Inside Story of the Second Russian Revolution*. London: Little, Brown.

Fukuyama, Francis, 1992. *The End of History and the Last Man*. New York: Free Press.

Furtak, Robert K., ed., 1990. *Elections in Socialist States*. New York: Harvester Wheatsheaf, 20–52.

Gans-Morse, Jordan, 2004. "Searching for Transitologists," *Post-Soviet Affairs*, 20, 4, 320–349.

Gerschenkron, Alexander, 1962. *Economic Backwardness in Historical Perspective*. Cambridge, MA: Harvard University Press.

Gibson, James L., 2001. "The Russian Dance with Democracy," *Post-Soviet Affairs*, 16, 2, 129–158.

Gibson, James L. and Duch, Raymond M., 1993. "Emerging Democratic Values in Soviet Political Culture." In Arthur H. Miller, et al., *Public Opinion and Regime Change: The New Politics of Post-Soviet Societies*. Boulder, CO: Westview Press, 69–94.

Goskomstat, 2005. *Natsional'nyi sostav naseleniya*. www.perepis2002.ru/ct/doc/TOM_04_01.xls.

Gurr, T. R., 1970. *Why Men Rebel*. Princeton: Princeton University Press.

Hankiss, Elemer, 1990. *East European Alternatives*. Oxford: Clarendon Press.

Hedlund, Stefan, 1999. *Russia's "Market" Economy: A Bad Case of Predatory Capitalism*. London: UCL Press.

Heller, Mikhail, 1988. *Cogs in the Soviet Wheel: The Formation of Soviet Man*. London: Collins Harvill.

Hermet, Guy, Rouquié, Alain and Rose, Richard, eds., 1978. *Elections Without Choice*. London: Macmillan.

Hill, Fiona and Gaddy, Clifford G., 2003. *The Siberian Curse: How Communist Planners Left Russia Out in the Cold*. Washington, DC: Brookings Institution Press.

Holmes, Stephen, 2003. "Potemkin Democracy." In T. K. Rabb and E. N. Suleiman, eds., *The Making and Unmaking of Democracy: Lessons from History and World Politics*. London: Routledge, 109–133.

Hosking, Geoffrey, 2001. *Russia and the Russians: A History*. Cambridge, MA: Harvard University Press.

2006. *Rulers and Victims: The Russians in the Soviet Union*. Cambridge, MA: Harvard University Press.

Hough, Jerry F., 1977. *The Soviet Union and Social Science Theory*. Cambridge, MA: Harvard University Press.

Howard, Marc Morjé, 2003. *The Weakness of Civil Society in Post-Communist Europe*. New York: Cambridge University Press.

Huntington, Samuel P., 1991. *The Third Wave: Democratization in the Late Twentieth Century*. Norman: University of Oklahoma Press.

Huskey, Eugene, 2001. "Overcoming the Yeltsin Legacy: Vladimir Putin and Russian Political Reform." In Archie Brown, ed., *Contemporary Russian Politics: A Reader*. Oxford: Oxford University Press, 82–98.

Hyden, Goran, Court, Julius and Mease, Kenneth, 2004. *Making Sense of Governance: Empirical Evidence from Sixteen Developing Countries*. Boulder, CO: Lynne Rienner.

IMF (International Monetary Fund), 1994. "Camdessus Expresses Confidence in Russian Economic Reform," *IMF Survey*, 4 April, 97–100.

Inglehart, Ronald, 1997. *Modernization and Postmodernization: Cultural, Economic and Political Change in Forty-One Societies*. Princeton: Princeton University Press.

Inkeles, Alex and Bauer, Raymond, 1959. *The Soviet Citizen: Daily Life in a Totalitarian Society*. Cambridge, MA: Harvard University Press.

Jack, Andrew, 2004. "Critics See No Room for Dissent in New Duma," *Financial Times*, 5 February.

Jacoby, Wade, 2004. *The Enlargement of the European Union and NATO*. New York: Cambridge University Press.

Jowitt, Kenneth, 1992. *New World Disorder: The Leninist Extinction*. Berkeley: University of California Press.

Karl, Terry Lynn, 2000. "Electoralism." In Richard Rose, ed., *The International Encyclopedia of Elections*. Washington, DC: CQ Press, 95–96.

Kelly, Catriona, 2005. *Comrade Pavlik: The Rise and Fall of a Soviet Boy Hero*. Cambridge: Granta.

Kinder, Donald and Kiewiet, D. R. 1981. "Sociotropic Politics: The American Case," *British Journal of Political Science*, 11, 129–161.

King, David, 1997. *The Commissar Vanishes: The Falsification of Photographs and Art in Stalin's Russia*. Edinburgh: Canongate.

Kirchheimer, Otto, 1965. "Confining Conditions and Revolutionary Breakthroughs," *American Political Science Review*, 59, 4, 964–974.

Kissinger, Henry, 1994. *Diplomacy*. New York: Simon and Schuster.

Klebnikov, Paul, 2000. *Godfather of the Kremlin: Boris Berezovsky and the Looting of Russia*. New York: Harcourt, Brace.

Kornai, Janos, 1992. *The Socialist System: The Political Economy of Communism*. Princeton: Princeton University Press.

Ledeneva, Alena V., 1998. *Russia's Economy of Favours*. Cambridge: Cambridge University Press.

Lentini, Peter, ed., 1995. *Elections and Political Order in Russia*. Budapest: Central European University Press.

Levi, Margaret, 1997. "A Model, a Method and a Map." In Mark I. Lichbach and Alan S. Zuckerman, eds., *Comparative Politics: Rationality, Culture and Structure*. New York: Cambridge University Press, 19–41.

Linz, Juan J., 1990. "Transitions to Democracy," *Washington Quarterly*, Summer, 143–164.

2000. *Totalitarian and Authoritarian Regimes.* Boulder, CO: Lynne Rienner.

Linz, Juan J. and Stepan, Alfred, eds., 1978. *The Breakdown of Democratic Regimes.* Baltimore: Johns Hopkins University Press.

1996. *Problems of Democratic Transition and Consolidation: Southern Europe, South America and Post-Communist Europe.* Baltimore: Johns Hopkins University Press.

Lipset, S. M. and Rokkan, Stein, eds., 1967. *Party Systems and Voter Alignments.* New York: Free Press.

Little, I. M. D., 1963. *A Critique of Welfare Economics.* Oxford: Clarendon Press.

Lopez-Claros, Augusto and Zadornov, Mikhail M., 2002. "Economic Reforms: Steady as She Goes," *Washington Quarterly*, 25, 1, 105–116.

Lukin, Alexander, 2000. *The Political Culture of the Russian "Democrats".* Oxford: Oxford University Press.

Lynch, Allen C., 2005. *How Russia Is Not Ruled.* New York: Cambridge University Press.

McFaul, Michael, 2001. *Russia's Unfinished Revolution.* Ithaca: Cornell University Press.

2005. "The Electoral System." In S. White, Z. Gitelman and R. Sakwa, eds., *Developments in Russian Politics 6.* Basingstoke: Macmillan, 61–79.

McFaul, Michael and Stoner-Weiss, Kathryn, 2004. "The Evolving Social Science of Postcommunism." In McFaul and Stoner-Weiss, eds., *After the Collapse of Communism.* New York: Cambridge University Press, 1–20.

Maddison, Angus, 1994. "Explaining the Economic Performance of Nations, 1820–1989." In W. J. Baumol, ed., *Convergence of Productivity, Cross-National Studies and Historical Evidence.* Oxford: Oxford University Press, 20–61.

Marer, Paul, Arvay, Janos, O'Connor, John, Schrenk, Martin and Swanson, Daniel, 1992. *Historically Planned Economies: A Guide to the Data.* Washington, DC: World Bank.

Marsden, Lee, 2005. *Lessons from Russia: Clinton and US Democracy Promotion.* Aldershot: Ashgate.

Mickiewicz, Ellen, 2006. "The Election News Story on Russian Teleision: A World Apart from Viewers," *Slavic Review*, 65, 1, 1–23.

Millar, James R., ed., 1987. *Politics, Work and Daily Life in the USSR: A Survey of Former Soviet Citizens.* New York: Cambridge University Press.

Miller, Arthur H. and Klobucar, Thomas F., 2000. "The Development of Party Identification in Post-Soviet Societies," *American Journal of Political Science*, 44, 4, 667–685.

Miller, William L., Grodeland, Ase B. and Koshechkina, Tatyana Y., 2001. *A Culture of Corruption.* Budapest: Central European University Press.

Mishler, William and Rose, Richard, 2002. "Learning and Re-Learning Regime Support: The Dynamics of Post-Communist Regimes," *European Journal of Political Research*, 41, 1, 5–36.

2005. "What Are the Political Consequences of Trust? A Test of Cultural and Institutional Theories in Russia," *Comparative Political Studies*, 38.

Mishler, William and Willerton, John P., 2003. "The Dynamics of Presidential Popularity in Post-Communist Russia: Cultural Imperative Versus Neo-Institutional Choice?," *Journal of Politics*, 65, 1, 111–131.

Morel, Laurence, 1996. "France: Towards a Less Controversial Use of the Referendum?" In M. Gallagher and Pier Vincenzo Uleri, eds., *The Referendum Experience in Europe*. Basingstoke: Macmillan, 66–85.

Munck, Gerardo and Verkuilen, Jay, 2002. "Conceptualizing and Measuring Democracy: Evaluating Alternative Indices," *Comparative Political Studies*, 35, 1, 5–34.

Munro, Neil, 2006. *Russia's Persistent Communist Legacy: Nostalgia, Reaction, and Reactionary Expectations*. Aberdeen: CSPP Studies in Public Policy No. 409.

Neumann, Iver B., 1996. *Uses of the Other: The East in European Identity Formation*. Manchester: Manchester University Press.

Norris, Pippa, ed., 1999. *Critical Citizens: Global Support for Democratic Governance*. Oxford: Oxford University Press.

North, Douglass, 1999. "In Anticipation of the Marriage of Political and Economic Theory." In James E. Alt, M. Levi and E. Ostrom, eds., *Competition and Cooperation*. New York: Russell Sage Foundation, 314–317.

O'Donnell, Guillermo, 1994. "Delegative Democracy," *Journal of Democracy*, 5, 1, 55–69.

O'Donnell, Guillermo and Schmitter, P. C., 1986. *Transitions from Authoritarian Rule: Tentative Conclusions About Uncertain Democracies*. Baltimore: Johns Hopkins University Press.

Ofer, Gur and Vinokur, Aaron, 1992. *The Soviet Household Under the Old Regime*. New York: Cambridge University Press.

Offe, Claus, 1996. *Varieties of Transition: The East Europe and East German Experience*. Cambridge: Polity.

OSCE (Organization for Security and Co-operation in Europe), 2004. *Russian Federation Presidential Election 14 March 2004*. Warsaw: OSCE/ODIHR Election Observation Mission Report.

Parsons, Talcott, 1967. *Sociological Theory and Modern Society*. New York: Free Press.

Petrov, Nikolai and Slider, Darrell, 2005. "Putin and the Regions." In Dale Herspring, ed., *Putin's Russia: Past Imperfect, Future Uncertain*. Lanham, MD: Rowman & Littlefield, 2nd edn., 237–258.

Pharr, Susan J., and Putnam, Robert D., eds., 2000. *Disaffected Democracies: What's Troubling the Trilateral Countries?* Princeton: Princeton University Press.

Pierson, Paul, 2004. *Politics in Time: History, Institutions and Social Analysis*. Princeton: Princeton University Press.

Plattner, Marc F., 1996. "The Democratic Moment." In Larry Diamond and Marc F. Plattner, eds., *The Global Resurgence of Democracy*. Baltimore: Johns Hopkins University Press, 2nd edn., 36–48.

Posusney, Marsha Pripstein, 2004. "Enduring Authoritarianism: Middle East Lessons for Comparative Theory," *Comparative Politics*, 36, 2, 127–138.

Pravda, Alex, 1978. "Elections in Communist Party States." In Hermet, et al., 1978, 169–195.

Pridham, Geoffrey, 2000. "Confining Conditions and Breaking with the Past: Historical Legacies and Political Learning in Transitions to Democracy," *Democratization*, 7, 2, 36–64.

Przeworski, Adam, 1991. *Democracy and the Market: Political and Economic Reform in Eastern Europe and Latin America*. Cambridge: Cambridge University Press.

Przeworski, Adam, Alvarez, Michael, Cheibub, Jose Antonio and Limongi, Fernando, 1996. "What Makes Democracies Endure," *Journal of Democracy*, 7, 1, 39–55.

Putin, Vladimir, 2000. *First Person*, with N. Gevorkyan, N. Timakova and A. Kolesnikov. London: Hutchinson.

2005. "Annual Address to the Federal Assembly: April 25." www.kremlin.ru/eng/text/speeches. Accessed April 27, 2005.

Putnam, Robert D., 1993. *Making Democracy Work*, with Robert Leonardi and Raffaella Y. Nanetti. Princeton: Princeton University Press.

2000. *Bowling Alone: The Collapse and Revival of American Community*. New York: Simon and Schuster.

Radkey, Oliver, 1950. *The Election of the Russian Constituent Assembly of 1917*. Cambridge, MA: Harvard University Press.

Raudenbush, Stephen W. and Bryk, Anthony S., 2002. *Hierarchical Linear Models: Applications and Data Analysis Methods*. Thousand Oaks, CA: Sage, 2nd edn.

Reddaway, Peter and Glinski, Dmitri, 2001. *The Tragedy of Russia's Reforms: Market Bolshevism Against Democracy*. Washington, DC: United States Institute of Peace Press.

Remington, Thomas F., 2005. "Putin, the Duma and Political Parties." In Dale Herspring, ed., *Putin's Russia: Past Imperfect, Future Uncertain*. Lanham, MD: Rowman & Littlefield, 2nd edn., 31–54.

2006. *Politics in Russia*. New York: Pearson Longman, 4th edn.

Riker, William, 1980. "Implications from the Disequilibrium of Majority Rule for the Study of Institutions," *American Political Science Review*, 74, 432–446.

Roberts, Andrew, 2004. "The State of Socialism: A Note on Terminology," *Slavic Review*, 63, 2, 349–368.

Roeder, Philip G., 1993. *Red Sunset: The Failure of Soviet Politics*. Princeton: Princeton University Press.

Rokkan, Stein, 1970. *Citizens, Elections, Parties*. Oslo: Universitetsforlaget.

Rose, Richard, 1969. "Dynamic Tendencies in the Authority of Regimes," *World Politics*, 21, 4, 612–628.

1993. "Contradictions Between Micro- and Macro-Economic Goals in Post-Communist Societies," *Europe–Asia* Studies, 45, 3, 419–444.

1995a. "Adaptation, Resilience and Destitution: Alternative Responses to Transition in the Ukraine," *Problems of Post-Communism*, 42, 6, 52–61.

1995b. "Freedom as a Fundamental Value," *International Social Science Journal*, 145, 457–471.

1995c. "Russia as an Hour-Glass Society: A Constitution Without Citizens," *East European Constitutional Review*, 4, 3, 34–42.

1996a. "Evaluating Benefits: The Views of Russian Employees." In Douglas Lippoldt, ed., *Social Benefits and the Russian Enterprise: A Time of Transition*. Paris: OECD, 39–60.

1996b. *What Is Europe? A Dynamic Perspective*. New York and London: Longman.

1997. "How Patient Are People in Post-Communist Societies?," *World Affairs*, 159, 3, 130–144.

1998. "What Is the Demand for Price Stability in Post-Communist Countries?," *Problems of Post-Communism*, 45, 2, 43–50.

1999. "Living in an Antimodern Society," *East European Constitutional Review*, 8, 1/2, 68–75.

2000a. "A Supply-Side View of Russia's Elections," *East European Constitutional Review*, 9, 1/2, 53–59.

2000b. "Uses of Social Capital in Russia: Modern, Pre-Modern and Anti-Modern," *Post-Soviet Affairs*, 16, 1, 33–57.

2002. "Economies in Transformation: A Multidimensional Approach to a Cross-Cultural Problem," *East European Constitutional Review*, 11, 4, 62–70.

2003. "Social Shocks, Social Confidence and Health." In Judyth Twigg and Kate Schecter, eds., *Social Cohesion and Social Capital in Russia*. Armonk, NY: M. E. Sharpe, 98–117.

2005. *Insiders and Outsiders: New Europe Barometer 2004*. Glasgow: CSPP Studies in Public Policy No. 404.

2006a. *Going Public with Private Opinions: Are Post-Communist Citizens Afraid to Say What They Think?* Aberdeen: CSPP Studies in Public Policy No. 408.

2006b. *Internet Diffusion Not Divide: A Proximity Model of Internet Take Off in Russia*. Oxford: Oxford Internet Institute Research Report No. 10.

Rose, Richard and Davies, Phillip, 1994. *Inheritance in Public Policy: Change Without Choice in Britain*. New Haven and London: Yale University Press.

Rose, Richard and Krassilnikova, Marina, 1996. *Relating Income to Consumer Durables in Russia*. Glasgow: CSPP Studies in Public Policy No. 296.

Rose, Richard and McAllister, Ian, 1990. *The Loyalty of Voters*. London: Sage Publications.

Rose, Richard and Mishler, William, 1996. "Representation and Leadership in Post-Communist Political Systems," *Journal of Communist Studies and Transition Politics*, 12, 2, 224–247.

2002. "Comparing Regime Support in Non-Democratic and Democratic Countries," *Democratization*, 9, 2, 1–20.

Rose, Richard, Mishler, William and Haerpfer, Christian, 1998. *Democracy and Its Alternatives: Understanding Post-Communist Societies*. Oxford: Polity Press and Baltimore: Johns Hopkins University Press.

Rose, Richard and Munro, Neil, 2002. *Elections Without Order: Russia's Challenge to Vladimir Putin*. New York: Cambridge University Press.

2003. *Elections and Parties in New European Democracies*. Washington, DC: CQ Press.

2006. *How Russians Differ in Their View of the World*. Aberdeen: CSPP Studies in Public Policy (in production).

Rose, Richard, Munro, Neil and Mishler, William, 2004. "Resigned Acceptance of an Incomplete Democracy: Russia's Political Equilibrium," *Post-Soviet Affairs*, 20, 3, 195–218.

Rose, Richard and Shin, Doh Chull, 2001. "Democratization Backwards: The Problem of Third-Wave Democracies," *British Journal of Political Science*, 31, 2, 331–354.

Rose, Richard and Tikhomirov, Evgeny, 1993. "Who Grows Food in Russia and Eastern Europe?," *Post-Soviet Geography*, 34, 2, 111–126.

Rose, Richard and Weller, Craig, 2003. "What Does Social Capital Add to Democratic Values?" In Gabriel Badescu and Eric Uslaner, eds., *Social Capital and the Transition to Democracy*. London and New York: Routledge, 200–218.

Rustow, Dankwart A., 1955. *The Politics of Compromise: A Study of Parties and Cabinet Government in Sweden*. Princeton: Princeton University Press.

Ryavec, Karl W., 2003. *Russian Bureaucracy: Power and Pathology*. Lanham, MD: Rowman & Littlefield.

Sachs, Jeffrey D. and Pistor, Katharina, eds., 1997. *The Rule of Law and Economic Reform in Russia*. Boulder, CO: Westview Press.

Sakwa, Richard, 2002. *Russian Politics and Society*. London: Routledge, 3rd edn.

Schedler, Andreas, ed., 2006. *Electoral Authoritarianism: The Dynamics of Unfree Competition*. Boulder, CO: Lynne Rienner.

Schmitter, P. C. and Karl, Terry Lynn, 1994. "The Conceptual Travels of Transitologists and Consolidologists," *Slavic Review*, 53, 1, 173–185.

Schumpeter, Joseph A., 1946. "The American Economy in the Interwar Years," *American Economic Review*, 36, supp., 1–10.

1952. *Capitalism, Socialism and Democracy*. London: George Allen & Unwin, 4th edn.

Seymour, Charles H. and Frary, Donald Paige, eds., 1918. *How the World Votes: The Story of Democratic Development in Elections*. Springfield, MA: C. A. Nichols Co., 1918, 2 vols.

Shelley, Louise I., 1996. *Policing Soviet Society: The Evolution of State Control*. London: Routledge.

Shevtsova, Lilia, 1999. *Yeltsin's Russia: Myths and Realities*. Washington, DC: Carnegie Endowment for International Peace.

Shlapentokh, Vladimir, 1987. *The Politics of Sociology in the Soviet Union*. Boulder, CO: Westview Press.

1989. *Public and Private Life of the Soviet People*. New York: Oxford University Press.

2001. *A Normal Totalitarian Society: How the Soviet Union Functioned and How It Collapsed*. Armonk, NY: M. E. Sharpe.

Shleifer, Andrei and Treisman, Daniel, 2004. "A Normal Country," *Foreign Affairs*, March/April, 20–38.

Silver, Brian D., 1987. "Political Beliefs of the Soviet Citizen: Sources of Support for Regime Norms." In Millar, 1987, 100–141.

Simon, Janos, 1996. *Popular Conceptions of Democracy in Postcommunist Europe*. Glasgow: CSPP Studies in Public Policy No. 273.

Smith, Gordon B., ed., 1999. *State-Building in Russia: The Yeltsin Legacy and the Challenge of the Future*. Armonk, NY: M. E. Sharpe.

Solzhenitsyn, A. I., 1974. *The Gulag Archipelago, 1918–1956: An Experiment in Literary Investigation*. London: Collins Harvill.

Steenbergen, Marco R. and Jones, Bradford S., 2002. "Modeling Multilevel Data Structures," *American Journal of Political Science*, 46, 1, 218–237.

Sternberger, Dolf and Vogel, Bernhard, eds., 1969. *Die Wahl der Parlamente*, vol. I, *Europa*. Berlin: Walter de Gruyter, 2 vols.

Stokes, Susan C., ed., 2001. *Public Support for Market Reforms in New Democracies*. New York: Cambridge University Press.

Summers, Lawrence H., 1991. "Lessons of Reform for the Baltics." Indianapolis: paper to Hudson Institute Conference, 29 October.

Taras, Ray, ed., 1997. *Postcommunist Presidents*. Cambridge: Cambridge University Press.

Tompson, William, 2004. "The Russian Economy Under Vladimir Putin." In Cameron Ross, ed., *Russian Politics Under Putin*. Manchester: Manchester University Press, 114–132.

Uleri, Pier Vincenzo, 2000. "Plebiscites and Plebiscitary Politics." In Richard Rose, ed., *International Encyclopedia of Elections*. Washington, DC: CQ Press, 199–202.

Umland, Andreas, 2005. "Zhirinovskii Enters Politics: A Chronology of the Emergence of the Liberal-Democratic Party of the Soviet Union, 1990–1991," *Journal of Slavic Military Studies*, 18, 15–30.

Vachudova, Milada Anna, 2005. *Europe Undivided: Democracy, Leverage and Integration After Communism*. Oxford: Oxford University Press.

VCIOM, 1997. *Russians Outside Russia: A 1991 VCIOM Survey*. Glasgow: CSPP Studies in Public Policy No. 283.

Wädekin, Karl-Eugen, 1994. "Agriculture." In Archie Brown, Michael Kaser and Gerald S. Smith, eds., *The Cambridge Encyclopedia of Russia and the Former Soviet Union*. Cambridge: Cambridge University Press, 399–403.

Watson, Roland, 2005. "I'll Be a Democrat – Well, Almost, Putin Tells Bush," *The Times* (London), 25 February.

Webb, Beatrice and Webb, Sidney, 1937. *Soviet Communism: A New Civilization*. London: Printed for Trade Union subscribers, 2nd edn.

Weber, Max, 1947. *The Theory of Social and Economic Organization*. Glencoe, IL: Free Press.

1948. *From Max Weber*, edited by H. H. Gerth and C. Wright Mills. London: Routledge.

Wedel, Janine R., 1986. *The Private Poland*. New York: Facts on File.

1998. *Collision and Collusion: The Strange Case of Western Aid to Eastern Europe, 1989–1998*. New York: St. Martin's Press.

Weil, Frederick D., 1987. "Cohorts, Regimes, and the Legitimation of Democracy: West Germany Since 1945," *American Sociological Review*, 52, 308–324.

Wesson, Robert, 1986. *The Russian Dilemma (Revised Edition)*. New York: Praeger Scientific.

White, Stephen, 1979. *Political Culture and Soviet Politics*. London: Macmillan.

White, Stephen, Rose, Richard and McAllister, Ian, 1997. *How Russia Votes*. Chatham, NJ: Chatham House.

Wilson, Andrew, 2005. *Virtual Politics: Faking Democracy in the Post-Soviet World*. New Haven: Yale University Press.

Winiecki, Jan, 1988. *The Distorted World of Soviet-Type Economics*. London: Routledge.

Wolff, Larry, 1994. *Inventing Eastern Europe*. Stanford: Stanford University Press.

Wyman, Matthew, 1997. *Public Opinion in Postcommunist Russia*. Basingstoke: Macmillan.

Yakovlev, Alexander N., 2002. *A Century of Violence in Soviet Russia*. New Haven: Yale University Press.

Young, H. Peyton, 1998. *Individual Strategy and Social Structure: An Evolutionary Theory of Institutions*. Princeton: Princeton University Press.

Z (Martin Malia), 1990. "To the Stalin Mausoleum," *Daedalus*, 119, 1, 295–344.

Zakaria, Fareed, 1994. "A Conversation with Lee Kwan Yew," *Foreign Affairs*, 73, 109–127.

Index